Practical Cooking

Baking

Practical Cooking

Baking

This is a Parragon Book
This edition published in 2002

Parragon
Queen Street House
4 Queen Street
Bath BA1 1HE, UK

ISBN: 0-75258-310-7 (Hardback)
ISBN: 0-75258-316-6 (Paperback)

Printed in China

NOTE

Cup measurements in this book are for American cups. Tablespoons are assumed tobe 15ml. Unless otherwise stated, milk is assumed to be full fat, eggs are medium and pepper is freshly ground black pepper.

Recipes using uncooked eggs should be avoided by infants, the elderly, pregnant women and anyone suffering from an illness.

Contents

Starters & Snacks

Savoury Meals

Savoury Meals (continued)

Vegetarian & Vegan Dishes

Desserts

Cakes & Bread

Biscuits

Introduction

It may be a daunting prospect to bake your own bread, pastries, biscuits and cakes instead of buying them at the supermarket, but once you have acquired the basic skills – and armed yourself with a few of the 'tricks' – it becomes fun, versatile and rewarding.

There are a few points that will ensure your baking session is successful, regardless of the type of recipe you have chosen. So, before you start:

- Read through the recipe carefully, and make sure you have the right ingredients – using plain flour when self-raising flour is specified, for example, may not produce the result you were expecting!
- Remember to preheat the oven to the required temperature.
- Make sure you are using the correct size and shape of tin or dish, because the quantities given in the recipe are for the size of the tin specified.
- Prepare the cookware before you start assembling any of the ingredients – grease or line tins, dishes or baking sheets as directed in the recipe.
- Weigh all the ingredients accurately, and do any basic preparation, such as chopping, slicing or grating, before you start cooking.
- Once you start cooking, follow the recipe step-by-step, in the order given. Using high-quality ingredients will give the best results – unbleached flours and unrefined sugars are all readily

available and are best for cakes, while fresh vegetables, fish and meat from a reliable supplier, and a good, extra virgin olive oil will make all the difference to your savoury bakes.

A few simple principles apply to making successful pastry, bread and cakes.

Pastry

- Metal tins, not porcelain dishes, are best for quiches and tarts.
- Use fat at room temperature, cut into small pieces.
- Use ice-cold water for mixing.
- Pastry benefits from cool ingredients, and cold hands.
- Always sieve the dry ingredients into a large mixing bowl, to incorporate air.
- Wrap the pastry in foil and allow it to 'rest' in the refrigerator for 30 minutes before using.

Bread

- Plan ahead – most bread recipes include one or two 'provings' (leaving the dough in a warm place to double its bulk).
- If the flour feels cool, warm it gently in an oven at a low temperature.
- Make sure the liquid is hand-hot, to activate the yeast.
- To knead dough, stretch it away from you with one hand while pulling it towards you with the other, then fold in the edges, give it a quarter turn, and repeat.
- To test whether bread is cooked, tap the base – it should sound hollow if it is done.

Cakes

- Using a loose-based tin will make it much easier to turn out the cake.
- Bring all the ingredients to room temperature before assembling.
- If possible, use a hand-held electric mixer for 'creaming' (beating together the butter and sugar until the mixture has a 'soft dropping' consistency).
- 'Fold in' the dry ingredients very gently, using a metal spoon or spatula in a figure-of-eight movement. This lets the air get to the mixture and stops the cake becoming too heavy.
- When the cake is cooked, it should feel springy when pressed lightly. Alternatively, insert a fine metal skewer into the centre of the cake – if it is cooked, the skewer should come out clean.

Regional Cooking

Trends in eating have changed enormously in recent years to fit in with a greater awareness of health and a busier lifestyle, becoming lighter, healthier and far more cosmopolitan. But one tradition has survived – the British afternoon tea – which many people around the world still enjoy today. Although it is often restricted to rest days and holidays, the aroma of freshly baked scones, biscuits, teabreads and cakes is as enticing as ever.

Teatime enthusiasts can progress through the year enjoying treats made with seasonal ingredients. Dark winter evenings may be cheered by a deliciously moist Orange, Banana & Cranberry Loaf; home-made Teacakes, laced with dried fruit and glazed with honey, served toasted, perhaps over a log fire; or a buttery, spicy Caraway Madeira.

Later in the year, the arrival of summer is celebrated by a leisurely tea in the garden. Cherry Scones, still warm from the oven, might be followed by Strawberry Roulade, a light sponge with a fruity fromage frais filling, topped with toasted almonds and dusted with icing sugar.

The onset of the cooler autumn days are lightened by the year's harvest. A glut of apples can be turned into a Spiced Apple Ring, or Apple Shortcakes – light scones filled with braised apples and whipped cream – while the addition of roasted pumpkin flesh makes an unusual and flavoursome Pumpkin Loaf.

At any time of year, the tea table can be enhanced by a plate of crisp, melting Shortbread Fantails, or one of the many fruitcake recipes – surely a good reason to start baking.

Equally appetizing, but in a totally different way, are the

Regional Cooking

baking aromas that float from the kitchen of an Italian cook. Here, pasta – in the form of lasagne, cannelloni or any of the wide variety of shapes – is often served mixed with a sauce of vegetables, fish or meat, topped with cheese and baked until golden. Spinach & Wild Mushroom Lasagne, Pasticcio and Prawn & Tuna Pasta Bake are just a few examples. Home-made bread is flavoured with olives, herbs, cheese, peppers or sun-dried tomatoes, and of course garlic is a favourite ingredient in many recipes.

From Italy, too, comes that universal favourite, pizza, said to have been created in Naples. A dough base, spread with a tomato sauce slowly reduced until thick, is topped with a mixture of vegetables and perhaps some Italian sausage, deliciously stringy Mozzarella cheese, olives, anchovies, a sprinkling of herbs and a drizzle of olive oil – the possible combinations are endless, and the end results are wonderful. A variation of this is Calzone – a pizza dough that completely enfolds the filling.

The basic recipe for risotto, a versatile Italian rice dish, can be combined with vegetables and cheese, bound with eggs and baked to make dishes such as Green Easter Pie.

To round off their meals, Italian cooks often make use of cream and soft, creamy cheeses in desserts, as in the fresh and tangy Lemon Mascarpone Cheesecake, which is studded with stem ginger, or the Sicilian Orange & Almond Cake, which is delicious served with cream.

Basic Recipes

Savoury Pastry

Makes 1 20-cm/8-inch savoury flan base.

6 tbsp butter, plus extra for greasing
175 g/6 oz plain flour
pinch of salt
2–3 tbsp water

1 Combine the flour and salt in a bowl, then rub in the butter. Add the water and work the mixture to a soft dough. Wrap in clingfilm and leave to chill for 30 minutes

2 Grease a 20-cm/8-inch flan tin. Roll out the dough and line the tin with it. Prick the dough with a fork, then cover with clingfilm and chill again for 30 minutes.

3 Preheat the oven to 200°C/400°F/Gas Mark 6. Line the pastry base with foil and then fill with baking beans. Bake in the preheated oven for 10–12 minutes, until golden.

4 Remove from the oven, discard the baking beans and foil, then bake in the oven for a further 10 minutes.

5 Remove from the oven, add your chosen filling and cook as directed.

Sweet Pastry

Makes 1 24-cm/9½-inch sweet flan base.

150 g/5 oz plain flour
25 g/1 oz caster sugar
125 g/4½ oz butter
1 tbsp water

1 Combine the flour and sugar in a bowl, then rub in the butter. Add the water and work the mixture to a soft dough. Wrap in clingfilm and leave to chill for 30 minutes

2 Grease a 24-cm/91/2-inch flan tin. Roll out the dough and line the tin with it. Prick the dough with a fork, then cover with clingfilm and chill again for 30 minutes.

3 Preheat the oven to 190°C/375°F/Gas Mark 5. Line the pastry base with foil and then fill with baking beans. Bake in the preheated oven for 15 minutes.

4 Remove from the oven discard the baking beans and foil, then bake for a further 15 minutes.

5 Remove from the oven, then add your chosen filling and cook as directed.

Basic Pizza Dough

Makes one 25-cm/10-inch pizza.

175 g/6 oz plain flour, plus extra for dusting
1 tsp salt
1 tsp easy-blend dried yeast
6 tbsp hand-hot water
1 tbsp olive oil

1 Sieve the flour and salt into a large bowl and add the yeast. Pour in the water and oil and mix to a dough. Knead for 5 minutes, then leave to 'prove' until doubled in size.

2 Knock out the air from the dough, then knead lightly. Roll it out on a lightly floured surface, ready for use.

Basic Pasta Dough

Makes about 250 g/9 oz pasta

125 g/4½ oz strong plain flour, plus extra for dusting
125 g/4½ oz fine semolina
1 tsp salt
1 tbsp olive oil
2 eggs
1–2 tbsp hot water

1 Sieve together the flour, semolina and salt in a bowl and make a well in the centre. Pour in the oil and add the eggs. Add 1 tablespoon of hot water and, using your fingertips, work to form a smooth dough. Sprinkle on a little more water if necessary to make the dough pliable.

2 Lightly dust a clean work surface with flour, then knead the dough until it is elastic and smooth. This can take 10–15 minutes. Dust the dough with more flour if your fingers become sticky.

3 Divide the dough into 2 equal pieces. Cover a work surface with a clean cloth or tea towel and dust it liberally with flour. Place one portion of the dough on the floured cloth and roll it out as thinly and evenly as possible, stretching the dough gently until the pattern of the weave shows through. Cover it with a cloth, then roll out the second piece in the same way

4 Use a ruler and a sharp knife to cut long, thin strips for noodles, or small confectionery cutters to cut rounds, star shapes or an assortment of other decorative shapes. Cover the dough shapes with a clean cloth and leave them in a cool place (not a refrigerator) for 30–45

minutes to become partly dry. To dry ribbons, place a tea towel over the back of a chair and hang the ribbons over it. Use this fresh pasta in the recipe of your choice.

Ragù Sauce

Makes about 500 ml/1 pint.

3 tbsp olive oil
40 g/1½ oz butter
2 large onions, chopped
4 celery sticks, thinly sliced
175 g/6 oz streaky bacon, chopped
2 garlic cloves, chopped
500 g/1 lb 2 oz minced beef
2 tbsp tomato purée
1 tbsp flour
400 g/14 oz canned chopped tomatoes
150 ml/5 fl oz beef stock
150 ml/5 fl oz red wine
2 tsp dried oregano
½ tsp freshly grated nutmeg
salt and pepper

1 Heat the oil and butter in a pan over a medium heat. Add the onions, celery and bacon and fry for 5 minutes, stirring constantly.

2 Stir in the garlic and beef and cook, stirring, until the meat has lost its redness. Lower the heat and simmer for 10 minutes, stirring occasionally.

3 Increase the heat to medium, stir in the tomato purée and the flour and cook for 1–2 minutes. Add the tomatoes, stock and wine and bring to the boil, stirring constantly. Season to taste, then stir in the oregano and nutmeg. Lower the heat, then cover and simmer for 45 minutes, stirring occasionally. The sauce is now ready to use.

Italian Cheese Sauce

Makes about 300 ml/10 fl oz.

2 tbsp butter
25 g/1 oz plain flour
300 ml/10 fl oz hot milk
pinch of nutmeg
pinch of dried thyme
2 tbsp white wine vinegar
3 tbsp double cream
55 g/2 oz grated mozzarella
55 g/2 oz grated Parmesan
1 tsp English mustard
2 tbsp soured cream
salt and pepper

1 Melt the butter in a pan and stir in the flour. Cook, stirring constantly, over a low heat until the roux is light in colour and crumbly in texture. Stir in the hot milk gradually then cook over a low heat, still stirring, for 10 minutes until thick and smooth.

2 Add the nutmeg, thyme and white wine vinegar and season to taste. Stir in the double cream and mix well, then add the cheeses, mustard and soured cream. Mix until the cheeses have melted and blended into the sauce.

Pesto Sauce

Makes about 300 ml/10 fl oz.

55 g/2 oz fresh parsley, finely chopped
2 garlic cloves, crushed
55 g/2 oz pine kernels, crushed
2 tbsp chopped fresh basil leaves
55 g/2 oz Parmesan cheese, freshly grated
150 ml/5 fl oz olive oil
white pepper

1 Put all the ingredients in a blender or food processor and process for 2 minutes. Alternatively, you can blend by hand using a pestle and mortar.

2 Season with white pepper, then transfer to a jug, cover with clingfilm, and store in the refrigerator before using.

How to Use This Book

Each recipe contains a wealth of useful information, including a breakdown of nutritional quantities, preparation and cooking times, and level of difficulty. All of this information is explained in detail below.

This amount of time represents the actual cooking time.

The nutritional information provided for each recipe is per serving or per portion. Optional ingredients, variations or serving suggestions have not been included in the calculations.

The number of chef's hats represents the difficulty of each recipe, ranging from easy (1 chef's hat) to difficult (5 chef's hats).

This amount of time represents the preparation of ingredients, including cooling, chilling and soaking times.

The ingredients for each recipe are listed in the order that they are used.

Baking 107

Braised Fennel & Linguine

This aniseed-flavoured vegetable gives that little extra punch to this delicious creamy pasta dish.

NUTRITIONAL INFORMATION

Calories	650	Sugars	6g
Protein	14g	Fat	39g
Carbohydrate	62g	Saturates	22g

20 mins 50 mins

SERVES 4

INGREDIENTS

- 6 fennel bulbs
- 150 ml/5 fl oz vegetable stock
- 2 tbsp butter
- 6 slices rindless smoked bacon, diced
- 6 shallots, quartered
- 2½ tbsp plain flour
- 100 ml/3½ fl oz double cream
- 1 tbsp Madeira
- 450 g/1 lb dried linguine pasta
- 1 tbsp olive oil
- salt and pepper

1 Trim the fennel bulbs, then peel off and reserve the outer layer of each. Cut the bulbs into quarters and put them in a large saucepan with the stock and the reserved outer layers.

2 Bring to the boil, lower the heat and simmer for 5 minutes.

3 Using a perforated spoon, transfer the fennel to a large dish. Discard the outer layers of the fennel bulbs. Bring the vegetable stock to the boil and allow to reduce by half. Set aside.

4 Melt the butter in a frying pan. Add the bacon and shallots and fry over a medium heat, stirring frequently, for 4 minutes. Add the flour, reduced stock, cream and Madeira and cook, stirring constantly, for 3 minutes or until the sauce is smooth. Season to taste with salt and pepper and pour over the fennel.

5 Bring a large saucepan of lightly salted water to the boil. Add the linguine and olive oil, bring back to the boil and cook for 8–10 minutes until tender but still firm to the bite. Drain and transfer to a deep ovenproof dish.

5 Add the fennel and sauce and braise in a preheated oven, 180°C/350°F/Gas Mark 4, for 20 minutes. Serve immediately.

COOK'S TIP

Fennel will keep in the salad drawer of the refrigerator for 2–3 days, but it is best eaten as fresh as possible. Cut surfaces turn brown quickly, so do not prepare it too much in advance of cooking.

The method is illustrated with step-by-step photographs, making the recipe easy to follow.

A full-colour photograph of the finished dish.

Variations and cook's tips provide useful information regarding ingredients or cooking techniques.

The method is clearly explained with step-by-step instructions that are easy to follow.

Starters & Snacks

With so many fresh ingredients readily available, it is very easy to create some deliciously different starters to make the perfect introduction to any meal. The ideas in this chapter are an inspiration to cook and a treat to eat, and

they give an edge to the appetite that makes the main course even more enjoyable. When choosing a starter, make sure that you provide a good balance of flavours, colours and textures that offer variety and contrast. Balance the nature of the recipes too – a rich main course is best preceded by a light starter to stimulate the tastebuds.

Aubergine Bake

This dish combines layers of aubergine, tomato sauce, mozzarella and Parmesan cheese to create a very tasty starter.

NUTRITIONAL INFORMATION

Calories	232	Sugars	8g
Protein	10g	Fat	18g
Carbohydrate	8g	Saturates	6g

5 mins — 45 mins

SERVES 4

INGREDIENTS

- 3–4 tbsp olive oil
- 2 garlic cloves, crushed
- 2 large aubergines
- 100 g/3½ oz mozzarella cheese, thinly sliced
- 200 ml/7 fl oz passata
- 50 g/1¾ oz Parmesan cheese, freshly grated

1 Heat 2 tablespoons of the olive oil in a large, heavy-based frying pan. Add the garlic and sauté over a low heat for 30 seconds.

2 Slice the aubergines lengthways. Add the slices to the pan and cook in the oil for 3–4 minutes on each side or until tender. (You will probably have to cook them in batches, so add the remaining oil as necessary.)

3 Remove the aubergines with a perforated spoon and drain on absorbent kitchen paper.

2

2

4

4 Place a layer of aubergine slices in a shallow ovenproof dish. Cover the aubergines with a layer of mozzarella and then pour over a third of the passata. Continue layering in the same order, finishing with a layer of passata on top.

5 Generously sprinkle the freshly grated Parmesan cheese evenly over the top of the dish and bake in a preheated oven, 200°C/400°F/Gas Mark 6, for about 25–30 minutes.

6 Transfer to serving plates and serve warm or chilled.

Baked Fennel

Fennel is used extensively in northern Italy. It is a very versatile vegetable, which is good cooked or used raw in salads.

NUTRITIONAL INFORMATION

Calories	111	Sugars	6g
Protein	7g	Fat	7g
Carbohydrate	7g	Saturates	3g

10 mins | 35 mins

SERVES 4

INGREDIENTS

- 2 fennel bulbs
- 2 celery sticks, cut into 7.5-cm/ 3-inch pieces
- 6 sun-dried tomatoes, halved
- 200 ml/7 fl oz passata
- 2 tsp dried oregano
- 50 g/1¾ oz Parmesan cheese, freshly grated

1 Using a sharp knife, trim the fennel, discarding any tough outer leaves, and cut the bulb into quarters.

2 Bring a large pan of water to the boil, add the fennel and celery and cook for 8–10 minutes or until just tender. Remove with a perforated spoon and drain.

3 Place the fennel pieces, celery and sun-dried tomatoes in a large ovenproof dish.

4 Mix the passata and oregano and pour the mixture over the fennel.

5 Sprinkle the surface evenly with the Parmesan cheese and bake in a preheated oven, 190°C/375°F/Gas Mark 5, for 20 minutes or until hot. Serve as a starter with fresh crusty bread or as a vegetable side dish.

1

3

4

Onion & Mozzarella Tarts

These individual tarts are delicious hot or cold, are great for lunchboxes or picnics and make a good dinner party starter.

NUTRITIONAL INFORMATION

Calories	327	Sugars	3g
Protein	5g	Fat	23g
Carbohydrate	25g	Saturates	9g

45 mins 45 mins

SERVES 4

INGREDIENTS

- 250g/9 oz packet puff pastry, defrosted if frozen
- 2 red onions
- 1 red pepper
- 8 cherry tomatoes, halved
- 100g/3½ oz mozzarella cheese, cut into chunks
- 8 sprigs fresh thyme

1 Roll out the pastry to make 4 x 7.5-cm/3-inch squares. Using a sharp knife, trim the edges of the pastry, reserving the trimmings. Leave the pastry to chill in the refrigerator for 30 minutes.

2 Place the pastry squares on a baking tray. Brush a little water along each edge of the pastry squares and use the reserved pastry trimmings to make a rim around each tart.

3 Cut the red onions into thin wedges and halve and deseed the pepper.

4 Place the onions and pepper in a roasting tin. Cook under a preheated grill for 15 minutes or until charred.

5 Place the roasted pepper halves in a polythene bag and leave to sweat for 10 minutes. When the pepper is cool enough to handle, peel off the skin and cut the flesh into strips.

6 Line the pastry squares with squares of foil. Bake in a preheated oven, 200°C/400°F/Gas Mark 6, for 10 minutes. Remove and discard the foil squares and bake the tart cases for a further 5 minutes.

7 Place the onions, pepper strips, tomatoes and cheese in each tart and sprinkle with the fresh thyme.

8 Return to the oven for 15 minutes or until the pastry is golden. Transfer to warmed serving plates if serving hot or to a cooling tray if serving cold.

1
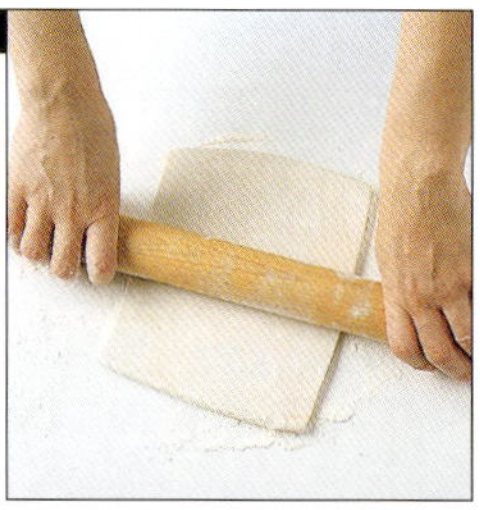

3

6

Stuffed Tomatoes

This is an impressive dinner-party dish – serve as a starter. You will find large tomatoes are easier to fill.

NUTRITIONAL INFORMATION

Calories	290	Sugars	5g
Protein	17g	Fat	23g
Carbohydrate	8g	Saturates	9g

5 mins

45 mins

SERVES 4

INGREDIENTS

- 6 large, firm tomatoes
- 4 tbsp unsalted butter
- 5 tbsp oil
- 1 medium onion, finely chopped
- 1 tsp finely chopped fresh root ginger
- 1 tsp fresh garlic, crushed
- 1 tsp pepper
- 1 tsp salt
- ½ tsp garam masala
- 450 g/1 lb minced lamb
- 1 green chilli, deseeded and finely chopped
- fresh coriander leaves

1

3

4

1 Rinse the tomatoes, cut off the tops and scoop out the flesh. Grease an ovenproof dish with the butter and place the tomatoes in it

2 Heat the oil in a pan and fry the onion until golden.

3 Lower the heat and add the ginger, garlic, pepper, salt and garam masala. Stir-fry the mixture for 3–5 minutes.

4 Add the minced lamb to the saucepan and fry for 10–15 minutes

5 Add the green chilli and fresh coriander leaves and continue stir-frying the mixture for 3–5 minutes.

6 Spoon the lamb mixture into the tomatoes and replace the tops. Cook the tomatoes in a preheated oven, 180°C/ 350°F/Gas Mark 4, for 15–20 minutes.

7 Transfer the tomatoes to serving plates and serve hot.

VARIATION

You could use the same recipe to stuff red or green peppers, if you prefer.

Pasta-stuffed Tomatoes

This unusual and inexpensive dish would make a good starter for eight people or a delicious light and summery lunch for four.

NUTRITIONAL INFORMATION

Calories	298	Sugars	4g
Protein	10g	Fat	20g
Carbohydrate	20g	Saturates	5g

15 mins | 35 mins

SERVES 8

INGREDIENTS

- 5 tbsp extra virgin olive oil, plus extra for greasing
- 8 beef tomatoes or large round tomatoes
- 115 g/4 oz dried ditalini or other very small pasta shapes
- 8 black olives, stoned and finely chopped
- 2 tbsp finely chopped fresh basil
- 1 tbsp finely chopped fresh parsley
- 55 g/2 oz Parmesan cheese, freshly grated
- salt and pepper
- fresh basil sprigs, to garnish

2

4

5

1 Brush a baking tray with olive oil. Slice the tops off the tomatoes and reserve to use as lids. If the tomatoes will not stand up, cut a thin slice off the bottom of each tomato.

2 Using a teaspoon, scoop out the tomato pulp into a sieve, but do not pierce the tomato shells. Invert the tomato shells on to kitchen paper, pat dry and then set aside to drain.

3 Bring a large saucepan of lightly salted water to the boil. Add the ditalini or other pasta and 1 tablespoon of the remaining olive oil and cook for 8–10 minutes or until tender, but still firm to the bite. Drain the pasta and set aside.

4 Put the olives, basil, parsley and Parmesan cheese into a large mixing bowl and stir in the drained tomato pulp. Add the pasta to the bowl. Stir in the remaining olive oil, mix together well and season to taste with salt and pepper.

5 Spoon the pasta mixture into the tomato shells and replace the lids. Arrange the stuffed tomatoes on the prepared baking tray and bake in a preheated oven, 190°C/375°F/Gas Mark 5, for 15–20 minutes.

6 Remove the tomatoes from the oven and set aside to cool until they are just warm.

7 Arrange the pasta-stuffed tomatoes on a serving dish, garnish with the basil sprigs and serve.

Mexican-Style Pizzas

Ready-made pizza bases are covered with a chilli-flavoured tomato sauce and topped with kidney beans, cheese and jalapeño chillies.

NUTRITIONAL INFORMATION

Calories	350	Sugars	8g
Protein	18g	Fat	10g
Carbohydrate	49g	Saturates	3g

10 mins 20 mins

SERVES 4

INGREDIENTS

- 4 ready-made individual pizza bases
- 1 tbsp olive oil
- 200 g/7 oz canned chopped tomatoes with garlic and herbs
- 2 tbsp tomato purée
- 200 g/7 oz canned kidney beans, drained and rinsed
- 115 g/4 oz sweetcorn kernels, defrosted if frozen
- 1–2 tsp chilli sauce
- 1 large red onion, shredded
- 100 g/3½ oz reduced-fat mature Cheddar cheese, grated
- 1 large green chilli, sliced into rings
- salt and pepper

1 Arrange the pizza bases on a baking tray and brush them lightly with the oil.

2 In a bowl, mix together the chopped tomatoes, tomato purée, kidney beans and sweetcorn and add chilli sauce to taste. Season with salt and pepper.

3 Spread the tomato and kidney bean mixture evenly over each pizza base to cover.

4 Top each pizza with shredded onion and sprinkle with some grated Cheddar cheese and a few slices of green chilli to taste.

5 Bake in a preheated oven, 220°C/425°F/Gas Mark 7, for about 20 minutes until the vegetables are tender, the cheese has melted and the base is crisp and golden.

6 Remove the pizzas from the baking tray and transfer to serving plates. Serve immediately.

1

3

4

COOK'S TIP

Serve a Mexican-style salad with this pizza. Arrange sliced tomatoes, fresh coriander leaves and a few slices of a small, ripe avocado on a platter. Sprinkle with fresh lime juice and coarse sea salt.

Cheese & Onion Pies

These crisp pies are filled with a tasty onion, garlic and parsley mixture, making them ideal for lunch boxes.

NUTRITIONAL INFORMATION

Calories	544	Sugars	9g
Protein	11g	Fat	36g
Carbohydrate	47g	Saturates	18g

15 mins — 35 mins

SERVES 4

INGREDIENTS

- 3 tbsp vegetable oil
- 4 onions, peeled and thinly sliced
- 4 garlic cloves, crushed
- 4 tbsp finely chopped fresh parsley
- 75 g/2¾ oz mature cheese, grated
- salt and pepper

PASTRY

- 175 g/6 oz plain flour
- ½ tsp salt
- 100 g/3½ oz butter, cut into small pieces
- 3–4 tbsp water

1 Heat the oil in a frying pan. Add the onions and garlic and fry for 10–15 minutes or until the onions are soft. Remove the pan from the heat and stir in the parsley and cheese and season to taste with salt and pepper.

2 To make the pastry, sieve the flour and salt into a mixing bowl. Add the butter and rub it in with your fingertips until the mixture resembles fine breadcrumbs. Gradually stir in the water and mix to a dough.

3 On a lightly floured surface, roll out the dough and divide it into 8 portions.

4 Roll out each portion to a 10-cm/ 4-inch round and use half of the rounds to line 4 individual tart tins.

5 Fill each round with a quarter of the cheese and onion mixture. Cover with the remaining 4 pastry rounds. Make a slit in the top of each tart with the point of a knife to allow steam to escape during cooking and seal the edges of the pies with the back of a teaspoon.

6 Bake in a preheated oven, 220°C/ 425°F/Gas Mark 7, for 20 minutes. Transfer the pies to warmed serving plates if serving hot or to a cooling rack if serving cold.

COOK'S TIP

You can prepare the onion filling in advance and store it in the refrigerator until required.

Garlic & Pine Kernel Tarts

A crisp lining of bread is filled with garlic butter and pine kernels to make a delightful and unusual light meal.

NUTRITIONAL INFORMATION

Calories	435	Sugars	1g
Protein	6g	Fat	39g
Carbohydrate	17g	Saturates	20g

20 mins   15 mins

SERVES 4

INGREDIENTS

- 4 slices wholemeal or Granary bread
- 50 g/1¾ oz pine kernels
- 150 g/5½ oz butter
- 5 garlic cloves, peeled and halved
- 2 tbsp fresh oregano, chopped, plus extra for garnish
- 4 stoned black olives, halved
- oregano leaves, to garnish

1 Using a rolling pin, flatten the bread slightly. Using a pastry cutter, cut out 4 circles of bread to fit your individual tart tins – they should measure about 10 cm/4 inches across. Reserve the offcuts of bread and leave them in the refrigerator for 10 minutes or until required.

2 Meanwhile, place the pine kernels on a baking tray. Toast the pine kernels under a preheated grill for 2–3 minutes or until golden.

3 Put the bread offcuts, pine kernels, butter, garlic and oregano into a food processor and blend for about 20 seconds. Alternatively, pound the ingredients by hand with a mortar and pestle. The mixture should have a rough texture.

4 Spoon the pine kernel butter mixture into the lined tin and top with the olives. Bake in a preheated oven, 200°C/400°F/Gas Mark 6, for 10–15 minutes or until golden.

5 Transfer the tarts to serving plates and serve warm, garnished with the fresh oregano leaves.

VARIATION

Puff pastry can be used for the tarts. Use 200 g/7oz puff pastry to line 4 tart tins. Leave the pastry to chill for 20 minutes. Line the tins with the pastry and foil and bake blind for 10 minutes. Remove the foil and bake for 3–4 minutes or until the pastry is set. Cool, then continue from step 2, adding 2 tablespoons breadcrumbs to the mixture.

Aubergines & Yogurt

This is an unusual Indian dish, in that the aubergines are first baked in the oven, then cooked in a saucepan.

NUTRITIONAL INFORMATION

Calories	147	Sugars	6g
Protein	3g	Fat	11g
Carbohydrate	8g	Saturates	1g

5 mins — 1 hr 5 mins

SERVES 4

INGREDIENTS

- 2 medium aubergines
- 4 tbsp oil
- 1 onion, sliced
- 1 tsp white cumin seeds
- 1 tsp chilli powder
- 1 tsp salt
- 3 tbsp natural yogurt
- ½ tsp mint sauce
- fresh mint leaves, to garnish

1 Rinse the aubergines and pat dry with kitchen paper.

2 Place the aubergines in an ovenproof dish. Bake in a preheated oven, 160°C/425°F/Gas Mark 3, for 45 minutes. Remove the baked aubergines from the oven and leave to cool.

3 Using a spoon, scoop out the aubergine flesh and reserve.

4 Heat the oil in a heavy-based saucepan. Add the onions and cumin seeds and fry over a medium heat, stirring, for 1–2 minutes.

5 Add the chilli powder, salt, yogurt and mint sauce to the saucepan and stir well to mix. Lower the heat.

6 Add the aubergine flesh to the onion and yogurt mixture and fry over a low heat. stirring constantly, for 5–7 minutes or until all of the liquid has been completely absorbed and the mixture is quite dry.

7 Transfer the aubergine and yogurt mixture to a warmed serving dish and garnish with fresh mint leaves. Serve immediately.

3

4

5

COOK'S TIP

Rich in protein and calcium, yogurt plays an important part in Indian cooking. Thick natural yogurt most closely resembles the yogurt made in many Indian homes.

Spinach & Ricotta Shells

This is a classic combination in which the smooth, creamy cheese balances the sharper taste of the spinach.

NUTRITIONAL INFORMATION

Calories	672	Sugars	10g
Protein	23g	Fat	26g
Carbohydrate	93g	Saturates	8g

5 mins 40 mins

SERVES 4

INGREDIENTS

- 400 g/14 oz dried lumache rigate grande pasta
- 5 tbsp olive oil
- 55 g/2 oz fresh white breadcrumbs
- 125 ml/4 fl oz milk
- 300 g/10½ oz frozen spinach, defrosted and drained
- 225 g/8 oz ricotta cheese
- pinch of freshly grated nutmeg
- 400 g/14 oz canned chopped tomatoes, drained
- 1 garlic clove, crushed
- salt and pepper

1 Bring a large saucepan of lightly salted water to the boil. Add the lumache and 1 tablespoon of the olive oil, bring back to the boil and cook for 8–10 minutes until just tender, but still firm to the bite. Drain the pasta, refresh under cold running water, drain again and set aside until required.

2 Put the breadcrumbs, milk and 3 tablespoons of the remaining olive oil in a food processor and process to combine.

3 Add the spinach and ricotta cheese to the food processor and process to a smooth mixture. Transfer to a bowl, stir in the nutmeg and season with salt and pepper to taste.

4 Mix together the tomatoes, garlic and the remaining oil and spoon the mixture into the base of a large ovenproof dish.

5 Using a teaspoon, fill the lumache with the spinach and ricotta mixture and arrange them on top of the tomato mixture in the dish. Cover and bake in a preheated oven, 180°C/350°F/Gas Mark 4, for 20 minutes. Serve hot straight from the dish.

2

3

5

COOK'S TIP

Ricotta is a creamy Italian cheese traditionally made from ewes' milk whey. It is soft and white, with a smooth texture and a slightly sweet flavour. It should be used within 2–3 days of purchase.

Tricolour Timballini

An unusual way of serving pasta, these cheese moulds are excellent with a crunchy salad for a light lunch.

NUTRITIONAL INFORMATION

Calories	529	Sugars	7g
Protein	18g	Fat	29g
Carbohydrate	46g	Saturates	12g

30 mins 1 hr

SERVES 4

INGREDIENTS

- 1 tbsp butter, softened
- 55 g/2 oz dried white breadcrumbs
- 175 g/6 oz dried tricolour spaghetti, broken into 5-cm/2-inch lengths
- 3 tbsp olive oil
- 1 egg yolk
- 125 g/4½ oz Gruyère cheese, grated
- 300 ml/10 fl oz Béchamel Sauce (see page 92)
- 1 onion, finely chopped
- 1 bay leaf
- 150 ml/5 fl oz dry white wine
- 150 ml/5 fl oz passata
- 1 tbsp tomato purée
- salt and pepper
- fresh basil leaves, to garnish

1

3

6

1 Grease four 175-ml/6-fl oz cup moulds or ramekins with the butter. Evenly coat the insides with half of the breadcrumbs.

2 Bring a pan of lightly salted water to the boil. Add the spaghetti and 1 tablespoon of oil and cook for 8–10 minutes or until just tender. Drain and transfer to a mixing bowl. Add the egg yolk and cheese to the pasta and season.

3 Pour the Béchamel Sauce into the bowl containing the pasta and mix. Spoon the mixture into the ramekins and sprinkle over the remaining breadcrumbs.

4 Stand the ramekins on a baking tray and bake in a preheated oven, 220°C/425°F/Gas Mark 7, for 20 minutes. Set aside for 10 minutes.

5 Meanwhile, make the sauce. Heat the remaining oil in a pan and gently fry the onion and bay leaf for 2–3 minutes.

6 Stir in the white wine, passata and tomato purée and season with salt and pepper to taste. Simmer gently for 20 minutes until thickened. Remove and discard the bay leaf.

7 Turn the timballini out on to serving plates, garnish with the basil leaves and serve with the tomato sauce.

Gnocchi Romana

This is a traditional Italian recipe but, for a less rich version, simply omit the eggs.

NUTRITIONAL INFORMATION

Calories	709	Sugars	9g
Protein	32g	Fat	41g
Carbohydrate	58g	Saturates	25g

1¼ hrs — 45 mins

SERVES 4

INGREDIENTS

- 700 ml/1¼ pints milk
- pinch of freshly grated nutmeg
- 6 tbsp butter, plus extra for greasing
- 225 g/8 oz semolina
- 125 g/4½ oz Parmesan cheese, freshly grated
- 2 eggs, beaten
- 55 g/2 oz Gruyère cheese, grated
- salt and pepper
- fresh basil sprigs, to garnish

1 Pour the milk into a large pan and bring to the boil. Remove the pan from the heat and stir in the nutmeg, 2 tablespoons of the butter and salt and pepper to taste.

2 Gradually stir the semolina into the milk, whisking to prevent lumps from forming, and return the pan to a low heat. Simmer, stirring constantly, for about 10 minutes or until very thick.

3 Beat 55 g/2 oz of grated Parmesan cheese into the semolina mixture, then beat in the eggs. Continue beating the mixture until smooth. Set the mixture aside for a few minutes to cool slightly.

4 Spread out the cooled semolina mixture in an even layer on a sheet of baking paper or in a large, oiled baking tin, smoothing the surface with a damp spatula – it should be 1 cm/½ inch thick. Set aside to cool completely, then chill in the refrigerator for 1 hour.

5 Once chilled, cut out rounds of gnocchi, measuring about 4 cm/1½ inches in diameter, using a plain, greased pastry cutter.

6 Grease a shallow ovenproof dish or 4 individual ovenproof dishes. Arrange the gnocchi trimmings over the base of the dish or dishes and then cover them with the rounds of gnocchi, overlapping them slightly.

7 Melt the remaining butter and drizzle it over the gnocchi. Sprinkle over the remaining Parmesan cheese, then sprinkle the Gruyère cheese evenly over the top of the dish.

8 Bake in a preheated oven, 200°C/400°F/Gas Mark 6, for 25–30 minutes, until the top is crisp and golden brown. Serve hot, garnished with the basil.

2

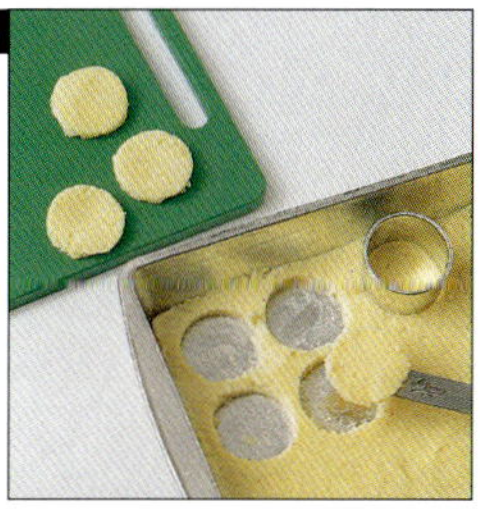
5

7

Three Cheese Bake

Serve this dish while the cheese is still hot and melted, as cooked cheese turns very rubbery if it is allowed to cool down.

NUTRITIONAL INFORMATION

Calories	710	Sugars	6g
Protein	34g	Fat	30g
Carbohydrate	80g	Saturates	16g

5 mins · 1 hr

SERVES 4

INGREDIENTS

- butter, for greasing
- 400 g/14 oz dried penne pasta
- 1 tbsp olive oil
- 2 eggs, beaten
- 350 g/12 oz ricotta cheese
- 4 sprigs fresh basil
- 100 g/3½ oz mozzarella or halloumi cheese, grated
- 70 g/2½ oz Parmesan cheese, freshly grated
- salt and pepper
- fresh basil leaves, to garnish (optional)

1 Lightly grease a large ovenproof dish with butter.

2 Bring a large pan of lightly salted water to the boil. Add the penne and olive oil and cook for 8–10 minutes until just tender, but still firm to the bite. Drain the pasta, set aside and keep warm.

3 Beat the eggs into the ricotta cheese and season to taste.

4 Spoon half of the penne into the base of the prepared dish and cover with half of the basil leaves.

5 Spoon over half of the ricotta cheese mixture. Sprinkle over the mozzarella or halloumi cheese and top with the remaining basil leaves. Cover with the remaining penne and then spoon over the remaining ricotta cheese mixture. Lightly sprinkle the freshly grated Parmesan cheese over the top.

6 Bake in a preheated oven, 190°C/375°F/Gas Mark 5, for 30–40 minutes until golden brown and the cheese topping is hot and bubbling. Garnish with fresh basil leaves, if liked, and serve the bake immediately.

3

4

5

VARIATION

Try substituting smoked Bavarian cheese for the mozzarella or halloumi and grated Cheddar cheese for the Parmesan, for a slightly different, but just as delicious flavour.

Mini Cheese & Onion Tarts

Serve these delicious little savoury tarts as finger food at buffets or drinks parties. They are also excellent for picnics.

NUTRITIONAL INFORMATION

Calories	114	Sugars	1g
Protein	3g	Fat	9g
Carbohydrate	7g	Saturates	5g

45 mins — 25 mins

SERVES 12

INGREDIENTS

PASTRY

- 100 g/3½ oz plain flour
- ¼ tsp salt
- 5½ tbsp butter, cut into small pieces
- 1–2 tbsp water

FILLING

- 1 egg, beaten
- 100 ml/3½ fl oz single cream
- 50 g/1¾ oz Red Leicester cheese, grated
- 3 spring onions, finely chopped
- salt
- cayenne pepper

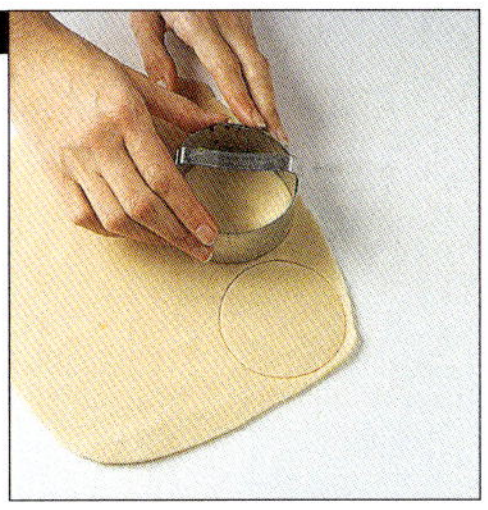

1 To make the pastry, sieve the flour and salt into a mixing bowl. Rub in the butter with your fingertips until the mixture resembles breadcrumbs. Stir in the water and mix to form a dough. Form the dough into a ball, cover with clingfilm and chill in the refrigerator for 30 minutes.

2 Roll out the pastry on a lightly floured surface. Using a 7.5-cm/3-inch biscuit cutter, stamp out 12 rounds from the pastry and line a tartlet tin.

3 To make the filling, whisk together the beaten egg, single cream, grated Red Leicester cheese and chopped spring onions in a mixing jug. Season to taste with salt and cayenne pepper.

4 Carefully pour the filling mixture into the pastry cases and bake in a preheated oven, 180°C/350°F/Gas Mark 4, for about 20–25 minutes or until the filling is just set and the pastry is golden brown. Transfer the tartlets to a warmed serving platter if serving warm or to a cooling tray if serving cold.

COOK'S TIP

If you use 175 g/6 oz of ready-made shortcrust pastry instead of making it yourself, these tarts can be made in minutes.

Mini Pizzas

Pizette, as they are known in Italy, are tiny pizzas. This quantity will make 8 individual pizzas, or 16 cocktail pizzas to go with drinks.

NUTRITIONAL INFORMATION

Calories	139	Sugars	1g
Protein	4g	Fat	6g
Carbohydrate	18g	Saturates	1g

$1\frac{1}{4}$ hrs — 15 mins

SERVES 8

INGREDIENTS

BASIC PIZZA DOUGH

- 2 tsp dried yeast
- 1 tsp sugar
- 250 ml/8 fl oz hand-hot water
- 350 g/12 oz strong plain flour
- 1 tsp salt
- 1 tbsp olive oil

TOPPING

- 2 courgettes
- 100 ml/$3\frac{1}{2}$ fl oz passata
- 75 g/$2\frac{3}{4}$ oz pancetta, diced
- 50 g/$1\frac{3}{4}$ oz black olives, stoned and chopped
- 1 tbsp mixed dried herbs
- 2 tbsp olive oil
- salt and pepper

1 Mix the yeast and sugar with 4 tablespoons of the water. Leave in a warm place for 15 minutes or until frothy.

2 Mix the flour with the salt and make a well in the centre. Add the oil, yeast mixture and remaining water. Mix into a smooth dough with a wooden spoon.

3 Turn the dough out on to a floured surface and knead for 4–5 minutes or until smooth. Return the dough to the bowl, cover with an oiled sheet of clingfilm and leave to rise for 30 minutes or until the dough has doubled in size.

4 Knead the dough for 2 minutes and divide into 8 balls. Roll out each portion thinly to form circles , then place them on an oiled baking tray, pushing out the edges until even. The dough should be no more than 5 mm/¼ inch thick because it will rise during cooking.

5 To make the topping, grate the courgettes finely. Cover them with absorbent kitchen paper and leave to stand for about 10 minutes to soak up some of the juices.

6 Spread 2–3 teaspoons of the passata over the pizza bases and top each with the grated courgettes, pancetta and olives. Season with pepper and add a sprinkling of mixed dried herbs to taste, then drizzle with olive oil.

7 Bake in a preheated oven, 200°C/400°F/Gas Mark 6, for 15 minutes or until crispy. Season with salt and pepper to taste and serve hot.

4

5

6

Vegetable Pasta Nests

These large pasta nests look impressive when presented filled with grilled mixed vegetables and taste absolutely delicious.

NUTRITIONAL INFORMATION

Calories	392	Sugars	1g
Protein	6g	Fat	28g
Carbohydrate	32g	Saturates	9g

25 mins 40 mins

SERVES 4

INGREDIENTS

- 175 g/6 oz dried spaghetti
- 1 aubergine, halved and sliced
- 1 courgette, diced
- 1 red pepper, deseeded and chopped diagonally
- 6 tbsp olive oil
- 2 garlic cloves, crushed
- 4 tbsp butter or margarine, melted, plus extra for greasing
- 15 g/½ oz dry white breadcrumbs
- salt and pepper
- fresh parsley sprigs, to garnish

3

5

6

1 Bring a saucepan of lightly salted water to the boil, add the pasta, bring back to the boil cook for 8–10 minutes until just tender. Drain and set aside.

2 Place the aubergine, courgette and pepper on a baking tray.

3 Mix the oil and garlic together and pour over the vegetables, tossing to coat all over.

4 Cook under a preheated hot grill for about 10 minutes, turning occasionally, until tender and lightly charred. Set aside and keep warm.

5 Divide the spaghetti among 4 lightly greased Yorkshire pudding tins. Using 2 forks, curl the spaghetti to form nests.

6 Brush the pasta nests with melted butter or margarine and sprinkle with the breadcrumbs. Bake in a preheated oven, 200°C/400°F/Gas Mark 6, for 15 minutes or until lightly golden. Remove the pasta nests from the tins and transfer to serving plates. Divide the grilled vegetables between the pasta nests, season to taste with salt and pepper and garnish with parsley sprigs.

COOK'S TIP

The Italian term *al dente* means 'to the bite' and describes cooked pasta that is not too soft, but still has a 'bite' to it.

Macaroni Bake

This warming and satisfying dish would make an excellent supper for a mid-week family meal on a dreary winter's day.

NUTRITIONAL INFORMATION

Calories	728	Sugars	11g
Protein	17g	Fat	42g
Carbohydrate	75g	Saturates	23g

15 mins 45 mins

SERVES 4

INGREDIENTS

- 450 g/1 lb dried short-cut macaroni
- 1 tbsp olive oil
- 4 tbsp beef dripping
- 450 g/1 lb potatoes, thinly sliced
- 450 g/1 lb onions, sliced
- 225 g/8 oz mozzarella cheese, grated
- 150 ml/5 fl oz double cream
- salt and pepper
- crusty brown bread and butter, to serve

1 Bring a large saucepan of lightly salted water to the boil. Add the macaroni and olive oil, bring back to the boil and cook for about 12 minutes or until the pasta is just tender but still firm to the bite. Drain the macaroni thoroughly and set aside.

2 Melt the beef dripping in a large flameproof casserole, then remove from the heat.

3 Make alternate layers of potatoes, onions, macaroni and grated mozzarella cheese in the casserole, seasoning well with salt and pepper between each layer and finishing with a layer of cheese on top. Finally, pour the cream over the top layer of cheese.

4 Bake in a preheated oven, 200°C/400°F/Gas Mark 6, for 25 minutes. Remove the casserole from the oven and carefully brown the top of the bake under a hot grill.

5 Serve the bake straight from the casserole with crusty brown bread and butter as a main course. Alternatively, serve as a vegetable accompaniment with your favourite main course.

VARIATION

For a stronger flavour, use *mozzarella affumicata*, a smoked version of this cheese, or Gruyère cheese, instead of the mozzarella.

Pancetta & Pecorino Cakes

This makes an excellent light meal when served with a topping of pesto or anchovy sauce and a crisp, green salad.

NUTRITIONAL INFORMATION

Calories	619	Sugars	4g
Protein	22g	Fat	29g
Carbohydrate	71g	Saturates	8g

20 mins — 25 mins

SERVES 4

INGREDIENTS

2 tbsp butter, plus extra for greasing
100 g/3½ oz pancetta, rind removed
225 g/8 oz self-raising flour
75 g/2¾ oz pecorino cheese, grated
150 ml/5 fl oz milk, plus extra for glazing
1 tbsp tomato ketchup
1 tsp Worcestershire sauce
400 g/14 oz dried farfalle pasta
1 tbsp olive oil
salt

TO SERVE

3 tbsp Pesto (see page 16) or anchovy sauce (optional)
green salad

1 Grease a baking tray with butter. Grill the pancetta until it is cooked. Allow the pancetta to cool, then chop finely.

2 Sieve together the flour and a pinch of salt into a mixing bowl. Add the butter and rub it in with your fingertips until the mixture resembles breadcrumbs. When the butter and flour have been thoroughly incorporated, add the pancetta and one-third of the grated cheese.

3 Mix together the milk, tomato ketchup and Worcestershire sauce and add to the dry ingredients, mixing to make a soft dough.

4 Roll out the dough on a lightly floured board to make an 18-cm/7-inch round. Brush with a little milk to glaze and cut into 8 wedges.

5 Arrange the dough wedges on the prepared baking tray and sprinkle over the remaining grated cheese. Bake in a preheated oven, 200°C/400°F/Gas Mark 6, for 20 minutes.

6 Meanwhile, bring a saucepan of lightly salted water to the boil. Add the farfalle and the oil and cook for 8–10 minutes until just tender, but still firm to the bite. Drain and transfer to a large serving dish. Top with the pancetta and pecorino cakes. Serve with the sauce of your choice and a green salad.

2

4

5

Fresh Tomato Tarts

These tomato-flavoured tarts should be eaten as fresh as possible to enjoy the flaky and crisp buttery puff pastry.

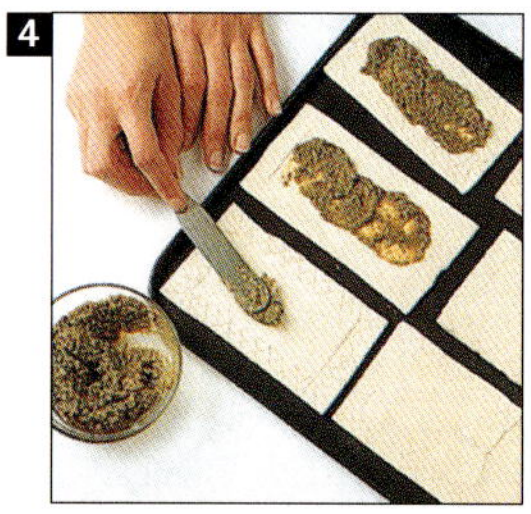

NUTRITIONAL INFORMATION

Calories	217	Sugars	3g
Protein	5g	Fat	14g
Carbohydrate	18g	Saturates	1g

35 mins · 20 mins

SERVES 6

INGREDIENTS

- 250 g/9 oz fresh ready-made puff pastry, defrosted if frozen
- 1 egg, beaten
- 2 tbsp Pesto (see page 16)
- 6 plum tomatoes, sliced
- salt and pepper
- fresh thyme leaves, to garnish (optional)

1 On a lightly floured surface, roll out the pastry to a rectangle measuring 30 x 25 cm/12 x 10 inches.

2 Cut the rectangle in half and divide each half into 3 pieces to make 6 even-size rectangles. Leave in the refrigerator to chill for 20 minutes.

3 Lightly score the edges of the pastry rectangles and brush them with the beaten egg.

4 Spread the Pesto over the rectangles, dividing it equally between them, leaving a 2½-cm/1-inch border around each one.

5 Arrange the tomato slices along the centre of each rectangle on top of the Pesto.

6 Season well with salt and pepper to taste and lightly sprinkle with fresh thyme leaves, if using.

7 Bake in a preheated oven, 200°C/400°F/Gas Mark 6, for 15–20 minutes until well risen and golden brown.

8 Transfer the tomato tarts to warm serving plates straight from the oven and serve while they are still piping hot.

VARIATION

Instead of individual tarts, roll the pastry out to form 1 large rectangle. Spoon over the Pesto and arrange the tomatoes over the top.

Provençal Tart

This tart is full of colour and flavour from the courgettes and red and green peppers. It makes a great change from a quiche Lorraine.

NUTRITIONAL INFORMATION

Calories	355	Sugars	5g
Protein	5g	Fat	29g
Carbohydrate	21g	Saturates	9g

10–15 mins   55 mins

SERVES 6

INGREDIENTS

- 250 g/9 oz fresh ready-made puff pastry, defrosted if frozen
- 3 tbsp olive oil
- 2 red peppers, deseeded and diced
- 2 green peppers, deseeded and diced
- 150 ml/5 fl oz double cream
- 1 egg
- 2 courgettes, sliced
- salt and pepper

1

2

6

1 Roll out the pastry on a lightly floured surface and line a 20-cm/8-inch loose-bottomed quiche/flan tin. Leave to chill in the refrigerator for 20 minutes.

2 Meanwhile, heat 2 tablespoons of the olive oil in a pan and fry the peppers over a low heat for about 8 minutes until softened, stirring frequently.

3 Whisk the double cream and egg together in a bowl and season to taste with salt and pepper. Stir in the cooked peppers.

4 Heat the remaining oil in a pan and fry the courgette slices over a medium heat, stirring frequently, for 4–5 minutes until lightly browned.

5 Pour the egg and pepper mixture into the pastry case.

6 Arrange the courgette slices around the edge of the tart.

7 Bake in a preheated oven, 180°C/350°F/Gas Mark 4, for 35–40 minutes or until just set and golden brown. Serve immediately or cool in the tin.

COOK'S TIP

This recipe could be used to make 6 individual tarts – use 15 x 10-cm/6 x 4-inch tins and bake them for 20 minutes.

Baked Tuna & Ricotta Rigatoni

Ribbed tubes of pasta are filled with the classic combination of tuna and ricotta cheese and then baked in a creamy sauce.

NUTRITIONAL INFORMATION

Calories	949	Sugars	5g
Protein	51g	Fat	48g
Carbohydrate	85g	Saturates	26g

10 mins　45 mins

SERVES 4

INGREDIENTS

butter, for greasing

450 g/1 lb dried rigatoni pasta

1 tbsp olive oil

200 g/7 oz canned flaked tuna, drained

225 g/8 oz ricotta cheese

125 ml/4 fl oz double cream

225 g/8 oz Parmesan cheese, freshly grated

125 g/4½ oz sun-dried tomatoes, drained and sliced

salt and pepper

1 Lightly grease a large ovenproof dish with butter.

2 Bring a large saucepan of lightly salted water to the boil. Add the rigatoni and olive oil, bring back to the boil and cook for 8–10 minutes until just tender, but still firm to the bite. Drain the pasta, rinse in cold water and set aside until cool enough to handle.

3 Meanwhile, in a bowl, mix together the flaked tuna and ricotta cheese until thoroughly combined into a soft paste. Spoon the mixture into a piping bag and use to fill the rigatoni. Arrange the filled pasta tubes side by side in a single layer in the prepared ovenproof dish.

4 To make the sauce, mix the cream and grated Parmesan cheese and season with salt and pepper to taste.

5 Spoon the sauce over the rigatoni and top with the sun-dried tomatoes, arranged in a criss-cross pattern. Bake in a preheated oven, 200°C/400°F/Gas Mark 6, for 20 minutes. Serve immediately straight from the dish.

VARIATION

For a vegetarian alternative to this recipe, simply substitute a mixture of stoned and chopped black olives and chopped walnuts for the tuna. Follow exactly the same cooking method.

Tuna Stuffed Tomatoes

Deliciously sweet roasted tomatoes are filled with home-made lemon mayonnaise and tuna in this unusual variation of a classic recipe.

NUTRITIONAL INFORMATION

Calories	196	Sugars	2g
Protein	9g	Fat	17g
Carbohydrate	2g	Saturates	3g

5–10 mins 25 mins

SERVES 4

INGREDIENTS

- 4 plum tomatoes
- 2 tbsp sun-dried tomato paste
- 2 egg yolks
- 2 tsp lemon juice
- finely grated rind of 1 lemon
- 4 tbsp olive oil
- 115g/4 oz canned tuna, drained
- 2 tbsp capers, rinsed
- salt and pepper

TO GARNISH

- 2 sun-dried tomatoes, cut into strips
- fresh basil leaves

1

3

5

1 Halve the tomatoes and scoop out the seeds. Divide the sun-dried tomato paste between the tomato halves and spread around the inside of the skin.

2 Place the tomatoes on a baking tray and roast in a preheated oven, 200°C/400°F/Gas Mark 6, for 12–15 minutes. Leave to cool slightly.

3 Meanwhile, make the mayonnaise. In a food processor, blend the egg yolks and lemon juice with the lemon rind until smooth. Once mixed and with the motor still running slowly, add the olive oil. Stop the processor as soon as the mayonnaise has thickened. Alternatively, use a hand whisk, beating the mixture continuously until it thickens.

4 Add the tuna and capers to the mayonnaise and season.

5 Spoon the tuna mayonnaise mixture into the tomato shells and garnish with sun-dried tomato strips and basil leaves. Return to the oven for a few minutes or serve chilled.

COOK'S TIP

For a picnic, do not roast the tomatoes, just scoop out the seeds and drain, cut side down, on absorbent kitchen paper for 1 hour, then fill with the mayonnaise mixture. They are firmer and easier to handle this way. If you prefer, shop-bought mayonnaise may be used instead – just stir in the lemon rind.

Roasted Seafood

Vegetables become deliciously sweet and juicy when they are roasted, and they go particularly well with fish and seafood.

NUTRITIONAL INFORMATION

Calories	280	Sugars	5g
Protein	15g	Fat	12g
Carbohydrate	28g	Saturates	2g

15 mins — 50 mins

SERVES 4

INGREDIENTS

- 600 g/1 lb 5 oz new potatoes
- 3 red onions, cut into wedges
- 2 courgettes, sliced into chunks
- 8 garlic cloves, peeled
- 2 lemons, cut into wedges
- 4 sprigs rosemary
- 4 tbsp olive oil
- 350 g/12 oz unpeeled prawns, preferably raw
- 2 small prepared squid, chopped into rings
- 4 tomatoes, quartered

1 Scrub the potatoes to remove any dirt. Cut any large potatoes in half. Place the potatoes in a large roasting tin, together with the onions, courgettes, garlic, lemon and rosemary sprigs.

2 Pour the olive oil into the roasting tin and toss to coat all of the vegetables. Cook in a preheated oven, 200°C/400°F/ Gas Mark 6, for 40 minutes, turning occasionally, until the potatoes are tender.

3 Once the potatoes are tender, add the prawns, squid rings and tomato quarters, tossing gently to coat them in the hot oil, and roast for 10 minutes. All of the vegetables should be cooked through and slightly charred for full flavour and all the prawns should have turned pink.

4 With a perforated spoon transfer the roasted seafood and vegetables to warmed individual serving plates and serve immediately.

1

1

2

VARIATION

Most vegetables are suitable for roasting in the oven. Try adding 450 g/1 lb pumpkin, squash or aubergine, if you prefer.

Pissaladière

This is a French variation of the classic Italian pizza but is made with ready-made puff pastry. It is perfect for outdoor eating.

NUTRITIONAL INFORMATION

Calories	290	Sugars	7g
Protein	7g	Fat	19g
Carbohydrate	25g	Saturates	1g

10 mins

55 mins

SERVES 8

INGREDIENTS

butter, for greasing

4 tbsp olive oil

700 g/1 lb 9 oz red onions, thinly sliced

2 garlic cloves, crushed

2 tsp caster sugar

2 tbsp red wine vinegar

350 g/12 oz fresh ready-made puff pastry, defrosted if frozen

salt and pepper

TOPPING

100 g/3½ oz canned anchovy fillets

12 stoned green olives

1 tsp dried marjoram

1 Lightly grease a Swiss roll tin. Heat the olive oil in a large, heavy-based saucepan. Add the onions and garlic and cook over a low heat for about 30 minutes, stirring occasionally.

2 Add the sugar and red wine vinegar to the pan and season with plenty of salt and pepper.

3 On a lightly floured surface, roll out the pastry to a rectangle about 33 x 23 cm/ 13 x 9 inches. Place the pastry rectangle in the prepared tin, pushing the pastry well into the corners of the tin.

4 Spread the onion mixture evenly over the pastry.

5 Arrange the anchovy fillets in a criss-cross pattern on top, place the green olives in between the anchovies, then sprinkle with the marjoram.

6 Bake in a preheated oven, 220°C/ 425°F/Gas Mark 7, for 20–25 minutes until the pissaladière is lightly golden. Serve piping hot, straight from the oven.

VARIATION

Cut the pissaladière into squares or triangles for easy finger food at a party or barbecue.

Creamy Ham Pizzas

This traditional pizza recipe uses a pastry case and a creamy sauce to make savoury flans. Grating the pastry gives it a lovely nutty texture.

NUTRITIONAL INFORMATION

Calories	628	Sugars	5g
Protein	19g	Fat	47g
Carbohydrate	35g	Saturates	16g

20 mins 40 mins

SERVES 4

INGREDIENTS

- 250 g/9 oz flaky pastry, well chilled
- 3 tbsp butter
- 1 red onion, chopped
- 1 garlic clove, chopped
- 5 tbsp plain white flour
- 300 ml/10 fl oz milk
- 50 g/1¾ oz Parmesan cheese, finely grated, plus extra for sprinkling
- 2 eggs, hard-boiled and cut into quarters
- 100 g/3½ oz Italian pork sausage, such as feline salame, cut into strips
- salt and pepper
- fresh thyme sprigs, to garnish

1 Fold the pastry in half and grate it into 4 individual flan tins measuring 10 cm/4 inches across. Using a floured fork, press the pastry flakes down so they are even, there are no holes and the pastry comes up the sides of the tins.

2 Line with foil and bake blind in a preheated oven, 220°C/425°F/Gas Mark 7, for 10 minutes. Reduce the heat to 200°C/400°F/Gas Mark 6, remove the foil and cook for 15 minutes or until golden and set.

3 Heat the butter in a pan. Add the onion and garlic and cook for 5–6 minutes or until softened.

4 Add the flour, stirring well to coat the onions. Gradually stir in the milk to make a thick sauce.

5 Season the sauce with salt and pepper to taste and then stir in the Parmesan cheese. Do not reheat once the cheese has been added or the sauce will become too stringy.

6 Spread the sauce over the pastry cases. Decorate with the egg and strips of sausage.

7 Sprinkle with a little extra Parmesan cheese, return to the oven and bake for 5 minutes, just to heat through.

8 Serve immediately, garnished with sprigs of fresh thyme.

COOK'S TIP

These pizzas are just as good cold, but do not prepare them too far in advance or the pastry will turn soggy.

Ham & Cheese Lattice Pies

These pretty lattice pies are equally delicious served hot or cold. They make a good picnic food served with salad.

NUTRITIONAL INFORMATION

Calories	257	Sugars	1g
Protein	8g	Fat	19g
Carbohydrate	16g	Saturates	5g

45 mins

20 mins

SERVES 6

INGREDIENTS

- 250 g/9 oz fresh ready-made puff pastry, defrosted if frozen
- 50 g/1¾ oz ham, finely chopped
- 125 g/4½ oz full-fat soft cheese
- 2 tbsp chopped fresh chives
- 1 egg, beaten
- 35 g/1¼ oz Parmesan cheese, freshly grated
- pepper

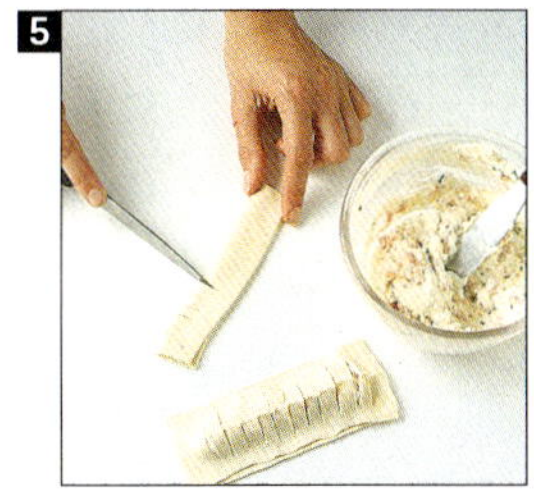

1 Roll out the pastry thinly on a lightly floured surface. Cut out 12 rectangles, each measuring 15 x 5 cm/6 x 2 inches.

2 Place the rectangles on greased baking trays and leave to chill in the refrigerator for 30 minutes.

3 Meanwhile, combine the ham, soft cheese and chives in a small bowl. Season with pepper to taste.

4 Spread the ham, cheese and chives mixture along the centre of 6 of the rectangles, leaving a 2.5-cm/1-inch border around each one. Brush the border with the beaten egg.

5 To make the lattice pattern, fold the remaining rectangles lengthways. Leaving a 2.5-cm/1-inch border, cut vertical lines across the folded edge of the pastry rectangles.

6 Unfold the latticed rectangles and place them over the rectangles topped with the ham and cheese mixture on the baking trays. Seal the pastry edges well and lightly sprinkle the pies with the Parmesan cheese.

7 Bake in a preheated oven, 180°C/350°F/Gas Mark 4, for 15–20 minutes. Serve hot or cold.

COOK'S TIP

These pies can be made in advance, frozen uncooked and baked fresh when required.

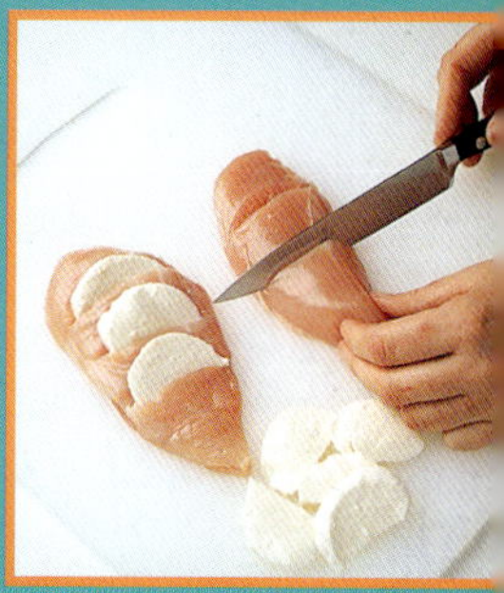

Savoury Meals

This chapter presents a mouthwatering array of savoury dishes to tempt any palate, including pies, pastries, tarts and flans, as well as a variety of delicious savoury bakes.

The choice is wide, including Cheese Pudding, Red Onion Tart Tatin and Asparagus & Cheese Tart. Fish fans can choose from a wide menu, including Smoky Fish Pie, Baked Scallops & Pasta, and Fillets of Red Mullet & Pasta. Meat and poultry dishes include Creamed Strips of Sirloin, Layered Meat Loaf and Italian Chicken Parcels.

Cheese Pudding

This savoury cheese pudding is very like a soufflé in texture, but it does not rise like a traditional soufflé.

NUTRITIONAL INFORMATION

Calories	483	Sugars	3g
Protein	15g	Fat	39g
Carbohydrate	20g	Saturates	24g

10 mins · 45 mins

SERVES 4

INGREDIENTS

- butter, for greasing
- 150 g/5½ oz fresh white breadcrumbs
- 100 g/3½ oz Gruyère cheese, grated
- 150 ml/5 fl oz hand-hot milk
- 125 g/4½ oz butter, melted
- 2 eggs, separated
- 2 tbsp chopped fresh parsley
- salt and pepper
- green salad, to serve

1 Grease a 1-litre/2-pint ovenproof dish.

2 Place the breadcrumbs and cheese in a bowl and mix. Pour the milk over the cheese and breadcrumb mixture and stir to mix. Add the melted butter, egg yolks, parsley and salt and pepper to taste. Mix well.

COOK'S TIP

For a slightly healthier alternative, make the cheese pudding with fresh wholemeal breadcrumbs instead of the white breadcrumbs.

3 Whisk the egg whites until firm, but not stiff. Gently fold the cheese mixture into the egg whites in a figure of eight movement.

4 Transfer the mixture to the prepared ovenproof dish and gently smooth the surface with a palette knife.

5 Bake the pudding in a preheated oven, 190°C/375°F/Gas Mark 5, for about 45 minutes or until golden and slightly risen, and a fine skewer inserted into the middle of the pudding comes out clean.

6 Serve the cheese pudding hot, with a green salad.

Red Onion Tart Tatin

Ready-made puff pastry works extremely well in this recipe and means you create a wonderful savoury tart in very little time.

2

3

5

NUTRITIONAL INFORMATION

Calories	398	Sugars	14g
Protein	5g	Fat	25g
Carbohydrate	40g	Saturates	7g

15 mins 50 mins

SERVES 4

INGREDIENTS

4 tbsp butter

6 tsp sugar

500 g/1 lb 2 oz red onions, peeled and quartered

3 tbsp red wine vinegar

2 tbsp fresh thyme leaves

250 g/8 oz ready-made puff pastry, defrosted if frozen

salt and pepper

1 Place the butter and sugar in a 23-cm/9-inch ovenproof frying pan and cook over a medium heat until melted and combined.

2 Add the red onion quarters and sweat them over a low heat, stirring occasionally, for 10–15 minutes until golden and caramelized.

3 Add the red wine vinegar and thyme leaves to the pan. Season with salt and pepper to taste, then simmer over a medium heat until the liquid has reduced and the red onion pieces are coated in the buttery sauce.

4 On a lightly floured surface, roll out the pastry to a circle slightly larger than the frying pan.

5 Place the pastry over the onion mixture and press down, tucking in the edges to seal it.

6 Bake in a preheated oven, 180°C/350°F/Gas Mark 4, for 20–25 minutes until the pastry is firm and golden brown. Remove the tart from the oven and leave to stand for 10 minutes.

7 To turn out, place a serving plate over the frying pan and, holding the m firmly together, carefully invert them both so that the pastry becomes the base of the tart. Serve the tart warm.

VARIATION

Replace the red onions with shallots, leaving them whole, if you prefer.

Asparagus & Cheese Tart

Fresh asparagus is now readily available all year round, so you can make this tasty supper dish at any time.

NUTRITIONAL INFORMATION	
Calories 360	Sugars 4g
Protein 11g	Fat 25g
Carbohydrate ...23g	Saturates 10g

5–10 mins

50 mins

SERVES 6

INGREDIENTS

- 250 g/9 oz fresh ready-made shortcrust pastry, defrosted if frozen
- 250 g/9 oz asparagus
- 1 tbsp vegetable oil
- 1 red onion, finely chopped
- 25 g/1 oz hazelnuts, chopped
- 200 g/7 oz goat's cheese
- 2 eggs, beaten
- 4 tbsp single cream
- salt and pepper

1 On a lightly floured surface, roll out the pastry and line a 24-cm/9½-inch loose-bottomed quiche/flan tin. Prick the base of the pastry with a fork and chill in the refrigerator for 30 minutes.

2 Line the pastry case with foil and baking beans and bake in a preheated oven, 190°C/375°F/Gas Mark 5, for about 15 minutes.

3 Remove the foil and baking beans and cook for a further 15 minutes.

4 Cook the asparagus in boiling water for 2–3 minutes, drain and cut into bite-size pieces.

5 Heat the oil in a small frying pan and fry the onion over a low heat, stirring occasionally, until soft and lightly golden. Spoon the asparagus, onion and hazelnuts into the prepared pastry case.

6 Beat together the cheese, eggs and cream until smooth or process in a blender until smooth. Season well with salt and pepper, then pour the mixture over the asparagus, onion and hazelnuts.

7 Bake in the oven for 15–20 minutes or until the cheese filling is just set. Serve warm or cold.

VARIATION

Omit the hazelnuts and sprinkle grated Parmesan cheese over the top of the tart just before cooking in the oven, if you prefer.

Celery & Onion Pies

These savoury celery and onion pies are quite irresistible, so it is probably a good idea to bake a double batch!

NUTRITIONAL INFORMATION

Calories	102	Sugars	1g
Protein	2g	Fat	6g
Carbohydrate	10g	Saturates	4g

1¼ hrs — 15–20 mins

MAKES 12

INGREDIENTS

PASTRY

- 125 g/4½ oz plain flour
- ½ tsp salt
- 2 tbsp butter, cut into small pieces
- 25 g/1 oz mature cheese, grated
- 3–4 tbsp water

FILLING

- 4 tbsp butter
- 125 g/4½ oz celery, finely chopped
- 2 garlic cloves, crushed
- 1 small onion, finely chopped
- 1 tbsp plain flour
- 50 ml/2 fl oz milk
- salt
- pinch of cayenne pepper

2

5

5

1 First, make the filling. Melt the butter in a frying pan. Add the celery, garlic and onion and fry over a moderate heat, stirring occasionally, for about 5 minutes or until softened.

2 Reduce the heat and stir in the flour, then the milk. Bring back to a simmer, then heat gently until the mixture is thick, stirring frequently. Season to taste with salt and cayenne pepper. Leave to cool.

3 To make the pastry, sieve the flour and salt into a mixing bowl and rub in the butter with your fingertips. Stir the cheese into the mixture together with the cold water and mix to form a dough.

4 Roll out three-quarters of the dough on a lightly floured surface. Using a 6-cm/2½-inch fluted biscuit cutter, cut out 12 circles. Line a tartlet tin with the pastry circles.

5 Divide the filling between the pastry cases. Roll out the remaining dough and, using a 5-cm/2-inch cutter, cut out 12 circles. Place the smaller circles on top of the pie filling and seal well. Make a slit in each pie and chill for 30 minutes.

6 Bake in a preheated oven, 220°C/425°F/Gas Mark 7, for 15-20 minutes. Leave to cool in the tin for 10 minutes before turning out. Serve warm.

Onion Tart

This crisp pastry case is filled with a tasty mixture of onions and cheese and baked until it melts in the mouth.

NUTRITIONAL INFORMATION

Calories	394	Sugars	7g
Protein	11g	Fat	27g
Carbohydrate	29g	Saturates	12g

5 mins | 55 mins

SERVES 4

INGREDIENTS

- 250 g/9 oz fresh ready-made shortcrust pastry, defrosted if frozen
- 3 tbsp butter
- 75 g/2¾ oz bacon, chopped
- 700 g/1lb 9 oz onions, peeled and thinly sliced
- 2 eggs, beaten
- 50 g/1¾ oz Parmesan cheese, freshly grated
- 1 tsp dried sage
- salt and pepper

1 Roll out the pastry on a lightly floured work surface and line a 24-cm/9½-inch loose-bottomed quiche/ flan tin.

2 Prick the base of the pastry with a fork and leave to chill in the refrigerator for 30 minutes.

3 Meanwhile, heat the butter in a saucepan, add the chopped bacon and sliced onions and sweat them over a low heat for about 25 minutes until tender. If the onion slices start to brown, add 1 tablespoon of water to the saucepan.

4 Add the beaten eggs to the onion mixture and stir in the grated cheese and sage and season with salt and pepper to taste.

5 Spoon the bacon and onion mixture into the prepared pastry case.

6 Bake in a preheated oven, 180°C/350°F/Gas Mark 4, for 20–30 minutes or until the filling has just set and the pastry is crisp and golden.

7 Leave to cool slightly in the tin, then serve the tart warm or cold.

2

3

5

VARIATION

For a vegetarian version of this tart, replace the bacon with the same amount of chopped mushrooms.

Pizza Margherita

Pizza means 'pie' in Italian. The fresh bread dough is not difficult to make but it does take a little time.

NUTRITIONAL INFORMATION

Calories	456	Sugars	7g
Protein	16g	Fat	13g
Carbohydrate	74g	Saturates	5g

1 hr

45 mins

SERVES 4

INGREDIENTS

PIZZA DOUGH

15 g/½ oz fresh yeast

½ tsp sugar

6 tbsp hand-hot water

1 tbsp olive oil

175 g/6 oz plain flour

1 tsp salt

TOPPING

400 g/14 oz canned tomatoes, chopped

2 garlic cloves, crushed

2 tsp dried basil

1 tbsp olive oil

2 tbsp tomato purée

100 g/3½ oz mozzarella cheese, diced

35 g/1¼ oz Parmesan cheese, freshly grated

salt and pepper

1

2

3

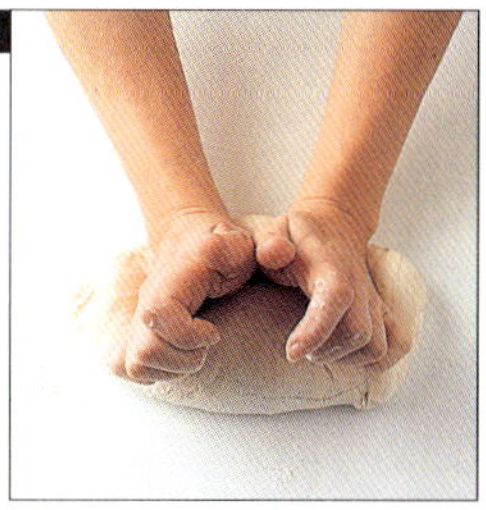

1 Mix together the yeast, sugar and 4 tablespoons of the water. Leave the yeast mixture in a warm place for 15 minutes or until frothy.

2 Mix the flour and salt and make a well in the centre. Add the oil, yeast mixture and remaining water. Mix to form a smooth dough.

3 Turn the dough out on to a floured surface and knead for 4–5 minutes or until smooth.

4 Return the dough to the bowl, cover with an oiled sheet of clingfilm and leave to rise for 30 minutes or until doubled in size.

5 Knead the dough for 2 minutes. Stretch the dough with your hands, then place it on an oiled baking tray, pushing out the edges until it forms an even circle. It should be no more than about 5 mm/¼ inch thick because it will rise during cooking.

6 To make the topping, place the tomatoes, garlic, dried basil and olive oil in a large, heavy-based frying pan and season to taste with salt and pepper. Simmer over a low heat for 20 minutes or until the sauce has thickened. Stir in the tomato purée, remove the pan from the heat and leave to cool slightly.

7 Spread the topping evenly over the pizza base almost to the rim. Top with the diced mozzarella and grated Parmesan cheese and bake in a preheated oven, 200°C/400°F/Gas Mark 6, for 20–25 minutes. Serve hot.

Gorgonzola & Pumpkin Pizza

A combination of blue Gorgonzola cheese, pumpkin and pears creates a colourful pizza. The wholemeal base adds a nutty flavour and texture.

NUTRITIONAL INFORMATION

Calories	470	Sugars	5g
Protein	17g	Fat	15g
Carbohydrate	72g	Saturates	6g

1¼ hrs — 35 mins

SERVES 4

INGREDIENTS

PIZZA DOUGH

- 7 g/¼ oz dried yeast
- 1 tsp sugar
- 250 ml/8 fl oz hand-hot water
- 175 g/6 oz plain wholemeal flour
- 175 g/6 oz strong plain white flour
- 1 tsp salt
- 1 tbsp olive oil

TOPPING

- 400 g/14 oz pumpkin or squash, peeled and cubed
- 1 tbsp olive oil
- 1 pear, cored, peeled and sliced
- 100 g/3½ oz Gorgonzola cheese
- 1 sprig fresh rosemary, to garnish

1 Place the yeast and sugar in a measuring jug and mix with 4 tablespoons of the water. Leave the yeast mixture in a warm place for about 15 minutes or until frothy.

2 Mix both of the flours with the salt and make a well in the centre. Add the oil, the yeast mixture and the remaining water. Using a wooden spoon, mix to form a dough.

3 Turn the dough out on to a floured surface and knead for 4–5 minutes or until smooth.

4 Return the dough to the bowl, cover with an oiled sheet of clingfilm and leave to rise for 30 minutes or until doubled in size.

5 Remove the dough from the bowl. Knead the dough for 2 minutes. Using a rolling pin, roll out the dough to form a long oval shape, then place it on an oiled baking tray, pushing out the edges until even. The dough should be no more than 5 mm/¼ inch thick because it will rise during cooking.

6 To make the topping, place the pumpkin in a shallow roasting tin. Drizzle with the olive oil and cook under a preheated grill for 20 minutes or until soft and lightly golden.

7 Top the dough with the pear and the pumpkin, brushing with the oil from the tin. Crumble over the Gorgonzola. Bake in a preheated oven, 200°C/400°F/Gas Mark 6, for 15 minutes or until the base is golden. Garnish with rosemary.

5

7

7

Tomato & Ricotta Pizza

This is a traditional dish from the Calabrian Mountains in southern Italy, where it is made with naturally sun-dried tomatoes and ricotta cheese.

NUTRITIONAL INFORMATION

Calories	274	Sugars	4g
Protein	8g	Fat	11g
Carbohydrate	38g	Saturates	4g

1¼ hrs 30 mins

SERVES 4

INGREDIENTS

1 quantity Basic Pizza Dough (see page 15)

TOPPING

4 tbsp sun-dried tomato paste

150g/5½ oz ricotta cheese

10 sun-dried tomatoes bottled in oil, drained

1 tbsp fresh thyme leaves

salt and pepper

1 Knead the Basic Pizza Dough on a floured surface for 2 minutes or until it is smooth and elastic.

2 Using a rolling pin, roll out the dough to form a circle, then transfer it to a lightly oiled baking tray, pushing out the edges until it forms an even circle. The dough should be no more than about 5 mm/¼ inch thick because it will rise during cooking.

3 Spread the sun-dried tomato paste evenly over the dough, then add spoonfuls of ricotta cheese dotting them over the top.

4 Cut the sun-dried tomatoes into thin strips and arrange these over the top of the pizza.

2

3

3

5 Finally, sprinkle the thyme leaves over the top of the pizza and season with salt and pepper to taste. Bake in a preheated oven, 200°C/ 400°F/Gas Mark 6, for 30 minutes or until the crust is golden. Serve hot.

COOK'S TIP

Sun-dried tomatoes are also available in packets. Before using, soak them in hot water until they are soft. Keep the tomato-flavoured soaking water to use in soups or sauces.

Mushroom Pizza

Juicy mushrooms and stringy mozzarella top this tomato-based pizza. Use wild mushrooms or a combination of wild and cultivated mushrooms.

NUTRITIONAL INFORMATION

Calories	302	Sugars	7g
Protein	10g	Fat	12g
Carbohydrate	41g	Saturates	4g

1¼ hrs — 45 mins

SERVES 4

INGREDIENTS

1 quantity Basic Pizza Dough (see page 15)

TOPPING

200 g/7 oz mushrooms

400g/14 oz canned chopped tomatoes

2 garlic cloves, crushed

1 tsp dried basil

1 tbsp olive oil

2 tbsp tomato purée

150 g/5½ oz mozzarella cheese, grated

salt and pepper

fresh basil leaves, to garnish

3

4

4

1 Knead the Basic Pizza Dough for 2 minutes.

2 Using a rolling pin, roll out the dough to form an oval or a circular shape, then place it on a lightly oiled baking tray, pushing out the edges until even. The dough should be no more than about 5 mm/¼ inch thick because it will rise during cooking.

3 Using a sharp knife, cut the mushrooms into slices.

4 To make the topping, place the tomatoes, garlic, dried basil and olive oil in a large, heavy-based frying pan and season to taste with salt and pepper. Simmer over a low heat for 20 minutes or until the sauce has thickened. Stir in the tomato purée, remove the pan from the heat and leave to cool slightly.

7 Spread the sauce over the base of the pizza, top with the mushrooms and scatter over the mozzarella. Bake in a preheated oven, 200°C/400°F/Gas Mark 6, for 25 minutes. Garnish with basil leaves.

COOK'S TIP

An easy way to intensify the mushroom flavour is to add a few dried porcini that have been soaked in hot water to the topping. Although they are expensive, you need only a few as the flavour is very concentrated.

Onion, Ham & Cheese Pizza

This pizza is a favourite of the Romans. It is slightly unusual because the topping is made without a tomato sauce base.

NUTRITIONAL INFORMATION

Calories	333	Sugars	8g
Protein	12g	Fat	14g
Carbohydrate	43g	Saturates	4g

1 hr — 40 mins

SERVES 4

INGREDIENTS

- 1 quantity Basic Pizza Dough (see page 15)

TOPPING

- 2 tbsp olive oil
- 250 g/9 oz onions, sliced into rings
- 2 garlic cloves, crushed
- 1 red pepper, deseeded and diced
- 100 g/3½ oz Parma ham, cut into strips
- 100 g/3½ oz mozzarella cheese, sliced
- 2 tbsp fresh rosemary, stalks removed and roughly chopped

3

3

5

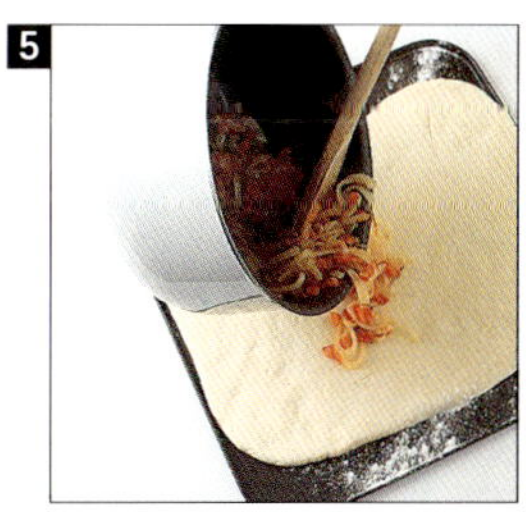

1 Knead the Basic Pizza Dough for 2 minutes.

2 Using a rolling pin, roll out the dough to form a square shape, then place it on a lightly oiled baking tray, pushing out the edges until even. The dough should be no more than about 5 mm/¼ inch thick because it will rise during cooking.

3 To make the topping, heat the olive oil in a heavy-based pan. Add the onions and garlic and cook over a low heat, stirring frequently, for 3 minutes. Add the red pepper and fry, stirring frequently, for 2 minutes.

4 Cover the pan and cook the vegetables over a low heat for 10 minutes, stirring occasionally, until the onions are slightly caramelized. Remove the pan from the heat and cool slightly.

5 Spread the topping evenly over the pizza base. Arrange the Parma ham, mozzarella and rosemary over the top.

6 Bake in a preheated oven, 200°C/400°F/Gas Mark 6, for 20–25 minutes. Serve hot.

COOK'S TIP

Parma ham, also known as prosciutto, is a classic, dry-cured, raw Italian ham. Other similar hams include prosciutto di San Daniele and prosciutto Veneto.

Tomato & Pepper Pizza

This pizza is made with a pastry base flavoured with cheese and topped with a delicious tomato sauce and roasted peppers.

NUTRITIONAL INFORMATION

Calories	611	Sugars	8g
Protein	14g	Fat	38g
Carbohydrate	56g	Saturates	21g

1½ hrs | 55 mins

SERVES 4

INGREDIENTS

- 225 g/8 oz plain flour
- 125 g/4½ oz butter, diced
- ½ tsp salt
- 35 g/1¼ oz dried grated Parmesan cheese
- 1 egg, beaten
- 2 tbsp cold water
- 2 tbsp olive oil
- 1 large onion, finely chopped
- 1 garlic clove, chopped
- 400 g/14 oz canned chopped tomatoes
- 4 tbsp tomato purée
- 1 red pepper, deseeded and halved
- 5 sprigs fresh thyme, stalks removed
- 6 black olives, stoned and halved
- 25 g/1 oz Parmesan cheese, freshly grated

1

1

3
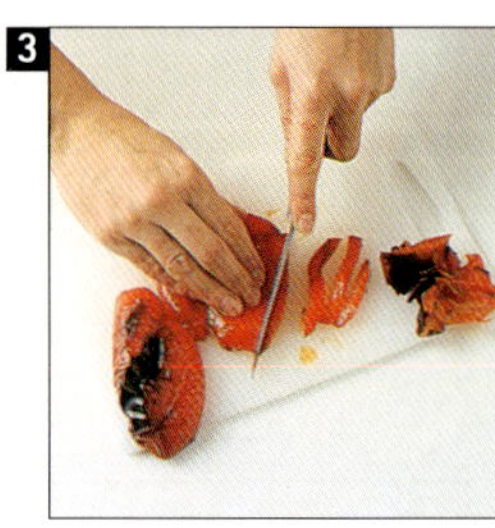

1 Sieve the flour into a bowl. Add the butter and rub in with the fingertips until the mixture resembles breadcrumbs. Stir in the salt and dried Parmesan. Add the egg and 1 tablespoon of the water and mix with a round-bladed knife. Add more water if necessary to make a soft dough. Form into a ball, cover with clingfilm and chill for 30 minutes.

2 Meanwhile, heat the oil in a frying pan and cook the onion and garlic for about 5 minutes or until golden. Add the tomatoes and cook for 8–10 minutes. Stir in the tomato purée.

3 Place the pepper, skin side up, on a baking tray and cook under a preheated grill for 15 minutes until charred. Place in a plastic bag and leave to sweat for 10 minutes. Peel off the skin and slice the flesh into thin strips.

4 Roll out the dough to fit a 23-cm/9-inch loose-bottomed fluted flan tin. Line with foil and bake in a preheated oven, 200°C/400°F/Gas Mark 6, for 10 minutes or until just set. Remove the foil and bake for a further 5 minutes until lightly golden. Leave to cool slightly.

5 Spoon the tomato sauce over the pastry base and top with the pepper, thyme, olives and fresh Parmesan. Return to the oven for 15 minutes or until the pastry is crisp. Serve warm or cold.

Green Easter Pie

This traditional Easter risotto pie is from Piedmont in northern Italy. Serve it warm or chilled in slices.

NUTRITIONAL INFORMATION

Calories	392	Sugars	3g
Protein	17g	Fat	17g
Carbohydrate	41g	Saturates	5g

25 mins 50 mins

SERVES 4

INGREDIENTS

- butter, for greasing
- 85 g/3 oz rocket leaves
- 2 tbsp olive oil
- 1 onion, chopped
- 2 garlic cloves, chopped
- 200 g/7 oz arborio rice
- 700 ml/1¼ pints hot chicken or vegetable stock
- 125 ml/4 fl oz white wine
- 50 g/1¾ oz Parmesan cheese, freshly grated
- 100 g/3½ oz frozen peas, defrosted
- 2 tomatoes, diced
- 4 eggs, beaten
- 3 tbsp fresh marjoram, chopped
- 50 g/1¾ oz fresh breadcrumbs
- salt and pepper

1 Lightly grease a 23-cm/9-inch deep cake tin and line the base.

2 Using a sharp knife, roughly chop the rocket leaves.

3 Heat the oil in a frying pan and fry the onion and garlic for 4–5 minutes or until softened.

4 Add the rice to the mixture in the frying pan, mix well to combine, then begin adding the stock a ladleful at a time. Wait until each ladleful of stock has been absorbed before adding the next.

5 Continue to cook the mixture, adding the wine, until the rice is tender. This will take at least 15 minutes. Remove the pan from the heat.

6 Stir in the Parmesan cheese, peas, rocket leaves, tomatoes, eggs and 2 tablespoons of the marjoram. Season to taste with salt and pepper.

7 Spoon the risotto into the prepared tin and level the surface by pressing down with the back of a wooden spoon.

8 Top with the breadcrumbs and the remaining marjoram.

9 Bake in a preheated oven, 180°C/350°F/Gas Mark 4, for 30 minutes or until set. Cut into slices and serve.

2

6

7

Spinach & Ricotta Pie

This puff pastry pie looks impressive, but it is actually fairly easy and quite quick to make. Serve it hot or cold.

NUTRITIONAL INFORMATION

Calories	545	Sugars	3g
Protein	19g	Fat	42g
Carbohydrate	25g	Saturates	13g

25 mins | 50 mins

SERVES 4

INGREDIENTS

- 225 g/8 oz spinach
- 25 g/1 oz pine kernels
- 100 g/3½ oz ricotta cheese
- 2 large eggs, beaten
- 50 g/1¾ oz ground almonds
- 40 g/1½ oz Parmesan cheese, freshly grated
- 250 g/9 oz puff pastry, defrosted if frozen
- 1 small egg, beaten

3

4

6

1 Rinse the spinach, place in a large pan and cook with just the water clinging to the leaves for 4–5 minutes until wilted. Drain thoroughly. When the spinach is cool enough to handle, squeeze out the excess liquid.

2 Place the pine kernels on a baking tray and lightly toast under a preheated grill for 2–3 minutes or until golden brown.

3 Place the ricotta, spinach and eggs in a bowl and mix together. Add the pine kernels, beat well, then stir in the ground almonds and Parmesan cheese.

4 Roll out the puff pastry and make 2 squares, 20 cm/8 inches wide. Trim the edges, reserving the pastry trimmings.

5 Place 1 pastry square on a baking tray. Spoon over the spinach mixture to within 1 cm/½ inch of the edge of the pastry. Brush the edges with beaten egg and place the second square over the top.

6 Using a round-bladed knife, press the pastry edges together by tapping along the sealed edge. Use the pastry trimmings to make a few leaves to decorate the pie.

7 Brush the pie with the beaten egg and bake in a preheated oven, 220°C/425°F/Gas Mark 8, for 10 minutes. Reduce the oven temperature to 190°C/375°F/Gas Mark 5 and bake for a further 25–30 minutes. Serve hot.

COOK'S TIP

Spinach must be washed very thoroughly in several changes of water to get rid of the grit and soil that can be trapped in it. Cut off any thick central ribs.

Spinach & Mushroom Lasagne

Always check the seasoning of vegetables – you can always add a little more to a recipe, but you cannot take it out once it has been added.

NUTRITIONAL INFORMATION

Calories	720	Sugars	9g
Protein	31g	Fat	52g
Carbohydrate	36g	Saturates	32g

20 mins | 40 mins

SERVES 4

INGREDIENTS

- 115 g/4 oz butter, plus extra for greasing
- 2 garlic cloves, finely chopped
- 115 g/4 oz shallots
- 225 g/8 oz wild mushrooms, such as chanterelles
- 450 g/1 lb spinach, cooked, drained and finely chopped
- 225 g/8 oz Cheddar cheese, grated
- ¼ tsp freshly grated nutmeg
- 1 tsp chopped fresh basil
- 6 tbsp plain flour
- 600 ml/1 pint hot milk
- 55 g/2 oz Cheshire cheese, grated
- 8 sheets pre-cooked lasagne
- salt and pepper

1 Lightly grease a large, rectangular or square ovenproof dish with a little butter.

2 Melt 55 g/2 oz of the butter in a large frying pan. Add the garlic, shallots and wild mushrooms and fry over a low heat, stirring occasionally, for 3 minutes.

3 Stir in the spinach, Cheddar cheese, nutmeg and basil. Season with salt and pepper to taste, remove from the heat and set aside.

4 Melt the remaining butter in a saucepan over a low heat. Add the flour and cook over a low heat, stirring constantly, for 1 minute. Gradually stir in the hot milk, whisking constantly until smooth and thickened. Remove the pan from the heat and stir in 25 g/1 oz of the Cheshire cheese and season to taste with salt and pepper.

5 Spread half of the mushroom and spinach mixture over the base of the prepared dish. Cover with a layer of lasagne and then with half of the cheese sauce. Repeat the layers and then sprinkle the remaining grated Cheshire cheese over the top.

6 Bake in a preheated oven, 200°C/400°F/Gas Mark 6, for 30 minutes or until golden brown. Serve hot.

2

3

5

VARIATION

You could substitute 4 peppers for the spinach. Roast them in a preheated oven, 200°C/400°F/Gas Mark 6, for 20 minutes. Rub off the skins under cold water, deseed and chop before using.

Vegetable Ravioli

It is important not to overcook the vegetable filling or it will become sloppy and unexciting, instead of firm to the bite and delicious.

NUTRITIONAL INFORMATION

Calories	622	Sugars	10g
Protein	12g	Fat	40g
Carbohydrate	58g	Saturates	6g

1½ hrs

55 mins

SERVES 4

INGREDIENTS

450 g/1 lb Basic Pasta Dough (see page 15)

1 tbsp olive oil

6 tbsp butter

150 ml/5 fl oz single cream

85 g/3 oz Parmesan cheese, freshly grated

fresh basil sprigs, to garnish

STUFFING

2 large aubergines

3 large courgettes

6 large tomatoes

1 large green pepper

1 large red pepper

3 garlic cloves

1 large onion

125 ml/4 fl oz olive oil

4½ tsp tomato purée

½ tsp chopped fresh basil

salt and pepper

1 To make the stuffing, cut the aubergines and the courgettes into 2.5-cm/1-inch chunks. Layer the aubergine pieces in a colander, sprinkle each layer with salt and set aside for 20 minutes. Rinse and drain, then pat dry on absorbent kitchen paper.

2 Blanch the tomatoes in boiling water for 2 minutes. Drain, peel and chop the flesh. Core and deseed the peppers and cut into 2.5-cm/1-inch dice. Chop the garlic and onion.

3 Heat the oil in a saucepan. Add the garlic and onion and fry over a low heat, stirring occasionally, for 3 minutes.

4 Stir in the aubergines, courgettes, tomatoes, peppers, tomato purée and basil. Season with salt and pepper to taste, cover and simmer for 20 minutes, stirring frequently.

5 Roll out the pasta dough and cut out 7.5-cm/3-inch rounds with a plain cutter. Put a spoonful of the vegetable stuffing on each round. Dampen the edges slightly and fold the pasta rounds over, pressing together to seal.

6 Bring a saucepan of salted water to the boil. Add the ravioli and the oil and cook for 3–4 minutes. Drain and transfer to a greased ovenproof dish, dotting each layer with butter. Pour over the cream and sprinkle over the Parmesan cheese. Bake in a preheated oven, 200°C/400°F/Gas Mark 6, for 20 minutes. Garnish and serve hot.

1

2

4

Vegetable Lasagne

This rich, baked pasta dish is packed full of vegetables, tomatoes and Italian mozzarella cheese and makes a delightful change.

NUTRITIONAL INFORMATION

Calories	510	Sugars	14g
Protein	17g	Fat	38g
Carbohydrate	28g	Saturates	14g

50 mins 50 mins

SERVES 6

INGREDIENTS

1 kg/2 lb 4 oz aubergines

125 ml/4 fl oz olive oil

2 tbsp garlic and herb butter

450 g/1 lb courgettes, sliced

225 g/8 oz mozzarella cheese, grated

600 ml/1 pint passata

6 sheets pre-cooked green lasagne

600 ml/1 pint Béchamel Sauce (see page 92)

55 g/2 oz Parmesan cheese, freshly grated

1 tsp dried oregano

salt and pepper

1 Thinly slice the aubergines and place in a colander. Sprinkle with salt and set aside for 20 minutes. Rinse, drain and pat dry with kitchen paper.

2 Heat 4 tablespoons of the oil in a large frying pan. Fry half of the aubergine slices over a low heat for 6–7 minutes or until golden. Drain thoroughly on kitchen paper. Repeat with the remaining oil and aubergine slices.

3 Melt the garlic and herb butter in the frying pan. Add the courgettes and fry over a low heat, stirring occasionally,for 5–6 minutes until golden brown all over. Drain thoroughly on kitchen paper.

4 Place half of the aubergine and courgette slices in a large ovenproof dish. Season to taste with pepper and sprinkle over half of the grated mozzarella cheese. Spoon over half of the passata and top with 3 sheets of lasagne. Repeat the layering process, ending with a layer of lasagne sheets.

5 Spoon over the Béchamel Sauce and sprinkle the grated Parmesan cheese and oregano over the top. Put the dish on a baking tray and bake in a preheated oven, 220°C/425°F/Gas Mark 7, for 30–35 minutes or until golden brown. Serve immediately.

Vermicelli & Vegetable Flan

Lightly cooked vermicelli is pressed into a flan ring and baked with a creamy mushroom filling to make an attractive, as well as tasty dish.

NUTRITIONAL INFORMATION

Calories	528	Sugars	6g
Protein	15g	Fat	32g
Carbohydrate	47g	Saturates	17g

15 mins

1 hr

SERVES 4

INGREDIENTS

- 6 tbsp butter, plus extra for greasing
- 225 g/8 oz dried vermicelli or spaghetti
- 1 tbsp olive oil
- 1 onion, chopped
- 140 g/5 oz button mushrooms
- 1 green pepper, cored, deseeded and sliced into thin rings
- 150 ml/5 fl oz milk
- 3 eggs, lightly beaten
- 2 tbsp double cream
- 1 tsp dried oregano
- freshly grated nutmeg
- 15 g/½ oz Parmesan cheese, freshly grated
- salt and pepper
- tomato and basil salad, to serve (optional)

1 Generously grease a 20-cm/8-inch loose-bottomed flan tin with butter.

2 Bring a large pan of lightly salted water to the boil. Add the vermicelli and olive oil, bring back to the boil and cook for 8–10 minutes until tender, but still firm to the bite. Drain, return to the pan, add 2 tablespoons of the butter and shake the pan to coat the pasta.

3 Press the pasta on to the base and around the sides of the flan tin to make a flan case.

4 Melt the remaining butter in a frying pan over a medium heat. Add the onion and fry over a low heat, stirring occasionally, until it is translucent.

5 Add the mushrooms and pepper rings to the frying pan and cook, stirring, for 2–3 minutes. Spoon the onion, mushroom and pepper mixture into the flan case and press it evenly into the base.

6 Beat together the milk, eggs and cream, stir in the oregano and season to taste with nutmeg and pepper. Carefully pour this mixture over the vegetables and then sprinkle with the Parmesan cheese.

7 Bake the flan in a preheated oven, 180°C/350°F/Gas Mark 4 for about 40–45 minutes or until the filling has set.

8 Carefully slide the flan out of the tin and serve warm with a tomato and basil salad, if wished.

3

5

5

Filled Aubergines

Combined with tomatoes and melting mozzarella cheese, pasta makes a tasty filling for baked aubergine shells.

NUTRITIONAL INFORMATION

Calories	342	Sugars	6g
Protein	11g	Fat	16g
Carbohydrate	40g	Saturates	4g

25 mins

55 mins

SERVES 4

INGREDIENTS

- 225 g/8 oz dried penne or other short pasta shapes
- 4 tbsp olive oil, plus extra for brushing
- 2 aubergines
- 1 large onion, chopped
- 2 garlic cloves, crushed
- 400 g/14 oz canned chopped tomatoes
- 2 tsp dried oregano
- 55 g/2 oz mozzarella cheese, thinly sliced
- 25 g/1 oz Parmesan cheese, freshly grated
- 25 g/1 oz dry breadcrumbs
- salt and pepper
- salad leaves, to serve

1 Bring a large saucepan of lightly salted water to the boil. Add the pasta and 1 tablespoon of the olive oil, bring back to the boil and then cook for 8–10 minutes or until just tender, but still firm to the bite. Drain, return to the pan, cover and keep warm.

2 Cut the aubergines in half lengthways and score around the inside with a sharp knife, being careful not to pierce the shells. Scoop out the flesh with a spoon. Brush the insides of the shells with olive oil. Chop the flesh and set aside.

3 Heat the remaining oil in a frying pan. Fry the onion until translucent. Add the garlic and fry for 1 minute. Add the chopped aubergine and fry, stirring frequently, for 5 minutes. Add the tomatoes and oregano and season to taste with salt and pepper. Bring to the boil and simmer for 10 minutes, or until thickened. Remove the pan from the heat and stir in the pasta.

4 Brush a baking tray with oil and arrange the aubergine shells in a single layer. Divide half of the tomato and pasta mixture between them. Scatter over the slices of mozzarella, then pile the remaining tomato and pasta mixture on top. Mix the Parmesan cheese and breadcrumbs and sprinkle over the top, patting it lightly into the mixture.

5 Bake in a preheated oven, 200°C/400°C/Gas Mark 6, for about 25 minutes or until the topping is golden brown. Serve hot with a selection of mixed salad leaves.

2

3

4

Macaroni & Prawn Bake

This adaptation of an 18th-century Italian dish is baked until it is golden brown and sizzling, then cut into wedges, like a cake.

NUTRITIONAL INFORMATION

Calories	576	Sugars	6g
Protein	25g	Fat	35g
Carbohydrate	42g	Saturates	19g

20 mins — 1 hr 5 mins

SERVES 4

INGREDIENTS

- 350 g/12 oz short pasta shapes, such as short-cut macaroni
- 1 tbsp olive oil, plus extra for brushing
- 6 tbsp butter, plus extra for greasing
- 2 small fennel bulbs, thinly sliced, leaves reserved
- 175 g/6 oz mushrooms, thinly sliced
- 175 g/6 oz peeled, cooked prawns
- 600 ml/1 pint Béchamel Sauce (see page 92)
- pinch of cayenne
- 55 g/2 oz Parmesan cheese, freshly grated
- 2 large tomatoes, sliced
- 1 tsp dried oregano
- salt

1 Bring a large saucepan of lightly salted water to the boil. Add the pasta and 1 tablespoon of olive oil, bring back to the boil and cook for 8–10 minutes or until just tender, but still firm to the bite. Drain the pasta in a colander, return to the pan and dot with 2 tablespoons of the butter. Shake the pan well to coat the pasta, cover and keep warm.

2 Melt the remaining butter in a large saucepan over a medium heat and fry the fennel for 3–4 minutes, stirring occasionally, until it begins to soften. Stir in the mushrooms and fry for 2 minutes. Stir in the prawns, remove the pan from the heat and set aside until required.

3 Make the Béchamel Sauce and season to taste with cayenne. Remove the pan from the heat and stir in the reserved vegetable and prawn mixture and the pasta.

4 Grease a round, shallow ovenproof dish. Pour in the pasta mixture and spread evenly. Sprinkle with the Parmesan and arrange the tomato slices in a ring around the edge of the dish. Brush the tomato with olive oil and sprinkle with the dried oregano.

5 Bake in a preheated oven, 180°C/350°F/Gas Mark 4, for 25 minutes or until golden brown. Serve hot.

Pasta & Prawn Parcels

This is the ideal dish when you have unexpected guests because the parcels can be prepared in advance, then put in the oven when you are ready to eat.

NUTRITIONAL INFORMATION

Calories	640	Sugars	1g
Protein	50g	Fat	29g
Carbohydrate	42g	Saturates	4g

15 mins · 30 mins

SERVES 4

INGREDIENTS

- 450 g/1 lb dried fettuccine
- 150 ml/5 fl oz Pesto Sauce (see page 16)
- 4 tsp extra virgin olive oil
- 750 g/1 lb 10 oz large raw prawns, peeled and deveined
- 2 garlic cloves, crushed
- 125 ml/4 fl oz dry white wine
- salt and pepper

3

3

4

1 Cut out 4 x 30-cm/12-inch squares of greaseproof paper.

2 Bring a large saucepan of lightly salted water to the boil. Add the fettuccine and cook for 2–3 minutes, until just softened. Drain and set aside.

3 Mix together the fettuccine and half of the Pesto Sauce. Spread out the paper squares and put 1 tsp olive oil in the middle of each. Divide the fettuccine between the the squares, then divide the prawns and place on top of the fettuccine.

4 Mix together the remaining Pesto Sauce and the garlic and spoon it over the prawns. Season each parcel with salt and pepper to taste and sprinkle with the white wine.

5 Dampen the edges of the greaseproof paper and wrap the parcels loosely, twisting the edges to seal.

6 Place the parcels on a baking tray and bake in a preheated oven at 200°C/400°F/Gas Mark 6 for 10–15 minutes until piping hot and the prawns have changed colour. Transfer the parcels to 4 individual serving plates and serve.

COOK'S TIP

Traditionally, these parcels are designed to look like money bags. The resemblance is more effective with greaseproof paper than with foil.

Seafood Lasagne

You can use any fish and any sauce you like in this recipe: try smoked finnan haddock and whisky sauce or cod with cheese sauce.

NUTRITIONAL INFORMATION

Calories	790	Sugars	23g
Protein	55g	Fat	32g
Carbohydrate	74g	Saturates	19g

30 mins 45 mins

SERVES 4

INGREDIENTS

- 450 g/1 lb finnan haddock fillet, skin removed and flesh flaked
- 115 g/ 4 oz prawns
- 115 g/4 oz sole fillet, skin removed and flesh sliced
- juice of 1 lemon
- 4 tbsp butter
- 3 leeks, very thinly sliced
- 6 tbsp plain flour
- about 600 ml/1 pint milk
- 2 tbsp clear honey
- 200g/7 oz mozzarella cheese, grated
- 450g/1 lb pre-cooked lasagne
- 55 g/2 oz Parmesan cheese, freshly grated
- pepper

1

3

3

1 Put the haddock fillet, prawns and sole fillet into a large bowl and season with pepper and lemon juice according to taste. Set aside while you make the sauce.

2 Melt the butter in a large saucepan. Add the leeks and cook over a low heat, stirring occasionally, for 8 minutes until softened. Add the flour and cook, stirring constantly, for 1 minute. Gradually stir in enough milk to make a thick, creamy sauce.

3 Blend in the honey and mozzarella cheese and cook for a further 3 minutes. Remove the pan from the heat and mix in the fish and prawns.

4 Make alternate layers of fish sauce and lasagne in an ovenproof dish finishing with a layer of fish sauce on top. Generously sprinkle over the grated Parmesan cheese and bake in a preheated oven,180°C/350°F/Gas Mark 4, for 30 minutes. Serve immediately.

VARIATION

For a cider sauce, substitute 1 finely chopped shallot for the leeks, 300 ml/10 fl oz cider and 300 ml/10 fl oz double cream for the milk and 1 teaspoon mustard for the honey. For a Tuscan sauce, substitute 1 chopped fennel bulb for the leeks; omit the honey.

Seafood Pizza

Make a change from the standard pizza toppings – this dish is piled high with seafood baked with a red pepper and tomato sauce.

NUTRITIONAL INFORMATION

Calories	248	Sugars	7g
Protein	27g	Fat	6g
Carbohydrate	22g	Saturates	2g

25 mins 55 mins

SERVES 4

INGREDIENTS

145 g/5 oz standard pizza base mix

4 tbsp chopped fresh dill or 2 tbsp dried dill

fresh dill, to garnish

SAUCE

1 large red pepper

400 g/14 oz canned chopped tomatoes with onion and herbs

3 tbsp tomato purée

salt and pepper

TOPPING

350 g/12 oz assorted cooked seafood, defrosted if frozen

1 tbsp capers in brine, drained

25 g/1 oz stoned black olives in brine, drained

25 g/1 oz low-fat mozzarella cheese, grated

15 g/½ oz Parmesan cheese, freshly grated

2

3

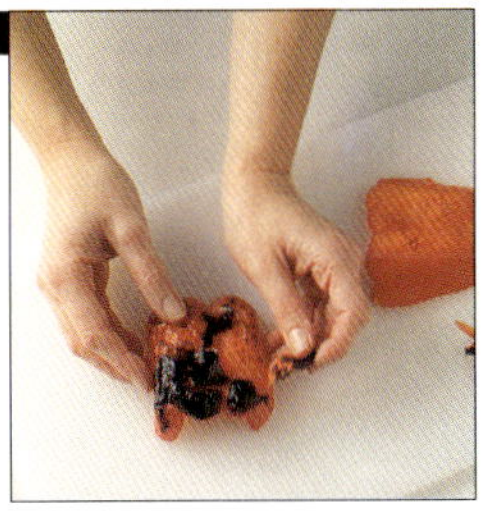

5

1 Place the pizza base mix in a bowl and stir in the chopped or dried dill. Make the dough according to the instructions on the packet.

2 Line a baking tray with baking paper. Press the pizza dough into an even round measuring about 25 cm/10 inches in diameter on the prepared baking tray. Set aside to prove.

3 Preheat the grill to hot. To make the sauce, halve and deseed the pepper and arrange on a grill rack. Cook for about 8–10 minutes until softened and charred. Leave to cool slightly, peel off the skin and chop the flesh.

4 Place the tomatoes and pepper in a saucepan. Bring to the boil, lower the heat and simmer for 10 minutes until thickened. Stir in the tomato purée and season to taste with salt and pepper.

5 Spread the sauce over the pizza base and top with the seafood. Sprinkle over the capers and olives, top with the cheeses and bake in a preheated oven, 200°C/400°F/Gas Mark 6 for 25–30 minutes. Garnish with sprigs of fresh dill and serve hot.

Smoky Fish Pie

This flavoursome and colourful fish pie is perfect for a light supper. The addition of smoked salmon gives it a touch of luxury.

NUTRITIONAL INFORMATION

Calories	523	Sugars	15g
Protein	58g	Fat	6g
Carbohydrate	63g	Saturates	2g

15 mins | 1 hr

SERVES 4

INGREDIENTS

- 900 g/2 lb smoked haddock or cod fillets
- 600 ml/1 pint skimmed milk
- 2 bay leaves
- 115 g/4 oz button mushrooms, quartered
- 115 g/4 oz frozen peas
- 115 g/4 oz frozen sweetcorn kernels
- 675 g/1½ lb potatoes, diced
- 5 tbsp low-fat natural yogurt
- 4 tbsp chopped fresh parsley
- 60 g/2 oz smoked salmon, sliced into thin strips
- 3 tbsp cornflour
- 25 g/1 oz smoked cheese, grated
- salt and pepper

1 Place the fish in a pan and add the milk and bay leaves. Bring to the boil, cover and simmer for 5 minutes. Add the mushrooms, peas and sweetcorn, bring back to a simmer, cover and cook for 5–7 minutes. Leave to cool.

1

2 Place the potatoes in a saucepan, cover with water, bring to the boil and cook for 8 minutes. Drain well and mash with a fork or a potato masher. Stir in the yogurt, parsley and seasoning. Set aside.

2

3 Using a slotted spoon, remove the fish from the pan. Flake the cooked fish away from the skin and place in an ovenproof gratin dish. Reserve the cooking liquid.

4 Drain the vegetables, reserving the cooking liquid, and gently stir into the fish with the salmon strips.

5 Blend a little cooking liquid into the cornflour to make a paste. Transfer the rest of the liquid to a saucepan and add the paste. Heat through, stirring, until thickened. Discard the bay leaves and season to taste. Pour the sauce over the fish and vegetables and mix. Spoon over the mashed potato so that the fish is covered, sprinkle with cheese and bake in a preheated oven, 200°C/400°F/Gas Mark 6, for 25–30 minutes.

5

COOK'S TIP

If possible, use smoked haddock or cod that has not been dyed bright yellow or artificially flavoured to give the illusion of having been smoked.

Prawn Pasta Bake

This dish is ideal for a substantial supper. You can use whatever pasta you like, but the tricolour varieties will give the most colourful results.

NUTRITIONAL INFORMATION

Calories	723	Sugars	9g
Protein	56g	Fat	8g
Carbohydrate	114g	Saturates	2g

10 mins   50 mins

SERVES 4

INGREDIENTS

- 225 g/8 oz tricolour pasta shapes
- 1 tbsp vegetable oil
- 175 g/6 oz button mushrooms, sliced
- 1 bunch spring onions, trimmed and chopped
- 400 g/14 oz canned tuna in brine, drained and flaked
- 175 g/6 oz peeled prawns, defrosted if frozen
- 2 tbsp cornflour
- 425 ml/15 fl oz skimmed milk
- 4 medium tomatoes, thinly sliced
- 25 g/1 oz fresh breadcrumbs
- 25 g/1 oz reduced-fat Cheddar cheese, grated
- salt and pepper

TO SERVE

- wholemeal bread
- fresh salad

1 Bring a large saucepan of lightly salted water to the boil. Add the pasta, bring back to the boil and cook for 8–10 minutes until tender, but still firm to the bite. Drain well.

2 Meanwhile, heat the oil in a large frying pan. Add the mushrooms and all but a handful of the spring onions and cook over a low heat, stirring occasionally, for 4–5 minutes until softened.

3 Place the cooked pasta in a bowl and stir in the mushroom mixture, tuna and prawns.

4 Blend the cornflour with a little milk to make a paste. Pour the remaining milk into a saucepan and stir in the paste. Heat, stirring, until the sauce begins to thicken. Season well. Stir the sauce into the pasta mixture. Transfer to an ovenproof dish and place on a baking tray.

5 Arrange the tomato slices over the pasta and sprinkle with the breadcrumbs and cheese. Bake in a preheated oven, 190°C/375°F/Gas Mark 5, for 25–30 minutes until golden. Serve sprinkled with the reserved spring onions and accompanied with bread and salad.

Baked Scallops & Pasta

This is another wonderfully tempting seafood dish which delights the eye almost as much as the tastebuds.

NUTRITIONAL INFORMATION			
Calories	725	Sugars	2g
Protein	38g	Fat	48g
Carbohydrate	38g	Saturates	25g

20 mins | 30 mins

SERVES 4

INGREDIENTS

- 12 scallops
- 3 tbsp olive oil
- 350 g/12 oz small, dried wholemeal pasta shells
- 150 ml/5 fl oz fish stock
- 1 onion, chopped
- finely grated rind and juice of 2 lemons
- 150 ml/5 fl oz double cream
- 225 g/8 oz Cheddar cheese, grated
- salt and pepper
- crusty brown bread, to serve

4

5

5

1 Remove the scallops from their shells. Scrape off the skirt and the black intestinal thread. Reserve the white part (the flesh) and the orange part (the coral), if any. Very carefully ease the flesh and coral from the shell with a short, but very strong knife.

2 Wash the shells thoroughly and dry them well. Put the shells on a baking tray, sprinkle lightly with two-thirds of the olive oil and set aside.

3 Meanwhile, bring a large saucepan of lightly salted water to the boil. Add the pasta shells and remaining olive oil, bring back to the boil and cook for 8–10 minutes or until tender, but still firm to the bite. Drain well and spoon about 25 g/1 oz of pasta into each scallop shell.

4 Put the scallops, fish stock onion and lemon rind in an ovenproof dish and season to taste with pepper. Cover with foil and bake in a preheated oven, 180°C/350°F/Gas Mark 4, for 8 minutes.

5 Remove the dish from the oven. Remove the foil and, using a perforated spoon, transfer the scallops to the shells. Add 1 tablespoon of the cooking liquid to each shell, together with a drizzle of lemon juice and a little cream, and top with the grated cheese.

6 Increase the oven temperature to 230°C/450°F/Gas Mark 8 and return the scallops to the oven for a further 4 minutes.

7 Serve the scallops in their shells with crusty brown bread and butter.

Fresh Baked Sardines

Here, fresh sardines are baked with eggs, herbs, and vegetables to form a dish rather like an elaborate omelette.

NUTRITIONAL INFORMATION

Calories	690	Sugars	12g
Protein	63g	Fat	42g
Carbohydrate	17g	Saturates	15g

35 mins

20–25 mins

SERVES 4

INGREDIENTS

- 2 tbsp olive oil
- 2 large onions, sliced into rings
- 3 garlic cloves, chopped
- 2 large courgettes, cut into sticks
- 3 tbsp fresh thyme, stalks removed
- 8 sardine fillets or about 1 kg/2 lb 4 oz sardines, filleted
- 1 cup grated parmesan cheese
- 4 eggs, beaten
- 300 ml/10 fl oz milk
- salt and pepper

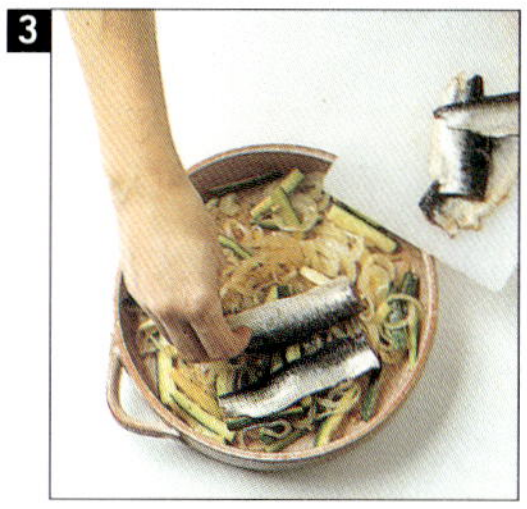

1 Heat 1 tablespoon of the olive oil in a frying pan. Add the onion rings and chopped garlic and fry over a low heat, stirring occasionally, for 2-3 minutes until soft and translucent.

2 Add the courgettes to the pan and cook, stirring occasionally, for about 5 minutes or until turning golden. Stir 2 tablespoons of the thyme leaves into the mixture and remove from the heat.

3 Place half the onions and courgettes in the base of a large ovenproof dish. Top with the sardine fillets and half the grated Parmesan cheese. Place the remaining onions and courgettes on top and sprinkle with the remaining thyme.

4 Mix the eggs and milk together in a bowl and season to taste with salt and pepper. Pour the mixture into the dish. Sprinkle the remaining Parmesan cheese over the top.

5 Bake in a preheated oven, 180°C/350°F/Gas Mark 4 for 20-25 minutes, or until golden and set. Serve the fresh baked sardines hot.

VARIATION

If you cannot find sardines that are large enough to fillet, use small mackerel instead.

Baked Trout Mexican-Style

Make this dish as hot or as mild as you like by adjusting the amount of green chilli. The red chillies are milder and add a pungency to the dish.

NUTRITIONAL INFORMATION

Calories	329	Sugars	5g
Protein	53g	Fat	10g
Carbohydrate	6g	Saturates	2g

10 mins — 30 mins

SERVES 4

INGREDIENTS

- 4 whole trout, 225 g/8 oz each
- 1 small bunch fresh coriander
- 4 shallots, finely chopped
- 1 small yellow pepper, deseeded and very finely chopped
- 1 small red pepper, deseeded and very finely chopped
- 2 green chillies, deseeded and finely chopped
- 1–2 red chillies, deseeded and finely chopped
- 1 tbsp lemon juice
- 1 tbsp white wine vinegar
- 2 tsp caster sugar
- salt and pepper
- fresh coriander, to garnish
- salad leaves, to serve

1 Wash the trout inside and out with cold running water and pat dry with kitchen paper. Season and stuff with coriander leaves.

2 Place the fish side by side in a shallow ovenproof dish. Sprinkle over the shallots, peppers and chillies.

3 Mix together the lemon juice, vinegar and sugar in a bowl. Spoon the mixture over the trout and season with salt and pepper. Cover the dish and bake in a preheated oven, 180°C/350°F/Gas Mark 4, for 30 minutes or until the fish is tender and the flesh is opaque.

4 Remove the the fish with a fish slice and drain. Transfer to warm serving plates and spoon the cooking juices over the fish. Garnish with fresh coriander and serve with salad leaves.

COOK'S TIP

Deseeding chillies reduces the degree of heat. However, this is not because the hot factor – capsaicin – is in the seeds, but because it is most concentrated in the flesh surrounding them. Removing the seeds removes most of the fiery flesh at the same time.

1

2

3

Smoked Cod Polenta

Using polenta as a crust for a gratin dish gives a lovely crispy outer texture and a smooth inside. It works well with smoked fish and chicken.

NUTRITIONAL INFORMATION

Calories	616	Sugars	3g
Protein	41g	Fat	24g
Carbohydrate	58g	Saturates	12g

30 mins 1¼ hrs

SERVES 4

INGREDIENTS

- 1.5 litres/2¾ pints water
- 350 g/12 oz instant polenta
- 200 g/7 oz chopped frozen spinach, defrosted
- 3 tbsp butter
- 50 g/1¾ oz pecorino cheese, grated
- 200 ml/7 fl oz milk
- 450 g/1 lb smoked cod fillet, skinned and boned
- 4 eggs, beaten
- salt and pepper

2

4

5

1 Bring the water to the boil in a large saucepan. Add the polenta and cook, stirring, for 30–35 minutes.

2 Stir the spinach, butter and half of the pecorino cheese into the polenta. Season to taste with salt and pepper.

3 Divide the cooked polenta between 4 individual ovenproof dishes, spreading it evenly across the bases and up the sides of the dishes.

4 In a frying pan, bring the milk to the boil. Add the fish and cook, turning once, for 8–10 minutes or until tender. Remove the fish with a perforated spoon.

5 Remove the pan from the heat. Pour the eggs into the milk in the pan and mix together.

6 Using a fork, flake the fish into smaller pieces and place it in the centre of the dishes.

7 Pour the milk and egg mixture over the fish.

8 Sprinkle with the remaining cheese and bake in a preheated oven, 190°C/375°F/Gas Mark 5, for 25–30 minutes or until set and golden. Serve hot.

VARIATION

Try using 350 g/12 oz cooked chicken breast with 2 tablespoons of chopped tarragon, instead of the smoked cod, if you prefer.

Italian Cod

Cod roasted with herbs and topped with a lemon and rosemary crust is a delicious main course that is perfect for a warm, summer's evening.

NUTRITIONAL INFORMATION

Calories	313	Sugars	0.4g
Protein	29g	Fat	20g
Carbohydrate	6g	Saturates	5g

10 mins — 35 mins

SERVES 4

INGREDIENTS

- 2 tbsp butter
- 50 g/1¾ oz wholemeal breadcrumbs
- 25 g/1 oz chopped walnuts
- grated rind and juice of 2 lemons
- 2 sprigs fresh rosemary, stalks removed
- 2 tbsp chopped fresh parsley
- 4 cod fillets, 150 g/5½ oz each
- 1 garlic clove, crushed
- 1 small red chilli, deseeded and diced
- 3 tbsp walnut oil
- salad leaves, to serve

1 Melt the butter in a large saucepan over a low heat.

2 Remove the pan from the heat and add the breadcrumbs, walnuts, the rind and juice of 1 lemon, half of the rosemary and half of the parsley.

3 Gently press the breadcrumb mixture over the top of the cod fillets. Place the cod fillets in a shallow, foil-lined roasting tin.

4 Bake in a preheated oven, 200°C/400°F/Gas Mark 6, for 25–30 minutes.

5 Mix the garlic, the remaining lemon rind and juice, rosemary and parsley and the chilli in a bowl. Beat in the walnut oil and mix to combine. Drizzle the dressing over the cod fillets as soon as they are cooked.

6 Transfer to warmed serving plates and serve with mixed salad leaves.

2

2

3

VARIATION

If preferred, the walnuts may be omitted from the crust. In addition, extra virgin olive oil can be used instead of walnut oil, if you prefer.

Orange Mackerel

Mackerel can be quite rich, but when it is stuffed with oranges and toasted ground almonds it is tangy and light.

NUTRITIONAL INFORMATION

Calories	623	Sugars	7g
Protein	42g	Fat	47g
Carbohydrate	8g	Saturates	8g

15 mins 35 mins

SERVES 4

INGREDIENTS

2 tbsp vegetable oil

4 spring onions, chopped

2 oranges

50 g/1¾ oz ground almonds

1 tbsp oats

50 g/1¾ oz mixed green and black olives, stoned and chopped

8 mackerel fillets

salt and pepper

crisp salad, to serve

1 Heat the oil in a frying pan. Add the spring onions and cook over a low heat for 2 minutes.

2 Finely grate the rind of the oranges, then, using a sharp knife, cut away the remaining skin and white pith.

3 Using a sharp knife, segment the oranges by cutting down either side of the membrane to loosen each segment. Do this over a plate so that you can catch and reserve any juices. Cut each orange segment in half.

4 Lightly toast the almonds under a preheated grill for 2–3 minutes or until golden; watch them carefully as they brown very quickly.

1

5

6

5 Mix the spring onions, oranges, ground almonds, oats and olives together in a bowl and season to taste with salt and pepper.

6 Spoon the orange mixture along the centre of each fillet. Roll up each fillet, securing it in place with a cocktail stick or skewer.

7 Bake in a preheated oven, 190°C/375°F/Gas Mark 5, for 25 minutes, until the fish is tender.

8 Transfer to serving plates and serve warm with a salad.

Cannelloni Filetti di Sogliola

This is a lighter dish than the better-known cannelloni stuffed with minced beef and would be ideal for an informal dinner party.

NUTRITIONAL INFORMATION

Calories	555	Sugars	4g
Protein	53g	Fat	21g
Carbohydrate	36g	Saturates	12g

20 mins

45 mins

SERVES 6

INGREDIENTS

- 12 small fillets of sole, 115 g/4 oz each
- 150 ml/5 fl oz red wine
- 6 tbsp butter
- 115 g/4 oz sliced button mushrooms
- 4 shallots, finely chopped
- 115 g/4 oz tomatoes, chopped
- 2 tbsp tomato purée
- 6 tbsp plain flour, sieved
- 150 ml/5 fl oz warm milk
- 2 tbsp double cream
- 6 dried cannelloni tubes
- 175 g/6 oz cooked, peeled prawns, preferably freshwater
- salt and pepper
- 1 sprig fresh fennel, to garnish

1 Brush the fillets with a little wine, season with salt and pepper and roll them up, skin side inwards. Secure with a skewer or cocktail stick.

2 Arrange the fish rolls in a single layer in a large frying pan, add the remaining red wine and poach for 4 minutes. Remove from the pan; reserve the liquid.

3 Melt the butter in another pan. Fry the mushrooms and shallots for 2 minutes, then add the tomatoes and tomato purée. Season the flour and stir it into the pan. Stir in the reserved cooking liquid and half the milk. Cook over a low heat, stirring, for 4 minutes. Remove from the heat and stir in the cream.

4 Bring a large saucepan of lightly salted water to the boil. Add the cannelloni and cook for about 8 minutes until tender, but still firm to the bite. Drain and set aside to cool.

5 Remove the skewers or cocktail sticks from the fish rolls. Put 2 sole fillets into each cannelloni tube together with 2–3 prawns and a little red wine sauce. Arrange the cannelloni in a single later in a large ovenproof dish, pour over the red wine sauce and bake in a preheated oven, 200°C/400°F/Gas Mark 6, for 20 minutes until cooked through and piping hot.

6 Serve the cannelloni immediately with the red wine sauce, garnished with the remaining prawns and a sprig of fresh fennel.

1

2

3

Spaghetti alla Bucaniera

Brill was once known as poor man's turbot, an unfair description as it is a delicately flavoured and delicious fish in its own right.

NUTRITIONAL INFORMATION

Calories	588	Sugars	5g
Protein	36g	Fat	18g
Carbohydrate	68g	Saturates	9g

25 mins   50 mins

SERVES 4

INGREDIENTS

- 85 g/3 oz plain flour
- 450 g/1 lb brill or sole fillets, skinned and chopped
- 450 g/1 lb hake fillets, skinned and chopped
- 6 tbsp butter
- 4 shallots, finely chopped
- 2 garlic cloves, crushed
- 1 carrot, diced
- 1 leek, finely chopped
- 300 ml/10 fl oz dry cider
- 300 ml/10 fl oz medium sweet cider
- 2 tsp anchovy essence
- 1 tbsp tarragon vinegar
- 450 g/1 lb dried spaghetti
- 1 tbsp olive oil
- salt and pepper
- chopped fresh parsley, to garnish
- crusty brown bread, to serve

1 Season the flour with salt and pepper. Sprinkle 25 g/1 oz of the seasoned flour on to a shallow plate. Gently press the fish pieces into the seasoned flour to coat thoroughly all over. Alternatively, put the flour in a plastic bag, add the fish pieces, a few at a time, and shake gently.

2 Melt the butter in a flameproof casserole. Add the fish fillets, shallots, garlic, carrot and leek and cook over a low heat, stirring frequently, for about 10 minutes.

3 Sprinkle over the remaining seasoned flour and cook, stirring constantly, for 2 minutes. Gradually stir in the cider, anchovy essence and tarragon vinegar and bring to the boil. Cover the casserole and transfer to a preheated oven, 180°C/350°F/Gas Mark 4, for 30 minutes.

4 About 15 minutes before the end of the cooking time, bring a large pan of lightly salted water to the boil. Add the spaghetti and olive oil, bring back to the boil and cook for about 12 minutes, until tender, but still firm to the bite. Drain the pasta thoroughly and transfer to a large, warmed serving dish.

5 Arrange the fish on top of the spaghetti and pour over the sauce. Garnish with chopped parsley and serve immediately with warm, crusty brown bread.

2

3

3

Fillets of Red Mullet & Pasta

This simple recipe perfectly complements the wonderfully sweet flavour and delicate texture of the fish.

NUTRITIONAL INFORMATION

Calories	457	Sugars	3g
Protein	39g	Fat	12g
Carbohydrate	44g	Saturates	5g

15 mins | 1 hr

SERVES 4

INGREDIENTS

1 kg/2 lb 4 oz red mullet fillets

300 ml/10 fl oz dry white wine

4 shallots, finely chopped

1 garlic clove, crushed

3 tbsp finely chopped mixed fresh herbs

finely grated rind and juice of 1 lemon

pinch of freshly grated nutmeg

3 anchovy fillets, roughly chopped

2 tbsp double cream

1 tsp cornflour

450 g/1 lb dried vermicelli

1 tbsp olive oil

salt and pepper

TO GARNISH

1 sprig fresh mint

lemon slices

lemon rind

1

2

3

1 Put the red mullet fillets in a large casserole. Pour over the wine and add the shallots, garlic, herbs, lemon rind and juice, nutmeg and anchovies. Season to taste with salt and pepper. Cover and bake in a preheated oven, 180°C/350°F/Gas Mark 4, for 35 minutes.

2 Transfer the mullet to a warm dish. Set aside and keep warm.

3 Pour the cooking liquid into a pan and bring to the boil. Simmer for 25 minutes, until reduced by half. Mix the cream and cornflour and stir into the sauce to thicken.

4 Meanwhile, bring a pan of lightly salted water to the boil. Add the vermicelli and oil, bring back to the boil and cook for 8–10 minutes until tender, but still firm to the bite. Drain the pasta and transfer to a warm serving dish.

5 Arrange the red mullet fillets on top of the vermicelli and pour over the sauce. Garnish with a fresh mint sprig, slices of lemon and strips of lemon rind and serve immediately.

Trout with Smoked Bacon

Most trout available nowadays is farmed rainbow trout. However, if you can, buy the superb-tasting wild brown trout for this recipe.

NUTRITIONAL INFORMATION

Calories	802	Sugars	8g
Protein	68g	Fat	36g
Carbohydrate	54g	Saturates	10g

35 mins 25 mins

SERVES 4

INGREDIENTS

butter, for greasing

4 whole trout, 275 g/9½ oz each, gutted and cleaned

12 anchovies in oil, drained and chopped

2 apples, peeled, cored and sliced

4 sprigs fresh mint

juice of 1 lemon

12 slices rindless smoked streaky bacon

450 g/1 lb dried tagliatelle

1 tbsp olive oil

salt and pepper

TO GARNISH

2 apples, cored and sliced

4 sprigs fresh mint

1 Grease a deep baking tray with butter.

2 Open up the cavities of each trout and rinse with warm salt water.

3 Season each cavity with salt and pepper. Divide the anchovies, sliced apples and mint sprigs between each of the cavities. Sprinkle the lemon juice into each cavity.

4 Carefully cover the whole of each trout, except the head and tail, with three slices of smoked bacon in a spiral.

5 Arrange the trout on the baking tray with the loose ends of bacon tucked underneath. Season with pepper and bake in a preheated oven, 200°C/400°F/Gas Mark 6, for 20 minutes, turning the trout over after 10 minutes.

6 Meanwhile, bring a large pan of lightly salted water to the boil. Add the tagliatelle and olive oil and cook for about 12 minutes until tender, but still firm to the bite. Drain the pasta and transfer to a large, warm serving dish.

7 Remove the trout from the oven and arrange on the tagliatelle. Garnish with sliced apples and fresh mint sprigs and serve immediately.

3

3

4

Smoked Haddock Casserole

This quick, easy and inexpensive dish would be ideal for a mid-week family supper, as it is both nourishing and filling.

NUTRITIONAL INFORMATION

Calories	525	Sugars	8g
Protein	41g	Fat	18g
Carbohydrate	53g	Saturates	10g

20 mins 45 mins

SERVES 4

INGREDIENTS

- 2 tbsp butter, plus extra for greasing
- 450 g/1 lb smoked haddock fillets, cut into 4 slices
- 600 ml/1 pint milk
- 2½ tbsp plain flour
- pinch of freshly grated nutmeg
- 3 tbsp double cream
- 1 tbsp chopped fresh parsley
- 2 eggs, hard-boiled and mashed to a pulp
- 450 g/1 lb dried fusilli pasta
- 1 tbsp lemon juice
- salt and pepper
- boiled new potatoes and beetroot, to serve

1 Thoroughly grease a casserole with butter. Put the haddock in the casserole and pour over the milk. Bake in a preheated oven, 200°C/400°F/Gas Mark 6, for about 15 minutes.

1

2 Carefully pour the cooking liquid into a jug without breaking up the fish. Set the fish aside in the casserole.

3 Melt the butter in a saucepan and stir in the flour. Gradually whisk in the reserved cooking liquid. Season to taste with salt, pepper and nutmeg. Stir in the cream, parsley and mashed hard-boiled egg and cook, stirring constantly, for 2 minutes.

3

4 Meanwhile, bring a large saucepan of lightly salted water to the boil. Add the fusilli and lemon juice, bring back to the boil and cook for 8–10 minutes until tender, but still firm to the bite.

5 Drain the pasta and spoon or tip it over the fish. Top with the egg sauce and return the casserole to the oven for 10 minutes.

5

6 Serve the casserole immediately with boiled new potatoes and beetroot.

VARIATION

You can use any type of dried pasta for this casserole. Try penne, conchiglie or rigatoni.

Quick Chicken Bake

This recipe is a type of cottage pie and is just as versatile. Add vegetables and herbs of your choice, depending on what you have at hand.

NUTRITIONAL INFORMATION

Calories	530	Sugars	8g
Protein	37g	Fat	23g
Carbohydrate	48g	Saturates	12g

1¾ hrs | 40 mins

SERVES 4

INGREDIENTS

- 500 g/1lb 2 oz minced chicken
- 1 large onion, finely chopped
- 2 carrots, finely diced
- 25 g/1 oz plain flour
- 1 tbsp tomato purée
- 300 ml/10 fl oz chicken stock
- pinch of fresh thyme
- 900 g/2 lb boiled potatoes, creamed with butter and milk and highly seasoned
- 85 g/3 oz grated Lancashire cheese
- salt and pepper
- peas, to serve

1 Dry-fry the minced chicken, onion and carrots in a non-stick saucepan over a low heat, stirring frequently, for about 5 minutes until the chicken has lost its pink colour.

2 Sprinkle the chicken with the flour and cook, stirring constantly, for a further 2 minutes.

3 Gradually blend in the tomato purée and stock, then simmer for about 15 minutes. Season to taste with salt and pepper and add the thyme.

4 Transfer the chicken and vegetable mixture to a casserole and set aside to cool completely.

5 Spoon the creamed potato over the chicken mixture and sprinkle with the Lancashire cheese. Bake in a preheated oven, 200°C/400°F/Gas Mark 6, for about 20 minutes, or until the cheese is bubbling and golden, then serve with the peas.

VARIATION

Instead of Lancashire cheese, you could sprinkle Cotswold cheese over the top. This is a tasty blend of Double Gloucester, onion and chives, and is ideal for melting as a topping. Alternatively, you could use a mixture of cheeses, depending on what you have available.

Italian Chicken Parcels

This cooking method makes the chicken aromatic and succulent, and reduces the oil needed as the chicken and vegetables cook in their own juices.

NUTRITIONAL INFORMATION

Calories	234	Sugars	5g
Protein	28g	Fat	12g
Carbohydrate	5g	Saturates	5g

25 mins 30 mins

SERVES 6

INGREDIENTS

- 1 tbsp olive oil
- 6 skinless chicken breast fillets
- 250 g/9 oz mozzarella cheese
- 500 g/1 lb 2 oz courgettes, sliced
- 6 large tomatoes, sliced
- 1 small bunch fresh basil or oregano
- pepper
- rice or pasta, to serve

1 Cut 6 pieces of foil, each measuring about 25 cm/10 inches square. Brush the foil squares lightly with oil and set aside until required.

2 Using a sharp knife, deeply slash each chicken breast 3 or 4 times at regular intervals.

3 Cut the mozzarella cheese into fairly thin slices and tuck the slices neatly between the slashes in each of the chicken breasts.

4 Divide the courgettes and tomatoes between the pieces of foil and season with pepper to taste. Tear or roughly chop the basil or oregano and scatter over the vegetables in each parcel.

5 Place the chicken on top of each pile of vegetables then wrap in the foil, tucking in the ends.

6 Place on a baking tray and bake in a preheated oven, 200°C/400°C/Gas Mark 6, for about 30 minutes.

7 To serve, unwrap each foil parcel and serve with rice or pasta.

3
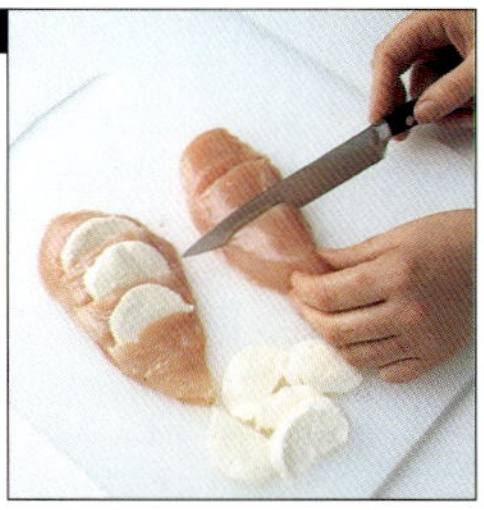

4

5

COOK'S TIP

To aid cooking, place the vegetables and chicken on the shiny side of the foil so that once the parcel is wrapped up the dull surface of the foil is facing outwards. This ensures that the heat is absorbed into the parcel and not reflected away from it.

Garlicky Chicken Cushions

Stuffed with creamy ricotta, spinach and garlic, then gently cooked in a rich tomato sauce, this chicken dish can be made ahead of time.

NUTRITIONAL INFORMATION

Calories	316	Sugars	6g
Protein	40g	Fat	13g
Carbohydrate	6g	Saturates	5g

10 mins

40 mins

SERVES 4

INGREDIENTS

- 4 part-boned chicken breasts
- 125 g/4½ oz frozen spinach, defrosted
- 150 g/5½ oz low-fat ricotta cheese
- 2 garlic cloves, crushed
- 1 tbsp olive oil
- 1 onion, chopped
- 1 red pepper, deseeded and sliced
- 425 g/15 oz canned chopped tomatoes
- 6 tbsp wine or chicken stock
- 10 stuffed olives, sliced
- salt and pepper
- flat leaf parsley sprigs, to garnish
- pasta, to serve

1 Make a slit between the skin and meat on one side of each chicken breast. Lift the skin to form a pocket, being careful to leave the skin attached to the other side.

2 Put the spinach into a sieve and press out the water with a spoon. Mix with the ricotta, half the garlic and seasoning.

3 Carefully spoon the spinach mixture under the skin of each chicken breast, then secure the edge of the skin with cocktail sticks.

4 Heat the oil in a frying pan, add the onion and fry for a minute, stirring. Add the remaining garlic and the red pepper and cook for 2 minutes. Stir in the tomatoes, wine or stock, olives and seasoning. Set the sauce aside and chill the chicken if preparing in advance.

5 Bring the sauce to the boil, pour into an ovenproof dish and arrange the chicken breasts on top in a single layer.

6 Cook, uncovered in a preheated oven, 200°C/400°F/Gas Mark 6, for about 35 minutes until the chicken is golden and cooked through. Test by making a slit in 1 of the chicken breasts with a skewer to make sure the juices run clear.

7 Spoon a little of the sauce over the chicken breasts, then transfer to serving plates and garnish with parsley. Serve with pasta.

1

3

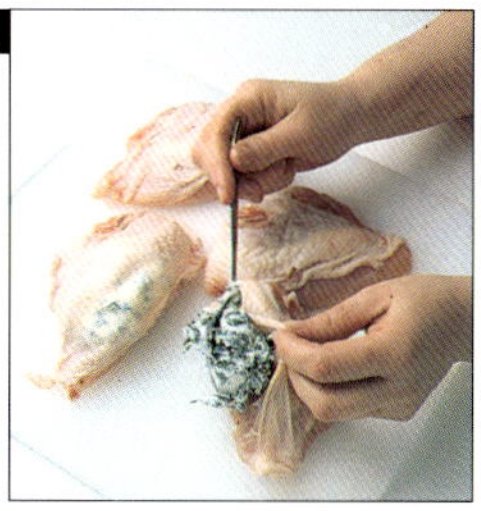

5

Parma-wrapped Chicken

Chicken breasts are stuffed with ricotta, nutmeg and spinach, then wrapped with wafer-thin slices of Parma ham and cooked in white wine.

NUTRITIONAL INFORMATION

Calories	426	Sugars	4g
Protein	44g	Fat	21g
Carbohydrate	9g	Saturates	8g

30 mins | 45 mins

SERVES 4

INGREDIENTS

- 125 g/4½ oz frozen spinach, defrosted
- 125 g/4½ oz ricotta cheese
- pinch of grated nutmeg
- 4 skinless, boneless chicken breasts, 175 g/6 oz each
- 4 slices Parma ham
- 2 tbsp butter
- 1 tbsp olive oil
- 12 small onions or shallots
- 125 g/4½ oz button mushrooms, sliced
- 1 tbsp plain flour
- 150 ml/5 fl oz dry white or red wine
- 300 ml/10 fl oz chicken stock
- salt and pepper
- carrot purée and green beans, to serve

2

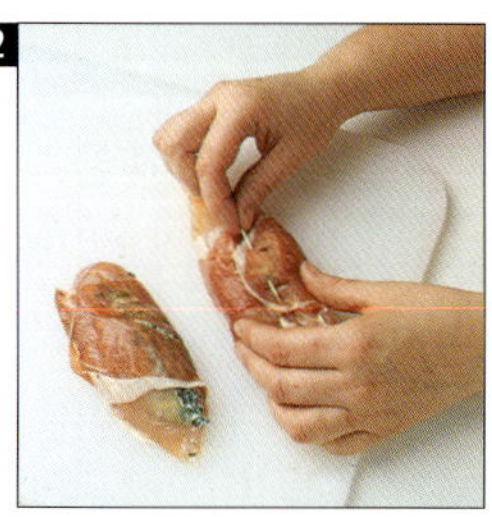

3

4

1 Put the spinach into a sieve and press out the water with a spoon. Mix with the ricotta and nutmeg and season with salt and pepper to taste.

2 Using a sharp knife, slit each chicken breast through the side and enlarge each cut to form a pocket. Fill with the spinach mixture, reshape the chicken breasts, wrap each breast tightly in a slice of ham and secure with cocktail sticks. Cover and chill in the refrigerator.

3 Heat the butter and oil in a heavy-based frying pan and brown over a low heat the chicken breasts for 2 minutes on each side. Transfer the chicken to a large, shallow ovenproof dish and keep warm until required.

4 Add the onions and mushrooms to the frying pan and fry over a medium heat, stirring occasionally, for 2–3 minutes until lightly browned. Stir in the flour, then gradually stir in the wine and stock. Bring to the boil, stirring constantly and cook until thickened. Season to taste with salt and pepper. Spoon the mixture around the chicken.

5 Cook the chicken, uncovered, in a preheated oven, 200°C/400°F/Gas Mark 6, for 20 minutes. Turn the breasts over and cook for a further 10 minutes. Remove the cocktail sticks and serve the chicken with the sauce, together with carrot purée and green beans.

Chicken with Green Olives

Olives are a popular flavouring for poultry and game in the Apulia region of Italy, where this recipe originates.

NUTRITIONAL INFORMATION

Calories	614	Sugars	6g
Protein	34g	Fat	30g
Carbohydrate	49g	Saturates	11g

15 mins

1½ hrs

SERVES 4

INGREDIENTS

- 3 tbsp olive oil
- 2 tbsp butter
- 4 chicken breasts, part boned
- 1 large onion, finely chopped
- 2 garlic cloves, crushed
- 2 red, yellow or green peppers, seeded and cut into large pieces
- 250 g/9 oz button mushrooms, sliced or quartered
- 175 g/6 oz tomatoes, peeled and halved
- 150 ml/5 fl oz dry white wine
- 175 g/6 oz stoned green olives
- 4–6 tbsp double cream
- 400 g/14 oz dried pasta
- salt and pepper
- chopped flat leaf parsley, to garnish

1

2

4

1 Heat 2 tbsp of the oil and the butter in a frying pan. Add the chicken breasts and fry until golden brown all over. Remove the chicken from the pan.

2 Add the onion and garlic to the pan and fry over a medium heat until beginning to soften. Add the peppers and mushrooms and cook for 2–3 minutes.

3 Add the tomatoes and season to taste with salt and pepper. Transfer the vegetables to a casserole and arrange the chicken on top.

4 Add the wine to the pan and bring to the boil. Pour the wine over the chicken. Cover and cook the casserole in a preheated oven, 180°C/350°F/Gas Mark 4, for 50 minutes.

5 Add the olives to the casserole and mix in. Pour in the cream, cover and return to the oven for 10–20 minutes.

6 Meanwhile, bring a large pan of lightly salted water to the boil. Add the pasta and the remaining oil, return to the boil and cook for 8–10 minutes or until tender, but still firm to the bite. Drain the pasta well and transfer to a warmed serving dish.

7 Arrange the chicken on top of the pasta, spoon over the sauce, garnish with the parsley and serve immediately. Alternatively, serve the chicken straight from the casserole, place the pasta in a large serving bowl and serve separately.

Chicken & Lobster on Penne

While this is certainly a special treat to get the tastebuds tingling, it is not quite so extravagant as it sounds.

NUTRITIONAL INFORMATION

Calories	696	Sugars	4g
Protein	59g	Fat	32g
Carbohydrate	45g	Saturates	9g

20 mins — 30 mins

SERVES 6

INGREDIENTS

- butter, for greasing
- 6 chicken suprêmes (see Cook's Tip)
- 450 g/1 lb dried penne rigate pasta
- 6 tbsp extra virgin olive oil
- 85 g/3 oz Parmesan cheese, freshly grated
- salt

FILLING

- 115 g/4 oz lobster meat, chopped
- 2 shallots, very finely chopped
- 2 figs, chopped
- 1 tbsp Marsala wine
- 25 g/1 oz fresh breadcrumbs
- 1 large egg, beaten
- salt and pepper

2

3

3

1 Grease 6 pieces of foil large enough to enclose each chicken suprême and lightly grease a baking tray.

2 Place all of the filling ingredients into a mixing bowl and blend together thoroughly with a spoon.

3 Cut a pocket in each chicken suprême with a sharp knife and fill with the lobster mixture. Wrap each chicken suprême in foil, place the parcels on the greased baking tray and bake in a preheated oven, 200°C/ 400°F/Gas Mark 6, for 30 minutes.

4 Meanwhile, bring a large pan of lightly salted water to the boil. Add the pasta and 1 tablespoon of the olive oil, bring back to the boil and cook for about 10 minutes or until tender, but still firm to the bite. Drain the pasta thoroughly and transfer to a large serving plate. Sprinkle over the remaining olive oil and the grated Parmesan cheese, then set aside and keep warm.

5 Carefully remove the foil from around the chicken suprêmes. Slice the suprêmes very thinly, arrange over the pasta and serve immediately.

COOK'S TIP

The cut of chicken known as suprême consists of the breast and wing. It is always skinned.

Italian Chicken Spirals

These little foil parcels retain all the natural juices of the chicken making a superb sauce for the pasta.

NUTRITIONAL INFORMATION

Calories	367	Sugars	1g
Protein	33g	Fat	12g
Carbohydrate	35g	Saturates	2g

20 mins 20–25 mins

SERVES 4

INGREDIENTS

4 skinless, boneless chicken breasts
25 g/1 oz fresh basil leaves
15 g/½ oz hazelnuts
1 garlic clove, crushed
250 g/9 oz wholemeal fusilli pasta
1 tbsp lemon juice
1 tbsp olive oil
2 sun-dried tomatoes in oil, drained or fresh tomatoes, diced
1 tbsp capers
55 g/2 oz stoned black olives
salt and pepper

1 Beat the chicken breasts with a rolling pin to flatten evenly.

2 Place the basil and hazelnuts in a food processor and process until finely chopped. Mix with the garlic and salt and pepper to taste.

3 Spread the basil mixture over the chicken breasts and roll up from one short end to enclose the filling. Wrap the chicken rolls tightly in foil so that they hold their shape, then seal the ends well. Place the rolls on a baking tray and bake in a preheated oven, 200°C/400°F/Gas Mark 6, for 20–25 minutes

4 Meanwhile, bring a large pan of lightly salted water to the boil. Add the fusilli, bring back to the boil and cook for 8–10 minutes or until it is tender, but still firm to the bite.

5 Drain the pasta and return to the pan with the lemon juice, olive oil, tomatoes, capers and olives. Heat through.

6 Check that the chicken is cooked through by piercing the rolls with a skewer to make sure that the juices run clear. Slice the chicken, arrange the slices over the pasta in a serving dish and serve.

2

3

5

COOK'S TIP

Sun-dried tomatoes have a wonderful, rich flavour, but if they're unavailable, use fresh tomatoes instead.

Mustard Baked Chicken

Chicken pieces are cooked in a succulent, mild mustard sauce, then coated in poppy seeds and served on a bed of fresh pasta shells.

NUTRITIONAL INFORMATION

Calories	652	Sugars	5g
Protein	51g	Fat	31g
Carbohydrate	46g	Saturates	12g

10 mins

35 mins

SERVES 4

INGREDIENTS

- 4 large or 8 small 8 chicken pieces
- 4 tbsp butter, melted
- 4 tbsp mild mustard (see Cook's Tip)
- 2 tbsp lemon juice
- 1 tbsp brown sugar
- 1 tsp paprika
- 3 tbsp poppy seeds
- 400 g/14 oz dried pasta shells
- 1 tbsp olive oil
- salt and pepper

1 Arrange the chicken pieces in a single layer in a large ovenproof dish.

2 Mix together the butter, mustard, lemon juice, sugar and paprika in a bowl and season with salt and pepper to taste. Brush the mixture over the upper surfaces of the chicken pieces and bake in a preheated oven, 200°C/400°F/Gas Mark 6, for 15 minutes.

3 Remove the dish from the oven and carefully turn over the chicken pieces. Coat the upper surfaces of the chicken with the remaining mustard mixture, sprinkle the chicken pieces with poppy seeds and return to the oven for a further 15 minutes.

4 Meanwhile, bring a large saucepan of lightly salted water to the boil. Add the pasta shells and olive oil, bring back to the boil and cook for 8–10 minutes or until tender, but still firm to the bite.

5 Drain the pasta thoroughly and divide between 4 warmed individual serving plates. Top the pasta with 1 or 2 of the chicken pieces, pour over the sauce and serve immediately.

COOK'S TIP

Dijon is the type of mustard most often used in cooking, as it has a clean and only mildly spicy flavour. German mustard has a sweet-sour taste, with Bavarian mustard being slightly sweeter. American mustard is mild and sweet.

Chicken & Ham Lasagne

You can use your favourite mushrooms, such as chanterelles or oyster mushrooms, for this delicately flavoured dish.

NUTRITIONAL INFORMATION

Calories	708	Sugars	17g
Protein	35g	Fat	35g
Carbohydrate	57g	Saturates	14g

40 mins

1¾ hrs

SERVES 4

INGREDIENTS

- butter, for greasing
- 14 sheets pre-cooked lasagne
- 900 ml/1½ pints Béchamel Sauce (see page 92)
- 85 g/3 oz Parmesan cheese, freshly grated

CHICKEN AND WILD MUSHROOM SAUCE

- 2 tbsp olive oil
- 2 garlic cloves, crushed
- 1 large onion, finely chopped
- 225 g/8 oz wild mushrooms, sliced
- 300 g/10½ oz minced chicken
- 85 g/3 oz chicken livers, finely chopped
- 115 g/4 oz Parma ham, diced
- 150 ml/5 fl oz Marsala wine
- 280 g/10 oz canned chopped tomatoes
- 1 tbsp chopped fresh basil leaves
- 2 tbsp tomato purée
- salt and pepper

2

3

4

1 To make the chicken and wild mushroom sauce, heat the olive oil in a large saucepan. Add the garlic, onion and mushrooms and cook, stirring frequently, for 6 minutes.

2 Add the minced chicken, chicken livers and Parma ham and cook over a low heat, stirring frequently, for about 12 minutes or until the meat has browned.

3 Stir the Marsala, tomatoes, basil and tomato purée into the mixture in the pan and cook for 4 minutes. Season with salt and pepper to taste, cover and simmer gently for 30 minutes. Uncover the pan, stir thoroughly and simmer for a further 15 minutes.

4 Lightly grease an ovenproof dish with butter. Arrange sheets of lasagne over the base of the dish, spoon over a layer of the chicken and wild mushroom sauce, then spoon over a layer of Béchamel Sauce. Place another layer of lasagne on top and repeat the process twice, finishing with a layer of Béchamel Sauce. Sprinkle over the grated cheese and bake in a preheated oven, 190°C/375°F/Gas Mark 5, for 35 minutes until golden brown and bubbling. Serve immediately.

Chicken Lasagne

This variation of the traditional beef dish has layers of pasta and chicken or turkey baked in red wine, tomatoes and a delicious cheese sauce.

NUTRITIONAL INFORMATION

Calories	550	Sugars	11g
Protein	35g	Fat	29g
Carbohydrate	34g	Saturates	12g

20 mins — 1¼ hrs

SERVES 4

INGREDIENTS

- 9 sheets fresh or dried lasagne
- butter, for greasing
- 1 tbsp olive oil
- 1 red onion, finely chopped
- 1 garlic clove, crushed
- 100 g/3½ oz mushrooms, wiped and sliced
- 350 g/12 oz chicken or turkey breast, cut into chunks
- 150 ml/5 fl oz red wine, diluted with 100 ml/3½ fl oz water
- 250 g/9 oz passata
- 1 tsp sugar

BECHAMEL SAUCE

- 5 tbsp butter
- 5 tbsp plain flour
- 600 ml/1 pint milk
- 1 egg, beaten
- 75 g/2¾ oz Parmesan cheese, freshly grated
- salt and pepper

1 Bring a large pan of lightly salted water to the boil. Add the sheets of lasagne and cook according to the instructions on the packet. Lightly grease a deep ovenproof dish.

2 Heat the oil in a pan. Add the onion and garlic and cook for 3–4 minutes. Add the mushrooms and chicken and stir-fry for 4 minutes or until the meat is golden brown.

3 Add the wine, bring to the boil, then lower the heat and simmer for 5 minutes. Stir in the passata and sugar and cook for 3–5 minutes until the meat is tender and cooked through. The sauce should have thickened, but still be quite runny.

4 To make the Béchamel Sauce, melt the butter in a pan, stir in the flour and cook for 2 minutes. Remove the pan from the heat and gradually add the milk, mixing to form a smooth sauce. Return the pan to the heat and bring to the boil, stirring until thickened. Leave to cool slightly, then beat in the egg and half of the cheese. Season to taste.

5 Place 3 sheets of lasagne in the base of the prepared dish and spread with half of the chicken mixture. Repeat the layers. Top with the last 3 sheets of lasagne, pour over the Béchamel Sauce and sprinkle with the grated Parmesan cheese. Bake in a preheated oven, 190°C/375°F/Gas Mark 5, for 30 minutes until golden and the pasta is cooked.

Spicy Roast Chicken

This chicken dish, ideal for dinner parties, is cooked in the oven – which is very rare in Indian cooking. The chicken can be boned, if desired.

NUTRITIONAL INFORMATION

Calories	586	Sugars	6g
Protein	34g	Fat	47g
Carbohydrate	8g	Saturates	12g

5 mins

50 mins

SERVES 4

INGREDIENTS

- 50 g/1¾ oz ground almonds
- 50 g/1¾ oz desiccated coconut
- 150 ml/5 fl oz vegetable oil
- 1 onion, finely chopped
- 1 tsp chopped fresh root ginger
- 1 tsp fresh garlic, crushed
- 1 tsp chilli powder
- 1½ tsp garam masala
- 1 tsp salt
- 150 ml/5 fl oz natural yogurt
- 4 chicken quarters, skinned
- green salad leaves, to serve

TO GARNISH

- fresh coriander leaves
- 1 lemon, cut into wedges

COOK'S TIP

If you want a spicier dish, add more chilli powder and garam masala.

1

3

5

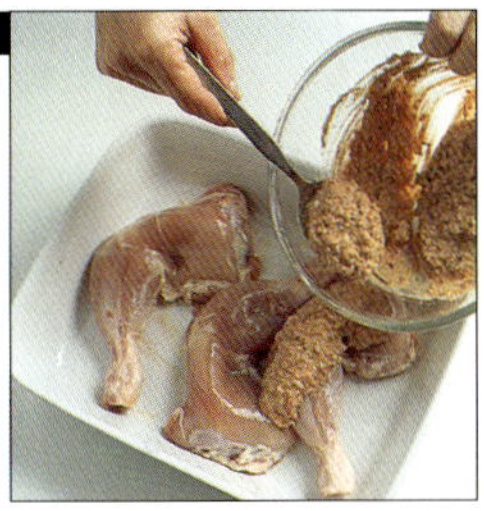

1 In a heavy-based saucepan, dry roast the ground almonds and coconut over a low heat and set aside.

2 Heat the oil in a frying pan and fry the onion over a low heat, stirring frequently, until golden brown.

3 Place the ginger, garlic, chilli powder, garam masala and salt in a bowl and mix with the yogurt. Add the almonds and coconut and mix well.

4 Add the onions to the spice mixture, blend and set aside.

5 Arrange the chicken quarters in the bottom of an ovenproof dish. Spoon the spice and yogurt mixture over the chicken sparingly.

6 Cook in a pre-heated oven, 160°C/325°F/Gas Mark 3, for 35–45 minutes. Check that the chicken is cooked thoroughly by piercing the thickest part of the meat with a sharp knife or a fine skewer – the juices will run clear when the chicken is cooked through. Transfer to a warmed serving dish, garnish with the coriander leaves and lemon wedges and serve with a salad.

Chicken with a Yogurt Crust

A spicy, Indian-style coating is baked around lean chicken to give a full flavour. Serve with a tomato, cucumber and coriander relish.

NUTRITIONAL INFORMATION

Calories	176	Sugars	5g
Protein	30g	Fat	4g
Carbohydrate	5g	Saturates	1g

10 mins | 35 mins

SERVES 4

INGREDIENTS

- 1 garlic clove, crushed
- 2 tsp finely chopped fresh root ginger
- 1 fresh green chilli, seeded and finely chopped
- 6 tbsp low-fat natural yogurt
- 1 tbsp tomato purée
- 1 tsp ground turmeric
- 1 tsp garam masala
- 1 tbsp lime juice
- 4 boneless, skinless chicken breasts, 125 g/4½ oz each
- salt and pepper
- wedges of lime or lemon, to serve

RELISH

- 4 tomatoes
- ¼ cucumber
- 1 small red onion
- 2 tbsp chopped fresh coriander

1 Place the garlic, ginger, chilli, yogurt, tomato purée, turmeric, garam masala and lime juice in a bowl and season with salt and pepper to taste. Mix thoroughly to combine all the ingredients.

2 Wash and the chicken breasts and pat dry with kitchen paper. Place them on a baking sheet.

3 Brush or spread the spicy yogurt mix all over the chicken and bake in a preheated oven, 190°C/375°F/Gas Mark 5, for 30–35 minutes until the meat is tender and cooked through.

4 Meanwhile, make the relish. Finely chop the tomatoes, cucumber and red onion and mix together with the chopped coriander in a small serving bowl. Season with salt and pepper to taste, cover with clingfilm and chill in the refrigerator until required.

5 Drain the cooked chicken on kitchen paper and serve hot with the relish and lime or lemon wedges. Alternatively, allow to cool, chill for at least 1 hour and serve sliced as part of a salad.

Crispy Stuffed Chicken

An attractive main course of chicken breasts filled with mixed peppers and set on a sea of red pepper and tomato sauce.

NUTRITIONAL INFORMATION

Calories	196	Sugars	4g
Protein	29g	Fat	6g
Carbohydrate	6g	Saturates	2g

20 mins

50 mins

SERVES 4

INGREDIENTS

4 boneless chicken breasts, 150 g/5½ oz each, skinned

4 sprigs fresh tarragon

½ small orange pepper, deseeded and sliced

½ small green pepper, deseeded and sliced

15 g/½ oz wholemeal breadcrumbs

1 tbsp sesame seeds

4 tbsp lemon juice

1 small red pepper, halved and deseeded

200 g/7 oz canned chopped tomatoes

1 small red chilli, deseeded and chopped

¼ tsp celery salt

salt and pepper

fresh tarragon, to garnish

1

3

5

1 Make a slit in each of the chicken breasts with a small, sharp knife to create a pocket. Season inside each pocket with salt and pepper.

2 Place a sprig of tarragon and a few slices of orange pepper and green pepper in each pocket. Place the chicken breasts on a non-stick baking tray and sprinkle the breadcrumbs and sesame seeds over them.

3 Spoon 1 tablespoon of lemon juice over each chicken breast and bake in a preheated oven, 190°C/375°F/Gas Mark 5, for 35–40 minutes until the chicken is tender and cooked through.

4 Meanwhile, preheat the grill to hot. Arrange the red pepper halves, skin side up, on the rack and cook for 5–6 minutes until the skin begins to char and blister. Set the grilled peppers aside to cool for about 10 minutes, then peel off the skins.

5 Put the red pepper in a blender, add the tomatoes, chilli and celery salt and process for a few seconds. Season to taste. Alternatively, finely chop the red pepper and press through a sieve with the tomatoes and chilli.

6 When the chicken is cooked, heat the sauce, spoon a little on to a warm plate and arrange a chicken breast in the centre. Garnish with tarragon and serve.

Chicken Pasta Bake

Tender lean chicken is baked with pasta in a creamy low-fat sauce which contrasts well with the fennel and the sweetness of the raisins.

NUTRITIONAL INFORMATION

Calories	380	Sugars	15g
Protein	39g	Fat	14g
Carbohydrate	27g	Saturates	6g

15 mins 45 mins

SERVES 4

INGREDIENTS

- 2 fennel bulbs
- 2 red onions, very thinly sliced
- 1 tbsp lemon juice
- 125 g/4½ oz button mushrooms
- 1 tbsp olive oil
- 225 g/8 oz dried penne pasta
- 55 g/2oz raisins
- 225 g/8 oz lean, boneless cooked chicken, skinned and shredded
- 375 g/13 oz low-fat soft cheese with garlic and herbs
- 125 g/4½ oz low-fat mozzarella cheese, thinly sliced
- 35 g/1¼ oz Parmesan cheese, freshly grated
- salt and pepper
- chopped fennel fronds, to garnish

1

5

6

1 Trim the fennel, reserving the green fronds, and slice the bulbs thinly.

2 Generously coat the onions in the lemon juice. Quarter the mushrooms.

3 Heat the oil in a large frying pan and fry the fennel, onion and mushrooms for 4–5 minutes, stirring, until just softened. Season well, transfer the mixture to a large bowl and set aside.

4 Bring a pan of lightly salted water to the boil and cook the penne according to the instructions on the packet until just cooked. Drain and mix the pasta with the vegetables.

5 Stir the raisins and chicken into the pasta mixture. Soften the soft cheese by beating it, then mix into the pasta and chicken – the heat from the pasta should make the cheese melt slightly.

6 Put the mixture into an ovenproof dish and place on a baking tray. Arrange slices of mozzarella over the top and sprinkle with the grated Parmesan.

7 Bake in a preheated oven, 200°C/400°F/Gas Mark 6, for 20–25 minutes until golden-brown.

8 Garnish with chopped fennel fronds and serve hot.

Chicken & Spinach Lasagne

A delicious pasta bake with all the colours of the Italian flag – red tomatoes, green spinach and pasta, and white chicken and sauce.

NUTRITIONAL INFORMATION

Calories	358	Sugars	12g
Protein	42g	Fat	9g
Carbohydrate	22g	Saturates	4g

25 mins 50 mins

SERVES 4

INGREDIENTS

- 350 g/12 oz frozen chopped spinach, defrosted and drained
- ½ tsp ground nutmeg
- 450 g/1 lb lean, cooked chicken meat, skinned and diced
- 4 sheets no-pre-cook lasagne verde
- 1½ tbsp cornflour
- 425 ml/15 fl oz skimmed milk
- 70 g/2½ oz Parmesan cheese, freshly grated
- salt and pepper

TOMATO SAUCE

- 400 g/14 oz canned chopped tomatoes
- 1 onion, finely chopped
- 1 garlic clove, crushed
- 150 ml/5 fl oz white wine
- 3 tbsp tomato purée
- 1 tsp dried oregano
- green salad, to serve

1

2

5

1 Preheat the oven to 200°C/400°F/Gas Mark 6. For the tomato sauce, place the tomatoes in a saucepan and stir in the onion, garlic, wine, tomato purée and oregano. Bring to the boil and simmer for 20 minutes until thick. Season well.

2 Drain the spinach again and spread it out on kitchen paper to make sure that as much water as possible is removed. Layer the spinach in the base of an ovenproof baking dish. Sprinkle with nutmeg and season.

3 Arrange the diced chicken over the spinach and spoon over the tomato sauce. Arrange the sheets of lasagne over the tomato sauce.

4 Blend the cornflour with a little of the milk to make a paste. Pour the remaining milk into a saucepan and stir in the cornflour paste. Heat for 2–3 minutes, stirring, until the sauce thickens. Season well.

5 Spoon the sauce over the lasagne and transfer the dish to a baking tray. Sprinkle the grated cheese over the sauce and bake in the oven for 25 minutes until golden brown. Serve with a green salad.

Turkey & Vegetable Loaf

This impressive-looking turkey loaf is flavoured with herbs and a layer of juicy tomatoes and covered with courgette ribbons.

NUTRITIONAL INFORMATION

Calories	165	Sugars	1g
Protein	36g	Fat	2g
Carbohydrate	1g	Saturates	0.5g

10 mins | 1¼ hrs

SERVES 6

INGREDIENTS

- 1 onion, finely chopped
- 1 garlic clove, crushed
- 900 g/2 lb lean minced turkey
- 1 tbsp chopped fresh parsley
- 1 tbsp chopped fresh chives
- 1 tbsp chopped fresh tarragon
- 1 egg white, lightly beaten
- 2 courgettes, 1 medium, 1 large
- 2 tomatoes
- salt and pepper
- tomato and herb sauce, to serve (optional)

1 Line a non-stick loaf tin with baking paper. Place the onion, garlic and turkey in a bowl, add the herbs and season to taste with salt and pepper. Mix together with your hands, then add the egg white to bind.

2 Press half of the turkey mixture into the base of the tin. Thinly slice the medium courgette and the tomatoes and arrange the slices over the meat. Top with the rest of the turkey mixture and press down firmly.

3 Cover with a layer of kitchen foil and place in a roasting tin. Pour in enough boiling water to come halfway up the sides of the loaf tin. Bake in a preheated oven, 190°C/375°F/GasMark5, for 1–1¼ hours, removing the foil for the last 20 minutes of cooking. Test that the loaf is cooked by inserting a skewer into the centre – the juices should run clear. The loaf will also shrink away from the sides of the tin.

4 Meanwhile, trim the large courgette. Using a vegetable peeler or hand-held metal cheese slice, cut the courgette lengthways into thin slices. Bring a saucepan of water to the boil and blanch the courgette ribbons for 1–2 minutes until just tender. Drain and keep warm.

5 Remove the turkey loaf from the tin and transfer to a warm serving platter. Drape the courgette ribbons over the turkey loaf and serve with a tomato and herb sauce, if liked.

2

3

4

Roast Duck with Apple

The richness of the duck meat contrasts well with the apricot sauce. If duckling portions are unavailable, use a whole bird cut into joints.

NUTRITIONAL INFORMATION

Calories	316	Sugars	38g
Protein	25g	Fat	6g
Carbohydrate	40g	Saturates	1g

10 mins 1½ hrs

SERVES 4

INGREDIENTS

- 4 duckling portions, 350 g/12 oz each
- 4 tbsp dark soy sauce
- 2 tbsp light muscovado sugar
- 2 red-skinned apples
- 2 green-skinned apples
- juice of 1 lemon
- 2 tbsp clear honey
- a few bay leaves
- salt and pepper
- assorted fresh vegetables, to serve

SAUCE

- 400 g/14 oz canned apricots in fruit juice
- 4 tbsp sweet sherry

1 Wash the duck and trim away any excess fat. Place on a wire rack over a roasting tin and prick all over with a fork or a clean, sharp needle.

1

2 Brush the duck with the soy sauce. Sprinkle over the sugar and season with pepper. Cook in a preheated oven, 190°C/375°F/Gas Mark 5, basting occasionally, for 50–60 minutes until the meat is cooked through – the juices should run clear when a skewer is inserted into the thickest part of the meat.

3 Meanwhile, core the apples and cut each into 6 wedges. Place in a small roasting tin and mix with the lemon juice and honey. Add a few bay leaves and season. Cook alongside the duck, basting occasionally, for 20–25 minutes until tender. Discard the bay leaves.

3

4 To make the sauce, place the apricots in a blender or food processor with the can juices and the sherry. Process until smooth. Alternatively, mash the apricots with a fork until smooth and mix with the juice and sherry.

4

5 Just before serving, heat the apricot purée in a small pan. Remove the skin from the duck and pat the flesh with kitchen paper to absorb any fat. Serve the duck with the apple wedges, apricot sauce and fresh vegetables.

VARIATION

Fruit complements duck perfectly. Use canned pineapple in natural juice for a delicious alternative.

Honey-Glazed Duck

Chinese-style duck is incredibly easy to prepare, but makes an impressive main course for a dinner party.

NUTRITIONAL INFORMATION

Calories	230	Sugars	9g
Protein	23g	Fat	9g
Carbohydrate	14g	Saturates	3g

2¼ hrs

30 mins

SERVES 4

INGREDIENTS

- 1 tsp dark soy sauce
- 2 tbsp clear honey
- 1 tsp garlic vinegar
- 2 garlic cloves, crushed
- 1 tsp ground star anise
- 2 tsp cornflour
- 2 tsp water
- 2 large boneless duck breasts, about 225g/8 oz each

TO GARNISH

- celery leaves
- cucumber wedges
- snipped chives

1 Mix the soy sauce, honey, garlic vinegar, garlic and star anise. Blend the cornflour with the water to form a smooth paste and stir it into the mixture.

2

4

5

2 Place the duck breasts in a shallow ovenproof dish. Brush with the soy marinade, turning them to coat completely. Cover and set aside to marinate in the refrigerator for at least 2 hours, or overnight.

3 Remove the duck from the marinade and cook in a preheated oven, 220°C/425°F/Gas Mark 7, for 20–25 minutes, basting frequently with the glaze.

4 Remove the duck from the oven and transfer to a preheated grill Grill for about 3–4 minutes to caramelize the top, without charring.

5 Remove the duck from the grill pan and cut it into thin slices. Arrange the duck slices on a warmed serving dish, garnish with celery leaves, cucumber wedges and snipped chives and serve immediately.

COOK'S TIP

If the duck begins to burn slightly while it is cooking in the oven, cover with foil. Check that the duck breasts are cooked through by inserting the point of a sharp knife into the thickest part of the flesh – the juices should run clear.

Pesto Baked Partridge

Partridge has a more delicate flavour than many game birds and this subtle sauce perfectly complements it.

NUTRITIONAL INFORMATION

Calories	895	Sugars	5g
Protein	79g	Fat	45g
Carbohydrate	45g	Saturates	18g

15 mins   40 mins

SERVES 4

INGREDIENTS

- 8 partridge pieces,115 g/4 oz each
- 4 tbsp butter, melted
- 4 tbsp Dijon mustard
- 2 tbsp lime juice
- 1 tbsp brown sugar
- 6 tbsp Pesto Sauce (see page 16)
- 450 g/1 lb dried rigatoni pasta
- 1 tbsp olive oil
- 115 g/4 oz Parmesan cheese, freshly grated
- salt and pepper

2

2

3

1 Arrange the partridge pieces, smooth side down, in a single layer in a large, ovenproof dish.

2 Mix together the butter, Dijon mustard, lime juice and brown sugar in a bowl. Season to taste with salt and pepper. Brush this mixture over the partridge pieces and bake in a preheated oven, 200°C/400°F/Gas Mark 6, for 15 minutes.

3 Remove the dish from the oven and coat the partridge pieces with 3 tablespoons of the Pesto Sauce. Return to the oven and bake for a further 12 minutes.

4 Remove the dish from the oven and carefully turn over the partridge pieces. Coat the top of the partridge with the remaining mustard mixture and return to the oven for a further 10 minutes.

5 Meanwhile, bring a large pan of lightly salted water to the boil. Add the rigatoni and olive oil and cook for 8–10 minutes until tender, but still firm to the bite. Drain and transfer to a serving dish. Toss the pasta with the remaining Pesto Sauce and the Parmesan cheese.

6 Serve the partridge with the pasta, pouring over the cooking juices.

VARIATION

You could also prepare young pheasant in the same way.

Pheasant Lasagne

This scrumptious and unusual baked lasagne is virtually a meal in itself. It is served with baby onions and green peas.

NUTRITIONAL INFORMATION

Calories	1038	Sugars	13g
Protein	65g	Fat	64g
Carbohydrate	54g	Saturates	27g

40 mins

1¼ hrs

SERVES 4

INGREDIENTS

- butter, for greasing
- 14 sheets pre-cooked lasagne
- 850 ml/1½ pints Béchamel Sauce (see page 92)
- 75 g/2¾ oz mozzarella cheese, grated

FILLING

- 225 g/8 oz pork fat, diced
- 2 tbsp butter
- 16 small onions
- 8 large pheasant breasts, thinly sliced
- 2½ tbsp plain flour
- 600 ml/1 pint chicken stock
- 1 bouquet garni
- 450 g/1 lb fresh peas, shelled
- salt

1 To make the filling, bring a saucepan of lightly salted water to the boil. Add the pork fat, bring back to the boil and simmer for 3 minutes, then drain and pat dry with kitchen paper.

2 Melt the butter in a large, heavy-based frying pan. Add the pork fat and onions to the pan and cook over a low heat, stirring occasionally, for about 3 minutes or until lightly browned.

3 Remove the pork fat and onions from the pan and set aside. Add the slices of pheasant and cook over a low heat for 12 minutes, until browned all over. Transfer to an ovenproof dish.

4 Stir the flour into the pan and cook until just brown, then blend in the stock. Pour the mixture over the pheasant, add the bouquet garni and cook in a preheated oven, 200°C/400°F/Gas Mark 6, for 5 minutes. Remove the bouquet garni. Add the onions, pork fat and peas and return to the oven for 10 minutes.

5 Put the pheasant and pork fat in a food processor and mince finely.

6 Lower the oven temperature to 190°C/375°F/Gas Mark 5. Grease an ovenproof dish with butter. Make layers of lasagne, pheasant sauce and Béchamel Sauce in the dish, ending with Béchamel Sauce. Sprinkle over the cheese and bake for 30 minutes.

2

3

5

Red Roast Pork in Soy Sauce

In this traditional Chinese dish the pork turns 'red' during cooking because it is basted in dark soy sauce.

NUTRITIONAL INFORMATION

Calories	268	Sugars	20g
Protein	26g	Fat	8g
Carbohydrate	22g	Saturates	3g

1¼ hrs

1¼ hrs

SERVES 4

INGREDIENTS

- 450 g/1 lb lean pork fillets
- 6 tbsp dark soy sauce
- 2 tbsp dry sherry
- 1 tsp Chinese five-spice powder
- 2 garlic cloves, crushed
- 2 tsp finely chopped fresh root ginger
- 1 large red pepper
- 1 large yellow pepper
- 1 large orange pepper
- 4 tbsp caster sugar
- 2 tbsp red wine vinegar

TO GARNISH

- spring onions, shredded
- fresh chives, snipped

2

5

7

1 Trim away any excess fat and silver skin from the pork and place in a shallow dish.

2 Mix together the soy sauce, sherry, Chinese five-spice powder, garlic and ginger. Spoon the mixture over the pork, turning it to coat, cover and set aside to marinate in the refrigerator for at least 1 hour or until required.

3 Drain the pork, reserving the marinade. Place the pork on a roasting rack over a roasting tin. Cook in a preheated oven, 190°C/375°F/Gas Mark 5, basting occasionally with the marinade, for 1 hour or until cooked through.

5 Meanwhile, halve and deseed the red, yellow and orange peppers. Cut each pepper half into 3 equal portions. Arrange them on a baking tray and bake alongside the pork for the last 30 minutes of cooking time.

6 Place the caster sugar and vinegar in a saucepan and heat gently until the sugar dissolves. Bring to the boil and simmer for 3–4 minutes until syrupy.

7 When the pork is cooked, remove it from the oven and brush with the sugar syrup. Leave for about 5 minutes, then slice and arrange on a serving platter with the peppers, garnished with the spring onions and chives.

Italian Calzone

A calzone is like a pizza in reverse – it resembles a large pasty with the dough on the outside and the filling on the inside.

NUTRITIONAL INFORMATION

Calories	405	Sugars	7g
Protein	19g	Fat	17g
Carbohydrate	48g	Saturates	5g

5 mins | 20 mins

SERVES 4

INGREDIENTS

1 quantity Basic Pizza Dough (see page 15)

FILLING

- 1 egg, beaten
- 1 tbsp tomato purée
- 25 g/1 oz Italian salami, chopped
- 25 g/1 oz mortadella, chopped
- 1 tomato, peeled and chopped
- 25 g/1 oz ricotta cheese
- 2 spring onions, chopped
- ¼ tsp dried oregano
- salt and pepper

1 Knead the dough and roll out on a lightly floured surface to form a 23-cm/9-inch circle.

2 Brush the edge of the dough with a little beaten egg.

3 Spread the tomato purée over the half of the circle nearest to you.

4 Scatter the salami, mortadella and chopped tomato on top.

5 Dot with the ricotta and sprinkle over the spring onions and oregano. Season with salt and pepper to taste.

6 Fold over the uncovered half of the dough to form a half-moon shape. Press the edges of the dough firmly together to prevent the filling from leaking out during cooking.

7 Carefully transfer the calzone to a baking tray and brush with beaten egg to glaze. Make a hole in the top in order to allow any steam to escape during the cooking time.

8 Bake in a preheated oven, 200°C/400°F/Gas Mark 6, for 20 minutes or until golden. Transfer to a warmed serving platter and serve immediately.

Stuffed Cannelloni

Cannelloni, the thick, round pasta tubes, make perfect containers for close-textured fillings of all kinds.

NUTRITIONAL INFORMATION

Calories	520	Sugars	5g
Protein	21g	Fat	39g
Carbohydrate	23g	Saturates	18g

30 mins 1¼ hrs

SERVES 4

INGREDIENTS

- 8 dried cannelloni tubes
- 1 tbsp olive oil
- 25 g/1 oz Parmesan cheese, freshly grated
- fresh herb sprigs, to garnish

FILLING

- 2 tbsp butter
- 300 g/10½ oz frozen spinach, defrosted and chopped
- 115 g/4 oz ricotta cheese
- 25 g/1 oz Parmesan cheese, freshly grated
- 55 g/2 oz chopped ham
- pinch of freshly grated nutmeg
- 2 tbsp double cream
- 2 eggs, lightly beaten
- salt and pepper

SAUCE

- 2 tbsp butter
- 2½ tbsp plain flour
- 300 ml/10 fl oz milk
- 2 bay leaves
- pinch of freshly grated nutmeg

1

3

5

1 To make the filling, melt the butter in a pan and stir-fry the spinach for 2–3 minutes. Remove from the heat and stir in the ricotta and Parmesan cheeses and the ham. Season to taste with nutmeg, salt and pepper. Beat in the cream and eggs to make a thick paste.

2 Bring a pan of lightly salted water to the boil. Add the pasta and the oil and cook for 10–12 minutes or until almost tender. Drain and set aside to cool.

3 To make the sauce, melt the butter in a pan. Stir in the flour and cook, stirring, for 1 minute. Gradually stir in the milk. Add the bay leaves and simmer, stirring, for 5 minutes. Add the nutmeg and salt and pepper to taste. Remove from the heat and discard the bay leaves.

4 Spoon the filling into a piping bag and fill the cannelloni.

5 Spoon a little sauce into the base of an ovenproof dish. Arrange the cannelloni in the dish in a single layer and pour over the remaining sauce. Sprinkle over the Parmesan cheese and bake in a preheated oven, 190°C/375°F/Gas Mark 5, for 40–45 minutes. Garnish with fresh herb sprigs and serve.

Tom's Toad-in-the-Hole

This unusual recipe uses chicken and Cumberland sausage which is then made into individual bite-size cakes.

NUTRITIONAL INFORMATION

Calories	470	Sugars	4g
Protein	28g	Fat	27g
Carbohydrate	30g	Saturates	12g

1¼ hrs | 30 mins

SERVES 4-6

INGREDIENTS

- 125 g/4½ oz plain flour
- pinch of salt
- 1 egg, beaten
- 200 ml/7 fl oz milk
- 5 tbsp water
- 2 tbsp beef dripping
- 250 g/9 oz chicken breasts
- 250 g/9 oz Cumberland sausage
- chicken or onion gravy, to serve (optional)

1 Mix the flour and salt in a bowl. make a well in the centre and add the beaten eggs.

2 Add half the milk and, using a wooden spoon, work in the flour slowly. Beat the mixture until smooth, then add the remaining milk and water. Beat again until the mixture is smooth. Let the mixture stand for at least 1 hour.

3 Add the dripping to individual Yorkshire pudding tins or to one large roasting tin. Cut up the chicken and sausage so that you get a generous piece in each individual tin or several scattered around the large tin.

4 Heat the tin or tins in a preheated oven, 220°C/425°F/Gas Mark 7, for about 5 minutes until very hot. Remove the tins from the oven and pour in the batter, leaving adequate space for the mixture to expand.

5 Return to the oven to cook for about 35 minutes until risen and golden brown. Do not open the oven door for at least 30 minutes.

6 Serve the toad-in-the-hole piping hot with chicken or onion gravy or simply on its own.

VARIATION

Use skinless, boneless chicken legs instead of chicken breast in the recipe. Cut up as directed. Instead of Cumberland sausage, use your favourite variety of sausage.

2

2

3

Braised Fennel & Linguine

This aniseed-flavoured vegetable gives that little extra punch to this delicious creamy pasta dish.

NUTRITIONAL INFORMATION

Calories	650	Sugars	6g
Protein	14g	Fat	39g
Carbohydrate	62g	Saturates	22g

20 mins   50 mins

SERVES 4

INGREDIENTS

- 6 fennel bulbs
- 150 ml/5 fl oz vegetable stock
- 2 tbsp butter
- 6 slices rindless smoked bacon, diced
- 6 shallots, quartered
- 2½ tbsp plain flour
- 100 ml/3½ fl oz double cream
- 1 tbsp Madeira
- 450 g/1 lb dried linguine pasta
- 1 tbsp olive oil
- salt and pepper

1 Trim the fennel bulbs, then peel off and reserve the outer layer of each. Cut the bulbs into quarters and put them in a large saucepan with the stock and the reserved outer layers.

2 Bring to the boil, lower the heat and simmer for 5 minutes.

3 Using a perforated spoon, transfer the fennel to a large dish. Discard the outer layers of the fennel bulbs. Bring the vegetable stock to the boil and allow to reduce by half. Set aside.

4 Melt the butter in a frying pan. Add the bacon and shallots and fry over a medium heat, stirring frequently, for 4 minutes. Add the flour, reduced stock, cream and Madeira and cook, stirring constantly, for 3 minutes or until the sauce is smooth. Season to taste with salt and pepper and pour over the fennel.

5 Bring a large saucepan of lightly salted water to the boil. Add the linguine and olive oil, bring back to the boil and cook for 8–10 minutes until tender but still firm to the bite. Drain and transfer to a deep ovenproof dish.

5 Add the fennel and sauce and braise in a preheated oven, 180°C/350°F/Gas Mark 4, for 20 minutes. Serve immediately.

COOK'S TIP

Fennel will keep in the salad drawer of the refrigerator for 2–3 days, but it is best eaten as fresh as possible. Cut surfaces turn brown quickly, so do not prepare it too much in advance of cooking.

Aubergine Pasta Cake

This dish would make a stunning dinner party dish, yet it contains simple ingredients and is easy to make.

NUTRITIONAL INFORMATION

Calories	201	Sugars	4g
Protein	14g	Fat	7g
Carbohydrate	22g	Saturates	4g

55 mins — 35 mins

SERVES 4

INGREDIENTS

- butter, for greasing
- 1 medium aubergine
- 300 g/10½ oz tricolour pasta shapes
- 125 g/4½ oz low-fat soft cheese with garlic and herbs
- 350ml/12 fl oz passata
- 70 g/2½ oz Parmesan cheese, freshly grated
- 1½ tsp dried oregano
- 25 g/1 oz dry white breadcrumbs
- salt and pepper

1 Grease and line a 20-cm/8-inch round spring-form cake tin.

2 Trim the aubergine and cut it lengthways into slices about 5 mm/¼ inch thick. Place in a bowl, sprinkle with salt and set aside for 30 minutes to remove any bitter juices. Rinse well under cold running water and drain.

3 Bring a saucepan of water to the boil and blanch the aubergine slices for 1 minute. Drain and pat dry with kitchen paper. Set aside.

4 Bring another large saucepan of lightly salted water to the boil. Add the pasta shapes, return to the boil and cook for 8–10 minutes until tender, but still firm to the bite. Drain well and return to the saucepan. Add the soft cheese and allow it to melt over the pasta.

5 Stir in the passata, Parmesan cheese, oregano and salt and pepper.

6 Arrange the aubergine over the base and sides of the tin, overlapping the slices and making sure there are no gaps.

7 Pile the pasta mixture into the tin, packing it down well, and sprinkle with the breadcrumbs. Bake in a preheated oven, 190°C/375°F/Gas Mark 5, for 20 minutes and then leave to stand for 15 minutes.

8 Loosen the cake round the edge with a palette knife and release from the tin. Turn out the pasta cake, aubergine side uppermost, and serve hot.

2

6

7

Fruity Lamb Casserole

The sweet spicy blend of cinnamon, coriander and cumin is the perfect foil for the tender lamb and apricots in this warming casserole.

NUTRITIONAL INFORMATION

Calories	384	Sugars	16g
Protein	32g	Fat	22g
Carbohydrate	17g	Saturates	9g

5 mins — 1¼ hrs

SERVES 4

INGREDIENTS

- 450 g/1 lb lean lamb, trimmed and cut into 2.5-cm/1-inch cubes
- 1 tsp ground cinnamon
- 1 tsp ground coriander
- 1 tsp ground cumin
- 2 tsp olive oil
- 1 red onion, finely chopped
- 1 garlic clove, crushed
- 400 g/14 oz canned chopped tomatoes
- 2 tbsp tomato purée
- 125 g/4½ oz no-soak dried apricots
- 1 tsp caster sugar
- 300 ml/10 fl oz vegetable stock
- salt and pepper
- 1 small bunch fresh coriander, to garnish
- brown rice, steamed couscous or bulgar wheat, to serve

1 Place the meat in a mixing bowl and add the cinnamon, coriander, cumin and oil. Mix thoroughly so that the lamb is well coated in the spices.

2 Heat a non-stick frying pan for a few seconds until it is hot, then add the spiced lamb. Reduce the heat and cook for 4–5 minutes, stirring, until browned all over. Using a perforated spoon, remove the lamb and transfer to a large ovenproof casserole.

3 Add the onion, garlic, tomatoes and tomato purée to the frying pan and cook, stirring occasionally, for 5 minutes. Season to taste with salt and pepper. Stir in the apricots and sugar, add the stock and bring to the boil.

4 Spoon the sauce over the lamb and mix well. Cover and cook in a preheated oven, 180°C/350°F/Gas Mark 4, for 1 hour, removing the lid of the casserole for the last 10 minutes.

5 Roughly chop the coriander and sprinkle over the casserole to garnish. Serve with brown rice, steamed couscous or bulgar wheat.

1

2

3

Hot Pot Chops

A hot pot is a lamb casserole made with carrots and onions and with a potato topping. The steaks used here are an interesting alternative.

NUTRITIONAL INFORMATION

Calories	250	Sugars	2g
Protein	27g	Fat	12g
Carbohydrate	8g	Saturates	5g

10 mins 30 mins

SERVES 4

INGREDIENTS

- 4 lean, boneless lamb leg steaks, 125 g/4½ oz each
- 1 small onion, thinly sliced
- 1 carrot, thinly sliced
- 1 potato, thinly sliced
- 1 tsp olive oil
- 1 tsp dried rosemary
- salt and pepper
- fresh rosemary, to garnish
- freshly steamed green vegetables, to serve

1 Using a small, sharp knife, trim any excess fat from the lamb steaks.

2 Season both sides of the steaks with salt and pepper to taste and arrange them on a baking tray.

3 Alternate layers of sliced onion, carrot and potato on top of each lamb steak, ending with a layer of potato.

4 Brush the tops of the potato lightly with oil, season well with salt and pepper to taste and then sprinkle with a little dried rosemary.

5 Bake the hot pot chops in a preheated oven, 180°C/350°F/Gas Mark 4, for 25–30 minutes until the lamb is tender and cooked through.

6 Drain the lamb on kitchen paper and transfer to a warmed serving plate.

7 Garnish with fresh rosemary and serve accompanied with a selection of steamed green vegetables.

1

3

4

VARIATION

This recipe would work equally well with boneless chicken breasts. Pound the chicken slightly with a meat mallet or covered rolling pin so that the pieces are the same thickness throughout.

Beef & Tomato Gratin

A satisfying bake of lean minced beef, courgettes and tomatoes cooked in a low-fat 'custard' with a cheesy crust.

NUTRITIONAL INFORMATION

Calories	278	Sugars	10g
Protein	29g	Fat	10g
Carbohydrate	20g	Saturates	5g

10 mins 1¼ hrs

SERVES 4

INGREDIENTS

- 350 g/12 oz lean minced beef
- 1 large onion, finely chopped
- 1 tsp dried mixed herbs
- 1 tbsp plain flour
- 300 ml/10 fl oz beef stock
- 1 tbsp tomato purée
- 2 large tomatoes, thinly sliced
- 4 courgettes, thinly sliced
- 2 tbsp cornflour
- 300 ml/10 fl oz skimmed milk
- 150 ml/5 fl oz low-fat fromage frais
- 1 egg yolk
- 70 g/2½ oz Parmesan cheese, freshly grated
- salt and pepper

TO SERVE

- crusty bread
- steamed vegetables

1 In a large, heavy-based frying pan, dry-fry the beef and onion over a low heat, stirring frequently, for 4–5 minutes until the meat is browned.

2 Stir in the dried mixed herbs, flour, beef stock and tomato purée and season to taste with salt and pepper. Bring to the boil, lower the heat and simmer gently for 30 minutes until the mixture has thickened.

3 Transfer the beef mixture to an ovenproof gratin dish. Cover with a layer of the sliced tomatoes and then add a layer of sliced courgettes.

4 Blend the cornflour with a little milk to make a smooth paste. Pour the remaining milk into a saucepan and bring to the boil. Add the cornflour mixture and cook, stirring, for 1–2 minutes until thickened. Remove from the heat and beat in the fromage frais and egg yolk. Season to taste with salt and pepper.

5 Spread the white sauce over the layer of courgettes. Place the dish on a baking sheet and sprinkle with grated Parmesan. Bake in a preheated oven, 190°C/375°F/Gas Mark 5, for about 25–30 minutes until the topping is golden brown and bubbling. Serve with crusty bread and steamed vegetables.

1

3

5

Rich Beef Stew

This slow-cooked beef stew is flavoured with an aromatic mixture of oranges, red wine and porcini mushrooms.

NUTRITIONAL INFORMATION

Calories	388	Sugars	15g
Protein	30g	Fat	21g
Carbohydrate	16g	Saturates	9g

45 mins | $1\frac{3}{4}$ hrs

SERVES 4

INGREDIENTS

- 1 tbsp vegetable oil
- 1 tbsp butter
- 225 g/8 oz baby onions, peeled and halved
- 600 g/1 lb 5 oz stewing steak, diced into 4-cm/1½-inch cubes
- 300 ml/10 fl oz beef stock
- 150 ml/5 fl oz red wine
- 4 tbsp chopped fresh oregano
- 1 tbsp sugar
- 1 orange
- 25 g/1 oz dried porcini or other mushrooms
- 225 g/8 oz fresh plum tomatoes
- cooked rice or potatoes, to serve

2

3

4

1 Heat the oil and butter in a large frying pan. Add the onions and fry over a low heat, stirring occasionally, for 5 minutes or until golden. Remove the onions with a perforated spoon, set aside and keep warm.

2 Add the beef to the pan and cook, stirring, for 5 minutes or until browned all over.

3 Return the onions to the frying pan and add the stock, wine, oregano and sugar, stirring to mix well. Transfer the mixture to a casserole.

4 Pare the rind from the orange and cut it into strips. Slice the orange flesh into rings. Add the orange rings and the rind to the casserole. Cook in a preheated oven, 180°C/350°F/Gas Mark 4, for 1¼ hours.

5 Meanwhile, soak the porcini mushrooms for 30 minutes in 4 tablespoons of warm water.

6 Peel and halve the tomatoes. Add the tomatoes, porcini mushrooms and their soaking liquid to the casserole. Cook for a further 20 minutes until the beef is tender and the juices thickened. Serve with cooked rice or potatoes.

Creamed Strips of Sirloin

This quick and easy dish tastes superb and would make a delicious treat for a special occasion.

NUTRITIONAL INFORMATION

Calories	796	Sugars	2g
Protein	29g	Fat	63g
Carbohydrate	26g	Saturates	39g

15 mins   30 mins

SERVES 4

INGREDIENTS

- 6 tbsp butter
- 450 g/1 lb sirloin steak, trimmed and cut into thin strips
- 175 g/6 oz button mushrooms, sliced
- 1 tsp mustard
- pinch of grated fresh root ginger
- 2 tbsp dry sherry
- 150 ml/5 fl oz double cream
- salt and pepper
- 4 slices hot toast, cut into triangles, to serve

PASTA

- 450 g/1 lb dried rigatoni pasta
- 2 tbsp olive oil
- 2 sprigs fresh basil
- 115 g/4 oz butter

1 Melt the butter in a large frying pan. Add the steak and fry over a low heat, stirring frequently, for 6 minutes. Using a perforated spoon, transfer the steak to an ovenproof dish and keep warm.

2 Add the sliced mushrooms to the frying pan and cook for 2–3 minutes in the juices remaining in the pan. Add the mustard and ginger and season to taste with salt and pepper. Cook for 2 minutes, then add the sherry and cream. Cook for a further 3 minutes, then pour the cream sauce over the steak.

3 Bake the steak and cream mixture in a preheated oven, 190°C/375°F/Gas Mark 5, for 10 minutes.

4 Meanwhile, cook the pasta. Bring a large saucepan of lightly salted water to the boil. Add the rigatoni, olive oil and 1 of the basil sprigs, bring back to the boil and cook for 8–10 minutes until tender, but still firm to the bite. Drain the pasta and transfer to a warm serving plate. Toss the pasta with the butter and garnish with a sprig of basil.

5 Serve the creamed steak strips with the pasta and triangles of warm toast.

1

2

2

COOK'S TIP

Dried pasta will keep for up to 6 months. Keep it in the packet and reseal it once you have opened it, or transfer the pasta to an airtight jar.

Fresh Spaghetti & Meatballs

This well-loved Italian dish is famous across the world. Make the most of it by using high-quality steak for the meatballs.

NUTRITIONAL INFORMATION

Calories	665	Sugars	9g
Protein	39g	Fat	24g
Carbohydrate	77g	Saturates	8g

45 mins

1¼ hrs

SERVES 4

INGREDIENTS

- 150 g/5½ oz brown breadcrumbs
- 150 ml/5 fl oz milk
- 2 tbsp butter
- 2½ tbsp wholemeal flour
- 200 ml/7 fl oz beef stock
- 400 g/14 oz canned chopped tomatoes
- 2 tbsp tomato purée
- 1 tsp sugar
- 1 tbsp finely chopped fresh tarragon
- 1 large onion, chopped
- 450 g/1 lb minced steak
- 1 tsp paprika
- 4 tbsp olive oil
- 450 g/1 lb fresh spaghetti
- salt and pepper
- fresh tarragon sprigs, to garnish

1 Place the breadcrumbs in a bowl, add the milk and set aside to soak for about 30 minutes.

2 Melt half of the butter in a pan. Add the flour and cook, stirring constantly, for 2 minutes. Gradually stir in the beef stock and cook, stirring constantly, for a further 5 minutes. Add the tomatoes, tomato purée, sugar and tarragon. Season well and simmer for 25 minutes.

3 Mix the onion, steak and paprika into the breadcrumbs and season to taste. Shape the mixture into 14 meatballs.

4 Heat the oil and remaining butter in a frying pan and fry the meatballs, turning, until brown all over. Place in a deep casserole, pour over the tomato sauce, cover and bake in a preheated oven, 180°C/350°F/Gas Mark 4, for 25 minutes.

5 Bring a large saucepan of lightly salted water to the boil. Add the fresh spaghetti, bring back to the boil and cook for about 2–3 minutes or until tender, but still firm to the bite.

6 Meanwhile, remove the meatballs from the oven and allow them to cool for 5 minutes. Serve the meatballs and their sauce with the spaghetti, garnished with tarragon sprigs.

Layered Meat Loaf

The cheese-flavoured pasta layer comes as a pleasant surprise inside this lightly spiced meat loaf.

NUTRITIONAL INFORMATION

Calories	412	Sugars	3g
Protein	21g	Fat	30g
Carbohydrate	15g	Saturates	13g

35 mins   1½ hrs

SERVES 6

INGREDIENTS

- 2 tbsp butter, plus extra for greasing
- 1 small onion, finely chopped
- 1 small red pepper, deseeded and chopped
- 1 garlic clove, chopped
- 450 g/1 lb minced beef
- 25 g/1 oz white breadcrumbs
- ½ tsp cayenne pepper
- 1 tbsp lemon juice
- ½ tsp grated lemon rind
- 2 tbsp chopped fresh parsley
- 85 g/3 oz dried short pasta, such as fusilli
- 1 tbsp olive oil
- 250 ml/8 fl oz Italian Cheese Sauce (see page 16)
- 4 bay leaves
- 175 g/6 oz fatty bacon, rinds removed
- salt and pepper
- salad leaves, to serve

2

2

4

1 Melt the butter in a pan over a medium heat and fry the onion and pepper for about 3 minutes. Stir in the garlic and cook for 1 minute.

2 Put the meat into a bowl and mash with a wooden spoon until sticky. Add the onion mixture, breadcrumbs, cayenne pepper, lemon juice, lemon rind and parsley. Season to taste with salt and pepper and set aside.

3 Bring a large pan of lightly salted water to the boil. Add the pasta and oil, bring back to the boil and cook for 8–10 minutes until tender. Drain and stir into the Italian Cheese Sauce.

4 Grease a 1-kg/2-lb 4-oz loaf tin and arrange the bay leaves in the base. Stretch the bacon slices with the back of a knife and line the base and sides of the tin with them. Spoon in half the meat mixture and smooth the surface. Cover with the pasta mixed with Italian Cheese Sauce, then spoon in the remaining meat mixture. Level the top and cover with foil.

5 Bake the meat loaf in a preheated oven, 180°C/350°F/Gas Mark 4, for 1 hour or until the juices run clear when a skewer is inserted into the centre and the loaf has shrunk away from the sides of the tin. Pour off any fat and turn out the loaf on to a serving dish. Serve with salad leaves.

Meatballs in Red Wine Sauce

A different twist is given to this traditional and ever-popular pasta dish with a rich, but subtle sauce.

NUTRITIONAL INFORMATION

Calories	811	Sugars	7g
Protein	30g	Fat	43g
Carbohydrate	76g	Saturates	12g

45 mins

1½ hrs

SERVES 4

INGREDIENTS

- 150 ml/5 fl oz milk
- 150 g/5½ oz fresh white breadcrumbs
- 2 tbsp butter
- 9 tbsp olive oil
- 225 g/8 oz sliced oyster mushrooms
- 2½ tbsp wholemeal flour
- 200 ml/7 fl oz beef stock
- 150 ml/5 fl oz red wine
- 4 tomatoes, peeled and chopped
- 1 tbsp tomato purée
- 1 tsp brown sugar
- 1 tbsp finely chopped fresh basil
- 12 shallots, chopped
- 450 g/1 lb minced steak
- 1 tsp paprika
- 450 g/1 lb dried egg tagliatelli pasta
- salt and pepper
- fresh basil sprigs, to garnish

1 Pour the milk into a bowl and soak the breadcrumbs in the milk for 30 minutes.

2 Heat half the butter and 4 tablespoons of the oil in a pan. Fry the mushrooms for 4 minutes, then stir in the flour and cook for 2 minutes. Add the stock and wine and simmer for 15 minutes. Add the tomatoes, tomato purée, sugar and basil. Season and simmer for 30 minutes.

3 Mix the shallots, steak and paprika with the breadcrumbs and season to taste. Shape the mixture into 14 meatballs.

4 Heat 4 tablespoons of the remaining oil and the rest of the butter in a large frying pan. Fry the meatballs, turning frequently, until brown all over. Transfer to a deep casserole, pour over the red wine and the mushroom sauce, cover and bake in a preheated oven, 180°C/350°F/Gas Mark 4, for 30 minutes.

5 Bring a pan of lightly salted water to the boil. Add the pasta and the remaining oil, bring back to the boil and cook for 8–10 minutes or until tender, but still firm to the bite. Drain and transfer to a serving dish. Remove the casserole from the oven and cool for 3 minutes. Pour the meatballs and sauce on to the pasta, garnish and serve.

3

3

4

Sicilian Spaghetti Cake

Any variety of long pasta, such as tagliatelle or fettuccine, could be used for this very tasty dish from Sicily.

NUTRITIONAL INFORMATION

Calories	876	Sugars	10g
Protein	37g	Fat	65g
Carbohydrate	39g	Saturates	18g

30 mins 50 mins

SERVES 4

INGREDIENTS

- 150 ml/5 fl oz olive oil, plus extra for brushing
- 2 aubergines
- 350 g/12 oz finely minced lean beef
- 1 onion, chopped
- 2 garlic cloves, crushed
- 2 tbsp tomato purée
- 400 g/14 oz canned chopped tomatoes
- 1 tsp Worcestershire sauce
- 1 tsp chopped fresh oregano or marjoram or ½ tsp dried oregano or marjoram
- 40 g/1½ oz stoned black olives, sliced
- 1 green, red or yellow pepper, deseeded and chopped
- 175 g/6 oz dried spaghetti
- 125 g/4½ oz Parmesan cheese, freshly grated
- salt and pepper

1 Brush a 20-cm/8-inch loose-bottomed round cake tin with oil and line the base with oiled baking paper. Cut the aubergines into slanting slices 5 mm/¼ inch thick. Heat some of the oil in a frying pan. Fry a few slices of aubergine at a time until lightly browned, turning once, and adding more oil as necessary. Drain on kitchen paper.

2 Put the minced beef, onion and garlic into a saucepan and dry-fry over a low heat, stirring frequently, until browned all over. Add the tomato purée, tomatoes, Worcestershire sauce and herbs and season to taste with salt and pepper. Simmer gently for 10 minutes, stirring occasionally, then add the olives and pepper and cook for 10 minutes.

3 Bring a large saucepan of lightly salted water to the boil. Add the pasta, bring back to the boil and cook for 8–10 minutes or until just tender, but still firm to the bite. Drain, turn the spaghetti into a bowl and mix in the meat mixture and Parmesan cheese, tossing together with 2 forks.

4 Lay overlapping slices of aubergine over the base and up the sides of the cake tin. Add the meat mixture and cover with the remaining aubergine slices.

5 Stand the cake tin in a roasting tin and cook in a preheated oven, 200°C/400°F/Gas Mark 6, for 40 minutes. Remove from the oven, leave to stand in the tin for 5 minutes, then loosen around the edges and invert on to a warmed serving dish, releasing the tin clip. Remove and discard the baking paper. Serve immediately.

1

3

4

Beef & Pasta Bake

The combination of Italian and Indian ingredients makes a surprisingly delicious recipe. Marinate the steak in advance to save time.

NUTRITIONAL INFORMATION

Calories	1050	Sugars	4g
Protein	47g	Fat	81g
Carbohydrate	37g	Saturates	34g

6¼ hrs — 1¼ hrs

SERVES 4

INGREDIENTS

- 900g/2 lb steak, cut into cubes
- 150 ml/5 fl oz beef stock
- 450g/1 lb dried macaroni
- 300 ml/10 fl oz double cream
- ½ tsp garam masala
- salt
- fresh coriander and flaked almonds, to garnish

KORMA PASTE

- 55 g/2 oz blanched almonds
- 6 garlic cloves
- 1½ tsp coarsely chopped fresh root ginger
- 6 tbsp beef stock
- 1 tsp ground cardamom
- 4 cloves, crushed
- 1 tsp cinnamon
- 2 large onions, chopped
- 1 tsp coriander seeds
- 2 tsp ground cumin seeds
- pinch of cayenne pepper
- 6 tbsp sunflower oil

1 To make the korma paste, grind the almonds finely using a pestle and mortar. Put the ground almonds and the rest of the korma paste ingredients into a food processor or blender and process to make a very smooth paste.

2 Put the steak in a shallow dish and spoon over the korma paste, turning to coat the steak well. Leave in the refrigerator to marinate for 6 hours.

3 Transfer the steak and korma paste to a large saucepan, and simmer over a low heat, adding a little beef stock if required, for 35 minutes.

4 Meanwhile, bring a large saucepan of lightly salted water to the boil. Add the macaroni, bring back to the boil and cook for 8–10 minutes until tender, but still firm to the bite. Drain the pasta thoroughly and transfer to a deep casserole. Add the steak, double cream and garam masala.

5 Bake in a preheated oven, 200°C/400°F/Gas Mark 6, for 30 minutes until the steak is tender. Remove the casserole from the oven and set aside to stand for about 10 minutes. Garnish the bake with fresh coriander and flaked almonds and serve hot.

1

2

3

Lasagne Verde

The sauce in this delicious baked pasta dish can also be used as an alternative sauce for Spaghetti Bologness.

NUTRITIONAL INFORMATION

Calories	619	Sugars	7g
Protein	29g	Fat	45g
Carbohydrate	21g	Saturates	19g

1¾ hrs   55 mins

SERVES 6

INGREDIENTS

Ragù Sauce (see page 15)

1 tbsp olive oil

225 g/8 oz lasagne verde

butter, for greasing

Béchamel Sauce (see page 92)

55 g/2oz Parmesan cheese, freshly grated

salt and pepper

green salad, tomato salad or black olives, to serve

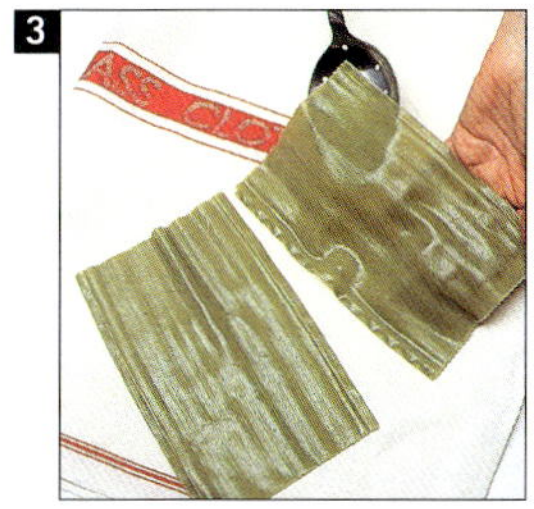

1 Make the Ragù Sauce as described on page 15, but cook for 10–12 minutes longer than the time given, in an uncovered pan, to allow the excess liquid to evaporate. It needs to be reduced to the consistency of a thick paste.

2 Have ready a large saucepan of boiling, salted water and add the olive oil. Drop the pasta sheets into the boiling water, a few at a time, and return the water to the boil before adding further pasta sheets. If you are using fresh lasagne, cook the sheets for a total of 8 minutes. If you are using dried or partly pre-cooked pasta, cook it according to the directions given on the packet.

3 Remove the pasta sheets from the saucepan with a perforated spoon. Spread them out in a single layer on clean, damp tea towels.

4 Grease a rectangular ovenproof dish, about 25–28 cm/10–11 inches long. To assemble the dish, spoon a little of the meat sauce into the prepared dish, cover with a layer of lasagne, then spoon over a little Béchamel Sauce and sprinkle with some of the cheese. Continue making layers in this way, covering the final layer of lasagne sheets with the remaining Béchamel Sauce.

5 Sprinkle on the remaining cheese and bake in a preheated oven, 190°C/375°F/Gas Mark 5, for 40 minutes or until the sauce is golden brown and bubbling. Serve with a green salad, a tomato salad, or a bowl of black olives.

Pasticcio

A recipe that has both Italian and Greek origins, this dish may be served hot or cold, cut into thick, satisfying squares.

NUTRITIONAL INFORMATION

Calories	590	Sugars	8g
Protein	34g	Fat	39g
Carbohydrate	23g	Saturates	16g

35 mins

1¼ hrs

SERVES 6

INGREDIENTS

225 g/8 oz fusilli, or other short pasta shapes
1 tbsp olive oil
4 tbsp double cream
salt
rosemary sprigs, to garnish

SAUCE

2 tbsp olive oil, plus extra for brushing
1 onion, thinly sliced
1 red pepper, deseeded and chopped
2 garlic cloves, chopped
625 g/1 lb 6 oz lean minced beef
400 g/14 oz canned chopped tomatoes
125 ml/4 fl oz dry white wine
2 tbsp chopped fresh parsley
50 g/1¾ oz canned anchovies, drained and chopped
salt and pepper

TOPPING

300 ml/10 fl oz natural yogurt
3 eggs
pinch of freshly grated nutmeg
40 g/1½ oz Parmesan cheese, freshly grated

1

4

5

1 To make the sauce, heat the oil in a large frying pan and fry the onion and red pepper for 3 minutes. Stir in the garlic and cook for 1 minute more. Stir in the beef and cook, stirring frequently, until it is no longer pink.

2 Add the tomatoes and wine, stir well and bring to the boil. Simmer, uncovered, for 20 minutes or until the sauce is fairly thick. Stir in the parsley and anchovies and season to taste.

3 Cook the pasta in a large pan of boiling salted water, adding the oil, for 8–10 minutes or until tender. Drain the pasta in a colander, then transfer to a bowl. Stir in the cream and set aside.

4 To make the topping, beat together the yogurt, eggs and nutmeg until well combined and season with salt and pepper to taste.

5 Brush a large, shallow ovenproof dish with oil. Spoon in half of the pasta mixture and cover with half of the meat sauce. Repeat these layers, then spread the topping evenly over the final layer. Sprinkle the grated Parmesan cheese evenly on top.

6 Bake in a preheated oven, 190°C/375°F/Gas Mark 5, for 25 minutes or until the topping is golden brown and bubbling. Garnish with sprigs of fresh rosemary and serve immediately.

Neapolitan Veal Cutlets

The delicious combination of apple, onion and mushroom perfectly complements the delicate flavour of veal.

NUTRITIONAL INFORMATION

Calories	1071	Sugars	13g
Protein	74g	Fat	59g
Carbohydrate	66g	Saturates	16g

20 mins 45 mins

SERVES 4

INGREDIENTS

- 200 g/7 oz butter
- 4 veal cutlets, 250 g/9 oz each, trimmed
- 1 large onion, sliced
- 2 apples, peeled, cored and sliced
- 175 g/6 oz button mushrooms
- 1 tbsp chopped fresh tarragon
- 8 black peppercorns
- 1 tbsp sesame seeds
- 400 g/14 oz dried marille pasta
- 100 ml/3½ fl oz extra virgin olive oil
- 2 large beef tomatoes, cut in half
- leaves of 1 sprig fresh basil
- 175 g/6 oz mascarpone cheese
- salt and pepper
- fresh basil leaves, to garnish

1 Melt 55 g/2 oz of the butter in a frying pan. Fry the veal over a low heat for 5 minutes on each side. Transfer to a dish and keep warm.

2 Add the onion and apples to the pan and fry over a low heat, stirring occasionally, for 5–8 minutes, until lightly browned. Transfer to a dish, place the veal on top and keep warm.

3 Melt the remaining butter in the pan. Add the mushrooms, tarragon and peppercorns and fry over a low heat for 3 minutes. Sprinkle over the sesame seeds.

4 Bring a pan of salted water to the boil. Add the pasta and 1 tablespoon of oil, bring back to the boil and cook for 8–10 minutes or until tender, but still firm to the bite. Drain and transfer to a plate.

5 Grill or fry the tomatoes and basil for 2–3 minutes.

6 Dot the pasta with the mascarpone cheese and sprinkle with the remaining olive oil. Place the onions, apples and veal cutlets on top of the pasta. Spoon the mushrooms, peppercorns and pan juices on to the cutlets, place the tomatoes and basil leaves around the edge and bake in a preheated oven, 150°C/300°F/Gas Mark 2, for 5 minutes.

7 Season to taste with salt and pepper, garnish with fresh basil leaves and serve immediately.

1

2

3

Vegetarian & Vegan

Anyone who ever thought that vegetarian meals were dull will be proved wrong by the rich variety of dishes in this chapter. You'll recognize influences from Middle Eastern

and Italian cooking, such as the Stuffed Vegetables, Roman Focaccia, and Sun-dried Tomato Loaf, but there are also traditional recipes such as Upside-down Cake and Fruit Crumble. They all make exciting treats at any time of year and for virtually any occasion. Don't be afraid to substitute your own personal favourite ingredients where ever appropriate.

Mushroom Cannelloni

Thick pasta tubes are filled with a mixture of seasoned chopped mushrooms and baked in a rich fragrant tomato sauce.

NUTRITIONAL INFORMATION

Calories	156	Sugar	8g
Protein	6g	Fats	1g
Carbohydrates	21g	Saturates	0.2g

35 mins 1½ hrs

SERVES 4

INGREDIENTS

- 350 g/12 oz chestnut mushrooms
- 1 onion, finely chopped
- 1 garlic clove, crushed
- 1 tbsp chopped fresh thyme
- ½ tsp ground nutmeg
- 4 tbsp dry white wine
- 50g/1¾ oz fresh white breadcrumbs
- 12 dried 'quick-cook' cannelloni tubes
- salt and pepper
- Parmesan shavings, to garnish (optional)

TOMATO SAUCE

- 1 large red pepper
- 200 ml/7 fl oz dry white wine
- 450 ml/16 fl oz passata
- 2 tbsp tomato purée
- 2 bay leaves
- 1 tsp caster sugar

1 Finely chop the mushrooms and place in a pan with the onion and garlic. Stir in the thyme, nutmeg and 4 tablespoons of wine. Bring to the boil, cover and simmer for 10 minutes.

2 Stir in the breadcrumbs to bind the mixture together and season with salt and pepper. Cool for 10 minutes.

3 Preheat the grill to hot. To make the sauce, halve and deseed the pepper, place on the grill rack and cook for 8–10 minutes until charred. Leave to cool for 10 minutes.

4 Once the pepper has cooled, peel off the charred skin. Chop the flesh and place in a food processor with the wine. Blend until smooth, and pour into a pan.

5 Mix the remaining sauce ingredients with the pepper and wine. Bring to the boil and simmer for 10 minutes. Discard the bay leaves.

6 Cover the base of an ovenproof dish with a thin layer of sauce. Fill the cannelloni with the mushroom mixture and place in the dish. Spoon over the remaining sauce, cover with foil and bake in a preheated oven, 200°C/400°f/Gas Mark 6, for 35–40 minutes. Garnish with Parmesan shavings, if using, and serve hot.

COOK'S TIP

Chestnut mushrooms, also known as champignons de Paris, are common cultivated mushrooms that may have brown or white caps.

Pasta & Bean Casserole

A satisfying winter dish, this is a slow-cooked, one-pot meal. The haricot beans need to be soaked overnight, so prepare well in advance.

NUTRITIONAL INFORMATION

Calories	323	Sugars	5g
Protein	13g	Fat	12g
Carbohydrate	41g	Saturates	2g

25 mins 3½ hrs

SERVES 6

INGREDIENTS

- 225 g/8 oz dried haricot beans, soaked overnight and drained
- 225 g/8 oz dried penne, or other short pasta shapes
- 6 tbsp olive oil
- 850 ml/1½ pints vegetable stock
- 2 large onions, sliced
- 2 garlic cloves, chopped
- 2 bay leaves
- 1 tsp dried oregano
- 1 tsp dried thyme
- 5 tbsp red wine
- 2 tbsp tomato purée
- 2 celery sticks, sliced
- 1 fennel bulb, sliced
- 125 g/4½ oz mushrooms, sliced
- 225 g/8 oz tomatoes, sliced
- 1 tsp dark muscovado sugar
- 50 g/1¾ oz dry white breadcrumbs
- salt and pepper

TO SERVE

- salad leaves
- crusty bread

1 Put the beans in a large pan, cover them with water and bring to the boil. Boil the beans rapidly for 20 minutes, then drain them and set aside.

2 Cook the pasta for only 3 minutes in a large pan of boiling salted water, adding 1 tablespoon of the oil. Drain in a colander and set aside.

3 Put the beans in a large flameproof casserole, pour on the vegetable stock and stir in the remaining olive oil, the onions, garlic, bay leaves, herbs, wine and tomato purée.

4 Bring to the boil, cover the casserole and cook in a preheated oven, 180°C/350°F/Gas Mark 4, for 2 hours.

5 Remove the casserole from the oven and add the reserved pasta, the celery, fennel, mushrooms and tomatoes and season to taste with salt and pepper.

6 Stir in the sugar and sprinkle on the breadcrumbs. Cover the casserole again, return to the oven and continue cooking for 1 hour. Serve hot with salad leaves and crusty bread.

3

5

6

Brazil Nut & Mushroom Pie

The button mushrooms give this wholesome vegan pie a wonderful aromatic flavour. The pie can be frozen uncooked and baked from frozen.

NUTRITIONAL INFORMATION

Calories	784	Sugars	5g
Protein	17g	Fat	58g
Carbohydrate	52g	Saturates	19g

45 mins 50 mins

SERVES 4

INGREDIENTS

PASTRY

- 225 g/8 oz plain wholemeal flour
- 100 g/3½ oz vegan margarine, cut into small pieces
- 4 tbsp water
- soya milk, to glaze

FILLING

- 2 tbsp vegan margarine
- 1 onion, chopped
- 1 garlic clove, finely chopped
- 125 g/4½ oz button mushrooms, sliced
- 1 tbsp plain flour
- 150 ml/5 fl oz vegetable stock
- 1 tbsp tomato purée
- 175 g/6 oz brazil nuts, chopped
- 75 g/2¾ oz fresh wholemeal breadcrumbs
- 2 tbsp chopped fresh parsley
- ½ tsp pepper

1 To make the pastry, sieve the flour into a mixing bowl and tip in the bran remaining in the sieve. Add the vegan margarine and rub in with your fingertips until the mixture resembles fine breadcrumbs. Stir in the water and bring together to form a dough. Wrap and chill in the refrigerator for 30 minutes.

2 To make the filling, melt half of the margarine in a frying pan. Add the onion, garlic and mushrooms and fry for 5 minutes until softened. Add the flour and cook for 1 minute, stirring constantly. Gradually add the stock, stirring until the sauce is smooth and beginning to thicken. Stir in the tomato purée, brazil nuts, breadcrumbs, parsley and pepper. Remove the pan from the heat and set aside to cool slightly.

3 On a lightly floured surface, roll out two-thirds of the pastry and use to line a 20-cm/8-inch loose-bottomed quiche/flan tin or pie dish. Spread the filling in the pastry case. Brush the edges of the pastry with soya milk. Roll out the remaining pastry to fit the top of the pie. Seal the edges, make a slit in the top of the pastry for steam to escape and brush with soya milk.

4 Bake in a preheated oven, 200°C/400°F/Gas Mark 6, for 30–40 minutes until golden brown.

2

2

2

Lentil & Red Pepper Flan

This savoury flan combines lentils and red peppers in a tasty wholemeal pastry case. This flan is suitable for vegans.

NUTRITIONAL INFORMATION

Calories	374	Sugars	5g
Protein	13g	Fat	17g
Carbohydrate	44g	Saturates	7g

15–20 mins

50 mins

SERVES 6

INGREDIENTS

PASTRY

225 g/8 oz plain wholemeal flour

100 g/3½ oz vegan margarine, cut into small pieces

4 tbsp water

FILLING

175 g/6 oz red lentils, rinsed

300 ml/10 fl oz vegetable stock

1 tbsp vegan margarine

1 onion, chopped

2 red peppers, deseeded and diced

1 tsp yeast extract

1 tbsp tomato purée

3 tbsp chopped fresh parsley

pepper

1 To make the pastry, sift the flour into a mixing bowl and tip in the bran remaining in the sieve. Add the vegan margarine and rub in with your fingertips until the mixture resembles fine breadcrumbs. Stir in the water and bring together to form a dough. Wrap and chill in the refrigerator for 30 minutes.

2 Meanwhile, make the filling. Put the lentils in a saucepan with the stock, bring to the boil and then simmer for 10 minutes until the lentils are tender and can be mashed to a purée.

3 Melt the margarine in a small pan, add the chopped onion and diced red peppers and fry until just soft.

4 Add the lentil purée, yeast extract, tomato purée and parsley. Season to taste with pepper. Mix until thoroughly combined.

5 On a lightly floured surface, roll out the dough and line a 24-cm/9½-inch loose-bottomed quiche tin. Prick the base of the pastry with a fork and spoon the lentil mixture into the pastry case.

6 Bake in a preheated oven, 200°C/400°F/Gas Mark 6, for 30 minutes until the filling is firm.

VARIATION

Add sweetcorn to the flan in step 4 for a colourful and tasty change, if you prefer.

Stuffed Vegetables

You can fill your favourite vegetables with this nutty-tasting combination of cracked wheat, tomatoes and cucumber.

NUTRITIONAL INFORMATION

Calories	194	Sugars	7g
Protein	5g	Fat	4g
Carbohydrate	36g	Saturates	0.5g

40 mins 25 mins

SERVES 4

INGREDIENTS

4 large beef tomatoes

4 courgettes

2 orange peppers

salt and pepper

FILLING

225 g/8 oz cracked wheat

¼ cucumber

1 red onion

2 tbsp lemon juice

2 tbsp chopped fresh coriander

2 tbsp chopped fresh mint

1 tbsp olive oil

2 tsp cumin seeds

warm pitta bread and hummus, to serve

1 Cut off the tops of the tomatoes and reserve. Using a teaspoon, scoop out the tomato pulp, chop and place in a bowl. Season the tomato shells with salt and pepper, then turn them upside down on absorbent kitchen paper.

1

2 Trim the courgettes and cut a V-shaped groove lengthways down each one. Finely chop the cut-out courgette flesh and add to the tomato pulp. Season the courgette shells with salt and pepper to taste and set aside. Halve the peppers. Leaving the stalks intact, cut out the seeds and discard. Season the pepper shells with salt and pepper to taste and set aside.

2

3 To make the filling, soak the cracked wheat according to the instructions on the packet. Finely chop the cucumber and add to the reserved tomato pulp and courgette mixture. Finely chop the red onion and add to the vegetable mixture with the lemon juice, herbs, olive oil, cumin and seasoning and mix together well.

2

4 When the wheat has soaked, mix with the vegetables and stuff into the tomato, courgette and pepper shells. Place the tops on the tomatoes, transfer to a roasting tin and bake in a preheated oven, 200°C/400°F/Gas Mark 6, for 20–25 minutes until cooked through. Drain and serve hot or warm with pitta bread and hummus.

COOK'S TIP

It is a good idea to blanch vegetables (except for tomatoes) before stuffing. Blanch peppers, courgettes and aubergines for 5 minutes.

Spicy Black-eyed Beans

A hearty casserole of black-eyed beans in a rich, sweet tomato sauce flavoured with treacle and mustard.

NUTRITIONAL INFORMATION

Calories	233	Sugars	21g
Protein	11g	Fat	4g
Carbohydrate	42g	Saturates	1g

15 mins

1½ hrs

SERVES 4

INGREDIENTS

- 350 g/12 oz dried black-eyed beans, soaked overnight in cold water
- 1 tbsp vegetable oil
- 2 onions, chopped
- 1 tbsp clear honey
- 2 tbsp treacle
- 4 tbsp dark soy sauce
- 1 tsp mustard powder
- 4 tbsp tomato purée
- 450 ml/16 fl oz vegetable stock
- 1 bay leaf
- 1 sprig each rosemary, thyme and sage
- 1 small orange
- 1 tbsp cornflour
- 2 red peppers, deseeded and diced
- pepper
- 2 tbsp chopped fresh flat-leaf parsley, to garnish
- crusty bread, to serve

1 Rinse the beans and place in a saucepan. Cover with water, bring to the boil and boil rapidly for 10 minutes. Drain and place in a casserole.

2 Meanwhile, heat the oil in a frying pan. Add the onions and fry over a low heat, stirring occasionally, for 5 minutes. Stir in the honey, treacle, soy sauce, mustard and tomato purée. Pour in the stock, bring to the boil and pour over the beans.

3 Tie the bay leaf and herbs together with a clean piece of string and add to the casserole containing the beans. Using a vegetable peeler, pare off 3 pieces of orange rind and mix into the beans, along with plenty of pepper. Cover and cook in a preheated oven, 150°C/300°F/Gas Mark 2, for 1 hour.

4 Squeeze the juice from the orange and blend with the cornflour to form a smooth paste. Stir into the beans, together with the red peppers. Cover the casserole and return to the oven for 1 hour, until the sauce is rich and thick and the beans are tender. Remove and discard the herbs and orange rind.

5 Garnish with chopped parsley and serve immediately with crusty bread.

1

2

3

Garlic & Sage Bread

This freshly made herb bread is an ideal accompaniment to salads and soups and is suitable for vegans.

NUTRITIONAL INFORMATION

Calories	207	Sugars	3g
Protein	9g	Fat	2g
Carbohydrate	42g	Saturates	0g

1¼ hrs

30 mins

MAKES 6

INGREDIENTS

- vegan margarine, for greasing
- 250 g/9 oz strong brown bread flour
- 1 sachet easy-blend dried yeast
- 3 tbsp chopped fresh sage
- 2 tsp sea salt
- 3 garlic cloves, finely chopped
- 1 tsp clear honey
- 150 ml/5 fl oz hand-hot water

1 Grease a baking tray. Sieve the flour into a large mixing bowl and stir in the bran remaining in the sieve.

2 Stir in the dried yeast, chopped sage and half of the sea salt. Reserve 1 teaspoon of the chopped garlic for sprinkling and stir the remainder into the bowl. Add the honey, together with the hand-hot water and mix together to form a dough.

3 Turn the dough out on to a lightly floured surface and knead it for about 5 minutes (alternatively, use an electric mixer with a dough hook).

4 Place the dough in a greased bowl, cover and leave to rise in a warm place until doubled in size.

5 Knead the dough again for a few minutes, shape it into a ring (see Cook's Tip) and place on the baking tray.

6 Cover and leave to rise for a further 30 minutes or until springy to the touch. Sprinkle with the rest of the sea salt and garlic.

7 Bake the loaf in a preheated oven, 200°C/400°F/Gas Mark 6, for 25–30 minutes. Transfer to a wire rack to cool before serving.

3

5

6

COOK'S TIP

Roll the dough into a long sausage and then curve it into a circular shape. You can omit the sea salt for sprinkling, if you prefer.

Roman Focaccia

Roman focaccia makes a delicious snack on its own or it can be served with soup, cheese and salad for a quick supper.

NUTRITIONAL INFORMATION

Calories	119	Sugars	2g
Protein	3g	Fat	2g
Carbohydrate	24g	Saturates	0.3g

1 hr

45 mins

Makes 16 squares

INGREDIENTS

- 10 g/¼ oz dried yeast
- 1 tsp granulated sugar
- 300 ml/10 fl oz hand-hot water
- 450 g/1 lb strong white flour
- 2 tsp salt
- 3 tbsp rosemary, chopped
- 2 tbsp olive oil
- 450 g/1 lb mixed red and white onions, sliced into rings
- 4 garlic cloves, sliced

1 Place the yeast and the sugar in a small bowl and mix with 100 ml/3½ fl oz of the water. Leave to ferment in a warm place for 15 minutes.

2 Mix the flour with the salt in a large bowl. Add the yeast mixture, half of the rosemary and the remaining water and mix to form a smooth dough. Knead the dough for 4 minutes. Cover the dough with oiled clingfilm and leave to rise for 30 minutes or until doubled in size.

3 Meanwhile, heat the oil in a large pan. Add the onions and garlic and fry over a low heat, stirring occasionally, for 5 minutes or until softened. Cover the pan and continue to cook for 7–8 minutes or until the onions are lightly caramelized.

4 Remove the dough from the bowl and knead it again for 1–2 minutes.

5 Roll the dough out to form a square shape. The dough should be no more than 5 mm/¼ inch thick because it will rise during cooking. Place the dough on a large baking tray, pushing out the edges until even.

6 Spread the onions over the dough, and sprinkle with the remaining chopped rosemary.

7 Bake in a preheated oven, 200°C/400°F/Gas Mark 6, for 25–30 minutes or until a golden brown colour. Cool slightly, cut the focaccia into 16 squares and serve immediately.

2

3

5

Sun-dried Tomato Loaf

This delicious tomato bread is great with cheese or soup or for making an unusual sandwich. This recipe makes one loaf.

2

5
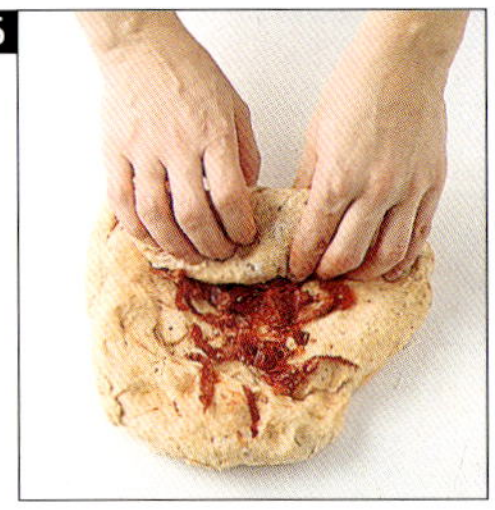

6

NUTRITIONAL INFORMATION

Calories	403	Sugars	5g
Protein	12g	Fat	2g
Carbohydrate	91g	Saturates	0.3g

1¾ hrs

35 mins

SERVES 4

INGREDIENTS

- 10 g/¼ oz dried yeast
- 1 tsp granulated sugar
- 300 ml/10 fl oz hand-hot water
- 450 g/1 lb strong white flour
- 1 tsp salt
- 2 tsp dried basil
- vegan margarine, for greasing
- 2 tbsp sun-dried tomato paste or tomato purée
- vegan margaraine, for greasing
- 12 sun-dried tomatoes in oil, drained and cut into strips

1 Place the yeast and sugar in a bowl and mix with 100 ml/3½ fl oz of the water. Leave to ferment in a warm place for 15 minutes.

2 Place the flour in a bowl and stir in the salt. Make a well in the dry ingredients and add the basil, yeast mixture, tomato paste and half of the remaining water. Using a wooden spoon, draw the flour into the liquid and mix to form a dough, adding the rest of the water a little at a time.

3 Turn out the dough on to a floured surface and knead for 5 minutes or until smooth. Cover with oiled clingfilm and leave in a warm place to rise for about 30 minutes or until doubled in size.

4 Lightly grease a 900-g/2-lb loaf tin with a little vegan margarine.

5 Remove the dough from the bowl and knead in the sun-dried tomatoes. Knead again for 2–3 minutes.

6 Place the dough in the prepared tin and leave to rise for 30–40 minutes or until it has doubled in size again. Bake in a preheated oven, 190°C/375°F/Gas Mark 5, for 30–35 minutes or until golden and the base sounds hollow when tapped. Cool on a wire rack.

COOK'S TIP

You could make mini sun-dried tomato loaves for children. Divide the dough into 8 equal portions, leave to rise and bake in mini-loaf tins for 20 minutes.

Roasted Pepper Bread

Peppers become marvellously sweet and mild when they are roasted and make this bread delicious.

NUTRITIONAL INFORMATION

Calories	426	Sugars	4g
Protein	12g	Fat	4g
Carbohydrate	90g	Saturates	1g

$1\frac{3}{4}$ hrs — 1 hr 5 mins

SERVES 4

INGREDIENTS

- vegan margarine, for greasing
- 1 red pepper, halved and deseeded
- 1 yellow pepper, halved and deseeded
- 2 sprigs rosemary
- 1 tbsp olive oil
- 10 g/$\frac{1}{4}$ oz dried yeast
- 1 tsp granulated sugar
- 300 ml/5 fl oz hand-hot water
- 450 g/1 lb strong white flour
- 1 tsp salt

1 Grease a 23-cm/9-inch deep round cake tin with vegan margarine.

2 Place the peppers and rosemary in a shallow roasting tin. Pour over the oil and roast in a preheated oven, 200°C/400°F/Gas Mark 6, for 20 minutes or until slightly charred. Remove the skin from the peppers and cut the flesh into slices.

3 Place the yeast and sugar in a small bowl and mix with 100 ml/$3\frac{1}{2}$ fl oz of hand-hot water. Leave to ferment in a warm place for 15 minutes.

4 Mix the flour and salt together in a large bowl. Stir in the yeast mixture and the remaining water and mix to form a smooth dough.

5 Knead the dough for about 5 minutes until smooth. Cover with oiled cling film and leave to rise for about 30 minutes or until doubled in size.

6 Cut the dough into 3 equal portions. Roll the portions into rounds slightly larger than the cake tin.

7 Place 1 round in the base of the tin so that it reaches up the sides of the tin by about 2 cm/$\frac{3}{4}$ inch. Top with half of the pepper mixture.

8 Place the second round of dough on top, followed by the remaining pepper mixture. Place the last round of dough on top, gently pushing the edges of the dough down the sides of the tin to enclose the peppers completely.

9 Cover the dough with oiled clingfilm and leave to rise for 30–40 minutes. Bake for 45 minutes until golden or the base sounds hollow when lightly tapped. Transfer to a wire rack to cool slightly and serve warm.

2

6

7

Apricot Slices

These vegan slices are ideal for children's lunches. They are full of flavour and made with healthy ingredients.

NUTRITIONAL INFORMATION

Calories	198	Sugars	13g
Protein	4g	Fat	9g
Carbohydrate	25g	Saturates	2g

50 mins   1 hr

MAKES 12

INGREDIENTS

PASTRY

- 100 g/3½ oz vegan margarine, cut into small pieces, plus extra for greasing
- 225 g/8 oz wholemeal flour
- 50 g/1¾ oz finely ground mixed nuts
- 4 tbsp water
- soya milk, to glaze

FILLING

- 225 g/8 oz dried apricots
- grated rind of 1 orange
- 300 ml/10 fl oz apple juice
- 1 tsp ground cinnamon
- 50 g/1¾ oz raisins

1 Lightly grease a 23-cm/9-inch square cake tin. To make the pastry, place the flour and nuts in a mixing bowl and rub in the margarine with your fingers until the mixture resembles breadcrumbs. Stir in the water and bring together to form a dough. Wrap and set aside to chill in the refrigerator for 30 minutes.

2 To make the filling, place the apricots, orange rind and apple juice in a pan and bring to the boil. Simmer for 30 minutes, until the apricots are mushy. Cool slightly, then process in a food processor or blender to a purée. Alternatively, press the mixture through a sieve. Stir in the cinnamon and raisins.

3 Divide the pastry in half, roll out one half and use to line the base of the tin. Spread the apricot purée over the top and brush the edges of the pastry with water. Roll out the rest of the dough to fit over the top of the apricot purée. Press down and seal the edges.

4 Prick the top of the pastry with a fork and brush with soya milk. Bake in a preheated oven, 200°C/400°F/Gas Mark 6, for 20–25 minutes until the pastry is golden. Leave to cool slightly before cutting into 12 bars. Serve either warm or cold.

1

2

3

COOK'S TIP

These slices will keep in an airtight container for 3-4 days.

Baked Cheesecake

This cheesecake has a rich creamy texture, but contains no dairy produce, as it is made with tofu.

NUTRITIONAL INFORMATION

Calories	282	Sugars	17g
Protein	9g	Fat	15g
Carbohydrate	29g	Saturates	4g

2¼ hrs 45 mins

SERVES 6

INGREDIENTS

- vegan margarine, for greasing
- 125 g/4½ oz digestive biscuits, crushed
- 4 tbsp vegan margarine, melted
- 50 g/1¾ oz chopped stoned dates
- 4 tbsp lemon juice
- rind of 1 lemon
- 3 tbsp water
- 350 g/12 oz firm tofu
- 150 ml/5 fl oz apple juice
- 1 banana, mashed
- 1 tsp vanilla essence
- 1 mango, peeled, stoned and chopped

1 Lightly grease an 18-cm/ 7-inch round loose-bottomed cake tin with vegan margarine.

2 Mix together the digestive biscuit crumbs and melted margarine in a bowl. Press the mixture into the base of the prepared tin.

3 Put the chopped dates, lemon juice, lemon rind and water into a saucepan and bring to the boil. Simmer for 5 minutes until the dates are soft, then mash them roughly with a fork.

4 Place the mixture in a blender or food processor, together with the tofu, apple juice, mashed banana and vanilla essence and process until the mixture is a thick, smooth purée.

5 Pour the tofu purée into the prepared biscuit crumb base and gently smooth the surface.

6 Bake in a preheated oven, 180°C/350°F/Gas Mark 4, for 30–40 minutes until lightly golden. Leave to cool in the tin, then chill thoroughly before serving.

7 Place the chopped mango in a blender and process until smooth. Serve it as a sauce with the cheesecake.

2

3

4

VARIATION

Silken tofu may be substituted for the firm tofu to give a softer texture; it will take 40–50 minutes to set.

Upside-down Cake

This recipe shows how a classic favourite can be adapted for vegans by using vegetarian margarine and oil instead of butter and eggs.

NUTRITIONAL INFORMATION

Calories	354	Sugars	31g
Protein	3g	Fat	15g
Carbohydrate	56g	Saturates	2g

15 mins — 50 mins

SERVES 6

INGREDIENTS

- 4 tbsp vegan margarine, cut into small pieces, plus extra for greasing
- 425 g/15 oz canned unsweetened pineapple pieces in fruit juice, drained, with the juice reserved
- 4 tsp cornflour
- 50 g/1¾ oz soft brown sugar
- 125 ml/4 fl oz water
- rind of 1 lemon

SPONGE

- 3½ tbsp sunflower oil
- 75 g/2¾ oz soft brown sugar
- 150 ml/5 fl oz water
- 150 g/5½ oz plain flour
- 2 tsp baking powder
- 1 tsp ground cinnamon

1 Grease a deep 18-cm/7-inch cake tin. Mix the reserved juice from the pineapple with the cornflour until it forms a smooth paste. Put the paste in a saucepan with the sugar, margarine and water and stir over a low heat until the sugar has dissolved. Bring to the boil and simmer for 2–3 minutes until thickened. Set aside to cool slightly.

2 To make the sponge, place the oil, sugar and water in a saucepan. Heat gently until the sugar has dissolved, but do not allow it to boil. Remove from the heat and leave to cool. Sift the flour, baking powder and ground cinnamon into a mixing bowl. Pour over the cooled sugar syrup and beat well to form a batter.

3 Place the pineapple pieces and lemon rind on the base of the prepared tin and pour over 4 tablespoons of the pineapple syrup. Spoon the sponge batter on top.

4 Bake in a preheated oven, 180°C/350°F/Gas Mark 4, for 35–40 minutes until set and a fine metal skewer inserted into the centre comes out clean. Invert on to a plate, leave to stand for 5 minutes, then remove the tin. Serve with the remaining syrup.

Date & Apricot Tart

There is no need to add any extra sugar to this filling because the dried fruit is naturally sweet. This tart is suitable for vegans.

NUTRITIONAL INFORMATION

Calories	359	Sugars	34g
Protein	7g	Fat	15g
Carbohydrate	53g	Saturates	2g

45 mins 50 mins

SERVES 8

INGREDIENTS

225 g/8 oz plain wholemeal flour
50 g/1¾ oz mixed nuts, ground
100 g/3½ oz vegan margarine, cut into small pieces
4 tbsp water
225 g/8 oz dried apricots, chopped
225 g/8 oz chopped stoned dates
425 ml/15 fl oz apple juice
1 tsp ground cinnamon
grated rind of 1 lemon
soya custard, to serve (optional)

1 Place the flour and ground nuts in a mixing bowl and rub in the margarine with your fingertips until the mixture resembles breadcrumbs. Stir in the water and bring together to form a dough. Wrap the dough and chill in the refrigerator for 30 minutes.

2 Meanwhile, place the apricots and dates in a saucepan, together with the apple juice, cinnamon and lemon rind. Bring to the boil, cover and simmer over a low heat for about 15 minutes until the fruit softens and can be mashed to a purée.

3 Reserve a small ball of pastry for making lattice strips. On a lightly floured surface, roll out the rest of the dough to form a round and use to line a 23-cm/9-inch loose-bottomed quiche tin.

4 Spread the date and apricot filling evenly over the base of the pastry case. Roll out the reserved pastry on a lightly floured surface and cut into strips 1 cm/½ inch wide. Cut the strips to fit the tart and gently twist them across the top of the fruit to form a decorative lattice pattern. Moisten the edges of the strips with water and seal them firmly around the rim of the tart.

5 Bake in a preheated oven, 200°/400°F/Gas Mark 6, for 25–30 minutes, until golden brown. Cut into slices and serve immediately with soya custard, if using.

2

4

4

Fruit Crumble

Any fruits in season can be used in this wholesome pudding. It is suitable for vegans as it contains no dairy produce.

NUTRITIONAL INFORMATION

Calories	426	Sugars	37g
Protein	8g	Fat	16g
Carbohydrate	67g	Saturates	4g

10 mins

30 mins

SERVES 6

INGREDIENTS

- vegan margarine, for greasing
- 6 dessert pears, peeled, cored, quartered and sliced
- 1 tbsp chopped stem ginger
- 1 tbsp dark muscovado sugar
- 2 tbsp orange juice

TOPPING

- 175 g/6 oz plain flour
- 75 g/2¾ oz vegan margarine, cut into small pieces
- 25 g/1 oz almonds, flaked
- 25 g/1 oz porridge oats
- 50 g/1¾ oz dark muscovado sugar
- soya custard, to serve

1 Lightly grease a 1-litre/2-pint ovenproof dish with vegan margarine.

2 Mix together the pears, ginger, muscovado sugar and orange juice in a large bowl. Spoon the mixture into the prepared dish.

3 To make the crumble topping, sift the flour into a mixing bowl. Add the margarine and rub in with your fingertips until the mixture resembles fine breadcrumbs. Stir in the flaked almonds, porridge oats and muscovado sugar. Mix until well combined.

4 Sprinkle the crumble topping evenly over the pear and ginger mixture in the dish.

5 Bake in a preheated oven, 190°C/375°F/Gas Mark 5, for 30 minutes, until the topping is golden and the fruit tender. Serve with soya custard, if using.

VARIATION

Stir 1 tsp ground mixed spice into the crumble mixture in step 3 for added flavour, if you prefer.

Eggless Sponge

This is a healthy and extremely tasty variation of the classic Victoria sponge cake, and is suitable for vegans.

NUTRITIONAL INFORMATION

Calories	273	Sugars	27g
Protein	3g	Fat	9g
Carbohydrate	49g	Saturates	1g

1¼ hrs | 30 mins

1 x 8" CAKE

INGREDIENTS

- vegan margarine, for greasing
- 225 g/8 oz self-raising wholemeal flour
- 2 tsp baking powder
- 175 g/6 oz caster sugar
- 6 tbsp sunflower oil
- 250 ml/8 fl oz water
- 1 tsp vanilla essence
- 4 tbsp strawberry or raspberry reduced-sugar spread
- caster sugar, for dusting

1 Grease 2 x 20-cm/8-inch sandwich cake tins and line the bases with baking paper.

2 Sieve the self-raising flour and baking powder into a large mixing bowl, stirring in any bran remaining in the sieve. Stir in the caster sugar.

3 Pour in the sunflower oil, water and vanilla essence. Mix well with a wooden spoon for about 1 minute until the mixture is smooth, then divide between the prepared tins.

4 Bake in a preheated oven, 180°C/ 350°F/Gas Mark 4, for 25–30 minutes until just firm to the touch.

3

3

3

5 Leave the sponges to cool in the tins before turning out and transferring to a wire rack.

6 To serve, remove the baking paper and place one of the sponges on a serving plate. Cover with the spread and place the other sponge on top.

7 Dust the eggless sponge cake with a little caster sugar before serving.

VARIATION

To make a chocolate-flavoured sponge, replace 15 g/½ oz of the flour with sifted cocoa powder. To make a citrus-flavoured sponge, add the grated rind of ½ lemon or orange to the flour in step 2. To make a coffee-flavoured sponge, replace 2 teaspoons of the flour with instant coffee powder.

Desserts

Confirmed pudding lovers feel a meal is lacking if there isn't a tempting dessert to finish off the menu. Yet it is often possible to combine indulgence with healthy

ingredients. A lot of the recipes in this chapter contain fruit, which is the perfect ingredient for healthy desserts that are still deliciously tempting, such as Blackberry Pudding, Raspberry Shortcake, One Roll Fruit Pie, Apple Tart Tatin and Baked Bananas. Some desserts are also packed full of protein-rich nuts, such as Pine Kernel Tart and Almond Cheesecakes.

Eve's Pudding

This is a popular family favourite pudding with soft apples on the bottom and a light buttery sponge on top.

NUTRITIONAL INFORMATION

Calories	365	Sugars	40g
Protein	5g	Fat	14g
Carbohydrate	58g	Saturates	7g

15 mins 45 mins

SERVES 6

INGREDIENTS

- 6 tbsp butter, plus extra for greasing
- 450 g/1 lb cooking apples, peeled, cored and sliced
- 75 g/2¾ oz granulated sugar
- 1 tbsp lemon juice
- 50 g/1¾ oz sultanas
- 75 g/2¾ oz caster sugar
- 1 egg, beaten
- 150 g/5½ oz self-raising flour
- 3 tbsp milk
- 25 g/1 oz flaked almonds
- custard or double cream, to serve

2

3

5

1 Grease an 900-ml/1½-pint ovenproof dish with butter.

2 Mix the apples with the sugar, lemon juice and sultanas. Spoon the mixture into the greased dish.

3 In a bowl, cream the butter and caster sugar together until pale. Add the egg, a little at a time.

4 Carefully fold in the self-raising flour and stir in the milk to give a soft, dropping consistency.

5 Spread the mixture over the apples and sprinkle with the flaked almonds.

6 Bake in a preheated oven, 180°C/350°F/Gas Mark 4, for 40–45 minutes until the sponge is golden brown.

7 Serve the pudding piping hot, accompanied by homemade custard or double cream.

COOK'S TIP

To increase the almond flavour of this pudding, add 25 g/1 oz ground almonds with the flour in step 4.

Queen of Puddings

A slightly different version of this old favourite made with the addition of orange rind and marmalade to give a delicious citrus flavour.

NUTRITIONAL INFORMATION

Calories	289	Sugars	46g
Protein	6g	Fat	8g
Carbohydrate	50g	Saturates	4g

25 mins — 45 mins

SERVES 8

INGREDIENTS

- 2 tbsp butter, plus extra for greasing
- 600 ml/1 pint milk
- 225 g/8 oz caster sugar
- finely grated rind of 1 orange
- 4 eggs, separated
- 75 g/2¾ oz fresh breadcrumbs
- 6 tbsp orange marmalade
- salt

1 Grease a 1.5-litre/2¾-pint ovenproof dish with butter.

2 To make the custard, heat the milk in a pan with the butter, 50 g/1¾ oz of the caster sugar and the grated orange rind until just warm.

3 Whisk the egg yolks in a bowl. Gradually pour the warm milk over the eggs, whisking constantly.

4 Stir the breadcrumbs into the pan, then transfer the mixture to the prepared dish and leave to stand for 15 minutes.

5 Bake in a preheated oven, 180°C/350°F/Gas Mark 4, for 20–25 minutes until the custard has just set. Remove the custard from the oven but do not turn the oven off.

6 To make the meringue, whisk the egg whites with a pinch of salt until they stand in soft peaks. Whisk in the remaining sugar, a little at a time.

7 Spread the orange marmalade over the cooked custard. Top with the meringue, spreading it right to the edges of the dish.

8 Return the pudding to the oven and bake for a further 20 minutes until the meringue is crisp and golden.

COOK'S TIP

If you prefer a crisper meringue, bake the pudding in the oven for an extra 5 minutes.

Bread & Butter Pudding

Everyone has their own favourite recipe for this dish. This one has added marmalade and grated apples for a really rich and unique taste.

NUTRITIONAL INFORMATION

Calories	427	Sugars	63g
Protein	9g	Fat	13g
Carbohydrate	74g	Saturates	7g

45 mins — 1 hr

SERVES 6

INGREDIENTS

- 5 tbsp butter, softened
- 4–5 slices of white or brown bread
- 4 tbsp chunky orange marmalade
- grated rind of 1 lemon
- 85–125 g/3–4½ oz raisins or sultanas
- 40 g/1½ oz chopped mixed peel
- 1 tsp ground cinnamon or mixed spice
- 1 cooking apple, peeled, cored and coarsely grated
- 85 g/3 oz light brown sugar
- 3 eggs
- 500 ml/18 fl oz milk
- 2 tbsp demerara sugar

2

5

6

1 Use the butter to grease an ovenproof dish and to spread on the slices of bread, then spread the bread with the marmalade.

2 Place a layer of bread in the base of the dish and sprinkle with the lemon rind, half the raisins or sultanas, half the mixed peel, half the spice, all of the apple and half the light brown sugar.

3 Add another layer of bread, cutting the slices so that they fit the dish.

4 Sprinkle over most of the remaining raisins or sultanas and the remaining peel, spice and light brown sugar, sprinkling it evenly over the bread. Top with a final layer of bread, again cutting to fit the dish.

5 Lightly beat together the eggs and milk and then carefully strain the mixture over the bread in the dish. If time allows, set aside to stand for 20–30 minutes.

6 Sprinkle the top of the pudding with the demerara sugar and scatter over the remaining raisins or sultanas and cook in a preheated oven, 200°C/400°F/Gas Mark 6, for 50–60 minutes, until risen and golden brown. Serve immediately if serving hot or allow to cool completely and then serve cold.

Plum Cobbler

This is a popular dessert which can be adapted to suit all types of fruit if plums are not available.

NUTRITIONAL INFORMATION

Calories	430	Sugars	46g
Protein	7g	Fat	12g
Carbohydrate	79g	Saturates	7g

10 mins

40 mins

SERVES 6

INGREDIENTS

butter, for greasing

1 kg/2 lb 4 oz plums, stoned and sliced

100 g/3 ½ oz caster sugar

1 tbsp lemon juice

250 g/9 oz plain flour

2 tsp baking powder

75 g/2¾ oz granulated sugar

1 egg, beaten

150 ml/5 fl oz buttermilk

75 g/2¾ oz butter, melted and cooled

double cream, to serve

1 Lightly grease a 2-litre/3½-pint ovenproof dish with butter.

2 In a large bowl, mix together the plums, caster sugar, lemon juice and 25 g/1 oz of the plain flour.

3 Spoon the coated plums into the bottom of the prepared ovenproof dish, spreading them out evenly.

4 Sift the remaining flour, together with the baking powder into a large bowl and add the granulated sugar. Stir well to combine.

5 Add the beaten egg, buttermilk and cooled melted butter. Mix everything gently together to form a soft dough.

6 Place spoonfuls of the dough on top of the fruit mixture until it is almost completely covered.

7 Bake the cobbler in a preheated oven, 190°C/375°F/Gas Mark 5, for about 35–40 minutes until golden brown and bubbling.

8 Serve the pudding piping hot, with double cream.

3

5

6

COOK'S TIP

If you cannot find buttermilk, try using soured cream.

Blackberry Pudding

A delicious dessert to make when blackberries are in abundance. If blackberries are unavailable, try using currants or gooseberries.

NUTRITIONAL INFORMATION

Calories	455	Sugars	47g
Protein	7g	Fat	18g
Carbohydrate	70g	Saturates	11g

15–20 mins 30 mins

SERVES 4

INGREDIENTS

- butter, for greasing
- 450 g/1 lb blackberries
- 75 g/2¾ oz caster sugar
- 1 egg
- 75 g/2¾ oz soft brown sugar
- 6 tbsp butter, melted
- 8 tbsp milk
- 125 g/4 ½ oz self-raising flour
- sugar, for sprinkling

1 Lightly grease a large 900-ml/1½-pint ovenproof dish with butter.

2 In a large mixing bowl, gently mix together the blackberries and caster sugar until well combined.

3

5

6

3 Transfer the blackberry and sugar mixture to the prepared dish.

4 Beat the egg and soft brown sugar in a separate mixing bowl. Stir in the melted butter and milk.

5 Sieve the flour into the egg and butter mixture and fold together lightly with a figure-of-eight movement to form a smooth batter.

6 Carefully spread the batter over the blackberry and sugar mixture in the ovenproof dish.

7 Bake the pudding in a preheated oven, 180°C/350°F/Gas Mark 4, for about 25–30 minutes until the topping is firm and golden.

8 Sprinkle the pudding with a little sugar and serve hot.

VARIATION

You can add 2 tablespoons of cocoa powder to the batter in step 5, if you prefer a chocolate flavour.

Raspberry Shortcake

For this lovely summery dessert, two crisp rounds of shortbread are sandwiched together with fresh raspberries and lightly whipped cream.

NUTRITIONAL INFORMATION

Calories	496	Sugars	14g
Protein	4g	Fat	41g
Carbohydrate	30g	Saturates	26g

40 mins

15 mins

SERVES 8

INGREDIENTS

- 100 g/3½ oz butter, cut into cubes, plus extra for greasing
- 175 g/6 oz self-raising flour
- 75 g/2¾ oz caster sugar
- 1 egg yolk
- 1 tbsp rose water
- 600 ml/1 pint whipping cream, lightly whipped
- 225 g/8 oz raspberries, plus a few extra for decoration

TO DECORATE

- icing sugar
- mint leaves

1 Lightly grease 2 baking trays with a little butter.

2 To make the shortcake, sieve the flour into a bowl.

3 Rub the butter into the flour with your fingers until the mixture resembles breadcrumbs.

4 Stir the sugar, egg yolk and rose water into the mixture and bring together with your fingers to form a soft dough. Divide the dough in half.

5 Roll each piece of dough to a 20-cm/8-inch round on a lightly floured surface. Carefully lift each one with the rolling pin on to a prepared baking tray. Crimp the edges of the dough.

6 Bake in a preheated oven, 190°C/375°F/Gas Mark 5, for 15 minutes until lightly golden. Transfer the shortcakes to a wire rack and leave to cool completely.

7 Mix the whipped cream with the raspberries and spoon the mixture on top of one of the shortcakes, spreading it out evenly. Top with the other shortcake round, dust with a little icing sugar and decorate with the extra raspberries and mint leaves.

3

4

5

COOK'S TIP

The shortcake can be made a few days in advance and stored in an airtight container until required.

Pavlova

This delicious dessert originated in Australia. Serve it with sharp fruits to balance the sweetness of the meringue.

NUTRITIONAL INFORMATION

Calories	354	Sugars	34g
Protein	3g	Fat	24g
Carbohydrate	34g	Saturates	15g

1 hr 10 mins · 1¼ hrs

MAKES 6

INGREDIENTS

- 3 egg whites
- 175 g/6 oz caster sugar
- 300 ml/10 fl oz double cream, lightly whipped
- fresh fruit of your choice (raspberries, strawberries, peaches, passion fruit, or cape gooseberries)
- salt

1 Line a baking sheet with a sheet of baking paper.

2 Whisk the egg whites with a pinch of salt in a large bowl until they form soft peaks.

3 Whisk in the sugar, a little at a time, whisking well after each addition until all of the sugar has been incorporated.

4 Spoon three-quarters of the meringue on to the baking sheet, forming a round 20-cm/8-inches in diameter.

5 Place spoonfuls of the remaining meringue all around the edge of the round so they join up to make a rim, creating a nest shape.

6 Bake in a preheated oven, 140°C/275°F/Gas Mark 1, for 1¼ hours.

7 Turn the heat off, but leave the pavlova in the oven until it is completely cold.

8 To serve, place the pavlova on a serving dish. Spread with the lightly whipped cream, then arrange the fresh fruit on top. Do not decorate the pavlova too far in advance or it will go soggy.

2

3

5

COOK'S TIP

If you are worried about making the round shape, draw a circle on the baking paper, turn the paper over, then spoon the meringue inside the outline.

One Roll Fruit Pie

This is an easy way to make a pie, once you have rolled out the pastry and filled it with fruit you just turn the edges of the pastry in!

NUTRITIONAL INFORMATION

Calories	229	Sugars	13g
Protein	4g	Fat	11g
Carbohydrate	30g	Saturates	7g

45 mins | 35 mins

SERVES 8

INGREDIENTS

PASTRY

- 100 g/3½ oz butter, cut into small pieces, plus extra for greasing
- 175 g/6 oz plain flour
- 1 tbsp water
- 1 egg, separated
- sugar cubes, crushed, for sprinkling

FILLING

- 600 g/1½ lb prepared fruit (rhubarb, gooseberries, plums, or damsons)
- 85 g/3 oz soft brown sugar
- 1 tbsp ground ginger

1 Grease a large baking sheet with a little butter.

2 To make the pastry, place the flour and butter in a mixing bowl and rub in the butter with your fingertips until the mixture resembles breadcrumbs. Add the water and work the mixture together until a soft pastry has formed. Wrap and chill in the refrigerator for 30 minutes.

3 On a lightly floured surface, roll out the chilled pastry to a round about 35 cm/14 inches in diameter.

4 Transfer the round to the centre of the greased baking tray. Brush the pastry with the egg yolk.

5 To make the filling, mix the prepared fruit with the brown sugar and ground ginger and pile it into the centre of the pastry.

6 Turn in the edges of the pastry all the way around. Brush the surface of the pastry with the egg white and sprinkle with the crushed sugar cubes.

7 Bake in a preheated oven, 200°C/400°F/Gas Mark 6, for 35 minutes or until golden brown. Transfer to a serving plate and serve warm.

2

4

6

COOK'S TIP

If the pastry breaks when shaping it into a round, don't panic – just patch and seal, as the overall effect of this tart is rough.

Fruit Crumble Tart

This tart has a double helping of flavours, with a fruit filling covered in a crumbly topping.

NUTRITIONAL INFORMATION

Calories	499	Sugars	26g
Protein	7g	Fat	30g
Carbohydrate	53g	Saturates	16g

1 hr 20 mins — 25 mins

SERVES 8

INGREDIENTS

PASTRY

- 150 g/5½ oz plain flour
- 25 g/1 oz caster sugar
- 125 g/4½ oz butter, cut into small pieces
- 1 tbsp water

FILLING

- 250 g/9 oz raspberries
- 450 g/1 lb plums, halved, stoned and roughly chopped
- 3 tbsp demerara sugar

TOPPING

- 125 g/4½ oz plain flour
- 75 g/2¾ oz demerara sugar
- 100 g/3½ oz butter, cut into small pieces
- 100 g/3½ oz chopped mixed nuts
- 1 tsp ground cinnamon

TO SERVE

- single cream

1 To make the pastry, place the flour, sugar and butter in a bowl and rub in the butter with your fingertips until the mixture resembles breadcrumbs. Add the water and work the mixture together until a soft dough has formed. Wrap and chill in the refrigerator for 30 minutes.

2 Roll out the pastry on a lightly floured surface and use to line the base of a 24-cm/9½-inch loose-bottomed quiche/flan tin. Prick the base of the pastry with a fork and chill in the refrigerator for about 30 minutes.

3 To make the filling, toss the raspberries and plums together with the sugar and spoon into the pastry case.

4 To make the crumble topping, combine the flour, sugar and butter in a bowl. Work the butter into the flour with your fingertips until the mixture resembles coarse breadcrumbs. Stir in the nuts and ground cinnamon.

5 Sprinkle the topping over the fruit and press down gently with the back of a spoon. Bake in a preheated oven, 200°C/400°F/Gas Mark 6, for 20–25 minutes until the topping is golden. Serve the tart with single cream.

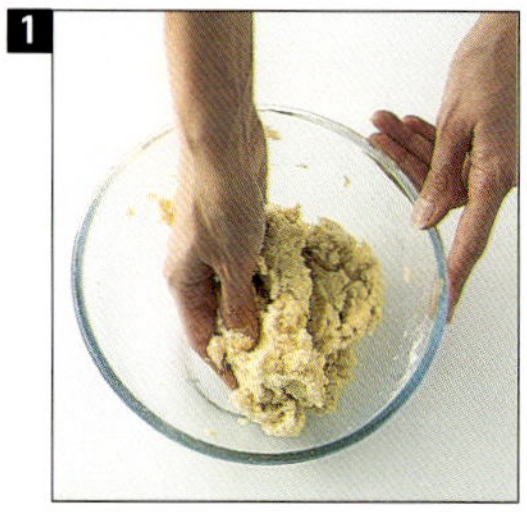

Cheese & Apple Tart

The chopped apples, dates and soft brown sugar combined with cheese make this a sweet tart with a savoury twist to it!

NUTRITIONAL INFORMATION

Calories	360	Sugars	26g
Protein	11g	Fat	18g
Carbohydrate	43g	Saturates	6g

15 mins 50 mins

SERVES 8

INGREDIENTS

- butter, for greasing
- 175 g/6 oz self-raising flour
- 1 tsp baking powder
- pinch of salt
- 75 g/2¾ oz soft brown sugar
- 100 g/3½ oz stoned dates, chopped
- 500 g/1lb 2 oz dessert apples, cored and chopped
- 50 g /1¾ oz walnuts, chopped
- 60 ml/2 fl oz sunflower oil
- 2 eggs
- 175 g/6 oz Red Leicester cheese, grated

2

3

5

1 Grease a 23-cm/9½-inch loose-bottomed quiche/flan tin and line with baking paper.

2 Sieve the flour, baking powder and salt into a bowl. Stir in the brown sugar, dates, apples and walnuts. Mix together until well combined.

3 Beat the oil and eggs together and add the mixture to the dry ingredients. Stir until well combined.

4 Spoon half of the mixture into the prepared tin and level the surface with the back of a spoon.

5 Sprinkle with the grated cheese, then spoon over the remaining cake mixture, spreading it evenly to the edges of the tin.

6 Bake in a preheated oven, 180°C/350°F/Gas Mark 4, for 45–50 minutes or until golden and firm to the touch.

7 Leave to cool slightly in the tin, then turn out and serve warm.

COOK'S TIP

This is a deliciously moist tart. Any leftovers should be stored in the refrigerator and heated to serve.

Apple Tart Tatin

This classic, French upside-down tart is always a popular choice for a comforting dessert at any time of year.

NUTRITIONAL INFORMATION

Calories	340	Sugars	23g
Protein	2g	Fat	22g
Carbohydrate	37g	Saturates	12g

15 mins 30 mins

SERVES 8

INGREDIENTS

- 125 g/4½ oz butter
- 125 g/4½ oz caster sugar
- 4 dessert apples, cored and quartered
- 250 g/9 oz shortcrust pastry dough, defrosted if frozen
- crème fraîche, to serve

1 Heat the butter and sugar in a 23-cm/9-inch ovenproof frying pan over a medium heat for about 5 minutes until the mixture is just beginning to caramelize. Remove the frying pan from the heat.

2 Arrange the apple quarters, skin side down, in the pan, taking care as the butter and sugar will be very hot. Place the frying pan back on the heat and simmer for 2 minutes.

3 On a lightly floured surface, roll out the pastry to form a circle just a little larger than the pan.

4 Place the pastry over the apples, press down and carefully tuck in the edges to seal the apples under the layer of pastry.

5 Bake in a preheated oven, 200°C/400°F/Gas Mark 6, for 20–25 minutes until the pastry is golden. Remove from the oven and set aside to cool for about 10 minutes.

6 Place a serving plate over the frying pan and invert so that the pastry forms the base of the turned-out tart. Serve warm with crème fraîche.

VARIATION

Replace the apples with pears, if you prefer. Leave the skin on the pears, cut them into quarters and then remove the core.

Treacle Tart

This is an old-fashioned pudding which still delights people time after time. It is very quick to make if you use ready-made pastry.

NUTRITIONAL INFORMATION

Calories	378	Sugars	36g
Protein	4g	Fat	17g
Carbohydrate	57g	Saturates	8g

50 mins

40 mins

SERVES 8

INGREDIENTS

- 250 g/9 oz shortcrust pastry dough, defrosted if frozen
- 350 g/12 oz golden syrup
- 125 g/4½ oz fresh white breadcrumbs
- 125 ml/4 fl oz double cream
- finely grated rind of ½ lemon or orange
- 2 tbsp lemon or orange juice
- custard, to serve

2

3

4

1 Roll out the pastry on a lightly floured surface to line a 20-cm/8-inch loose-bottomed quiche/flan tin, reserving the pastry trimmings. Prick the base of the pastry with a fork and leave to chill in the refrigerator for 30 minutes.

2 Cut out small shapes from the reserved pastry trimmings, such as leaves, stars or hearts, to decorate the top of the tart.

3 In a bowl, mix together the golden syrup, breadcrumbs, double cream and grated lemon or orange rind and lemon or orange juice.

4 Pour the mixture into the pastry case and decorate the edges of the tart with the pastry cut-outs.

5 Bake in a preheated oven, 190°C/375°F/Gas Mark 5, for 35–40 minutes or until the filling is just set.

6 Leave the tart to cool slightly in the tin. Turn out and serve warm with homemade custard.

VARIATION

Use the pastry trimmings to create a lattice pattern on top of the tart, if preferred.

Apple & Mincemeat Tart

The fresh apple brings out the flavour of the sweet rich mincemeat and makes it a beautifully moist filling for pies and tarts.

NUTRITIONAL INFORMATION

Calories	402	Sugars	44g
Protein	2g	Fat	19g
Carbohydrate	58g	Saturates	12g

1¼ hrs

50 mins

SERVES 8

INGREDIENTS

PASTRY

150 g/5½ oz plain flour

25 g/1 oz caster sugar

125 g/4½ oz butter, cut into small pieces

1 tbsp water

FILLING

411 g/14½ oz jar mincemeat

3 dessert apples, cored and grated

1 tbsp lemon juice

40 g/1½ oz golden syrup

3 tbsp butter

1. To make the pastry, place the flour and caster sugar in a large mixing bowl and rub in the butter with your fingertips until the mixture resembles breadcrumbs.

2. Add the water and work the mixture together until a soft dough has formed. Wrap and leave to chill in the refrigerator for 30 minutes.

3. On a lightly floured surface, roll out the dough and line a 24-cm/9½-inch loose-bottomed quiche/flan tin. Prick the dough with a fork and leave to chill for 30 minutes.

4. Line the pastry case with foil and baking beans. Bake the case in a preheated oven, 190°C/375°F/Gas Mark 5, for 15 minutes. Remove the foil and beans and cook the pastry case for for a further 15 minutes.

5. Combine the mincemeat with the apples and lemon juice and spoon into the baked pastry case.

6. Melt the syrup and butter together in a small saucepan over a low heat and pour it over the mincemeat mixture in the tart.

7. Return the tart to the oven and bake for about 20 minutes or until firm. Serve warm.

4

5

6

VARIATION

Add 2 tablespoons of sherry to spice up the mincemeat, if you wish.

Custard Tart

This is a classic egg custard tart which should be served as fresh as possible for the best flavour and texture.

NUTRITIONAL INFORMATION

Calories	268	Sugars	5g
Protein	5g	Fat	19g
Carbohydrate	20g	Saturates	12g

1¼ hrs

1 hr

SERVES 8

INGREDIENTS

PASTRY

150 g/5½ oz plain flour

25 g/1 oz caster sugar

125 g/4½ oz butter, cut into small pieces

1 tbsp water

FILLING

3 eggs

150 ml/5 fl oz single cream

150 ml/5 fl oz milk

freshly grated nutmeg

TO SERVE

whipping cream

3

4

7

1 To make the pastry, place the flour and sugar in a mixing bowl and rub in the butter with your fingertips until the mixture resembles breadcrumbs.

2 Add the water and mix together until a soft dough has formed. Wrap in clingfilm and chill in the refrigerator for about 30 minutes.

3 Roll out the dough to form a round slightly larger than a 24-cm/9½-inch loose-bottomed quiche/flan tin.

4 Line the tin with the dough, trimming off the edges. Prick the dough with a fork and leave to chill in the refrigerator for 30 minutes.

5 Line the pastry case with foil and baking beans.

6 Bake in a preheated oven, 190°C/375°F/Gas Mark 5, for 15 minutes. Remove the foil and baking beans and bake the pastry case for a further 15 minutes.

7 To make the filling, whisk together the eggs, cream, milk and nutmeg. Pour the filling into the prepared pastry case. Return the tart to the oven and cook for 25–30 minutes or until just set. Serve with whipping cream, if wished.

COOK'S TIP

Baking the pastry case blind ensures that the finished tart has a crisp base.

Lemon Tart

No-one will be able to resist this tart with its buttery pastry and a sharp, melt-in-the-mouth lemon filling.

NUTRITIONAL INFORMATION

Calories	363	Sugars	18g
Protein	5g	Fat	25g
Carbohydrate	32g	Saturates	15g

1 hr 50 mins — 50 mins

SERVES 8

INGREDIENTS

PASTRY

150 g/5½ oz plain flour

25 g/1 oz caster sugar

125 g/4½ oz butter, cut into small pieces

1 tbsp water

FILLING

150 ml/5 fl oz double cream

100 g/3½ oz caster sugar

4 eggs

grated rind of 3 lemons

175 ml/6 fl oz lemon juice

icing sugar, for dusting

1 To make the pastry, place the flour and sugar in a bowl and rub in the butter using your fingertips until the mixture resembles breadcrumbs. Add the water and mix until a soft dough has formed. Wrap in clingfilm and leave to chill for 30 minutes.

2 On a lightly floured surface, roll out the dough and line a 24-cm/9½-inch loose-bottomed quiche/flan tin. Prick the pastry with a fork and chill in the refrigerator for 30 minutes.

3 Line the pastry case with foil and baking beans and bake in a preheated oven, 190°C/375°F/ Gas Mark 5, for 15 minutes. Remove the foil and baking beans and cook the pastry case for a further 15 minutes.

4 To make the filling, whisk the cream, sugar, eggs, lemon rind and juice together until thoroughly combined. Place the pastry case, still in its tin, on a baking tray and pour in the filling (see Cook's Tip).

5 Bake the tart for about 20 minutes or until the filling is just set. Leave to cool, then remove the tart from the tin and dust lightly with icing sugar just before serving.

1

2

4

COOK'S TIP

To avoid any spillage, pour half of the filling into the pastry case, place in the oven and pour in the remaining filling.

Orange Tart

This is a variation of the classic lemon tart – in this recipe fresh breadcrumbs are used to create a thicker texture.

NUTRITIONAL INFORMATION

Calories	450	Sugars	17g
Protein	6g	Fat	31g
Carbohydrate	40g	Saturates	19g

1 hr 20 mins — 1¾ hrs

SERVES 6–8

INGREDIENTS

PASTRY

- 150 g/5½ oz plain flour
- 25 g/1 oz caster sugar
- 125 g /4½ oz butter, cut into small pieces
- 1 tbsp water

FILLING

- grated rind of 2 oranges
- 135 ml/4½ fl oz orange juice
- 50 g/1¾ oz fresh white breadcrumbs
- 2 tbsp lemon juice
- 150 ml/5 fl oz single cream
- 4 tbsp butter
- 50 g/1¾ oz caster sugar
- 2 eggs, separated
- salt

4

4

5

1 To make the pastry, place the flour and sugar in a bowl and rub in the butter with your fingertips until the mixture resembles breadcrumbs. Add the water and work the mixture together until a soft dough has formed. Wrap in clingfilm and chill in the refrigerator for 30 minutes.

2 Roll out the dough on a lightly floured surface and line a 24-cm/9½-inch loose-bottomed quiche/flan tin. Prick the pastry with a fork and chill in the refrigerator for 30 minutes.

3 Line the pastry case with foil and baking beans and bake in a preheated oven, 190°C/375°F/ Gas Mark 5, for 15 minutes. Remove the foil and beans and cook for a further 15 minutes.

4 To make the filling, mix the orange rind and juice and the breadcrumbs in a bowl. Stir in the lemon juice and cream. Melt the butter and sugar in a pan over a low heat. Remove the pan from the heat, add the egg yolks, a pinch of salt and the breadcrumb mixture and stir.

5 In a mixing bowl, whisk the egg whites with a pinch of salt until they form soft peaks. Fold them into the egg yolk mixture.

6 Pour the filling mixture into the pastry case. Bake in a preheated oven, 170°C/325°F/Gas Mark 3, for about 45 minutes or until just set. Leave to cool slightly and serve warm.

Coconut Cream Tart

Decorate this tart with some fresh tropical fruit, such as mango or pineapple, and extra desiccated coconut, toasted.

NUTRITIONAL INFORMATION	
Calories 740	Sugars 37g
Protein 9g	Fat 52g
Carbohydrate ...62g	Saturates 35g

2¼ hrs — 40 mins

SERVES 6–8

INGREDIENTS

PASTRY

- 150 g/5½ oz plain flour
- 25 g/1 oz caster sugar
- 125 g/4½ oz butter, cut into small pieces
- 1 tbsp water

FILLING

- 425 ml/15 fl oz milk
- 125 g/4½ oz creamed coconut
- 3 egg yolks
- 125 g/4½ oz caster sugar
- 50 g/1¾ oz plain flour, sifted
- 25 g/1 oz desiccated coconut
- 25 g/1 oz glacé pineapple, chopped
- 2 tbsp rum or pineapple juice
- 300 ml/10 fl oz whipping cream, whipped

1 To make the pastry, place the flour and sugar in a bowl and rub in the butter with your fingertips until the mixture resembles breadcrumbs. Add the water and work the mixture together until a soft dough has formed. Wrap in clingfilm and chill in the refrigerator for 30 minutes.

2 Roll out the dough on a lightly floured surface and line a 24-cm/9½-inch loose-bottomed quiche/flan tin. Prick the pastry with a fork and chill in the refrigerator for 30 minutes.

3 Line the pastry case with foil and baking beans and bake in a preheated oven, 190°C/375°F/Gas Mark 5, for 15 minutes. Remove the foil and baking beans and cook the pastry case for a further 15 minutes. Leave to cool.

4 To make the filling, pour the milk into a small saucepan and add the creamed coconut. Set over a low heat and bring to just below boiling point, stirring constantly until the coconut has melted. Remove the pan from the heat.

5 In a bowl, whisk the egg yolks with the sugar until pale and fluffy. Whisk in the flour. Pour the hot milk mixture over the egg mixture, stirring. Return the mixture to the pan and heat gently, stirring constantly, for 8 minutes until thick. Leave to cool.

6 Stir in the coconut, pineapple, rum or juice and spread the filling in the pastry case. Cover with the whipped cream and chill until required.

1

4

5

Pine Kernel Tart

This tart has a sweet filling made with creamy cheese and it is topped with pine kernels for a decorative finish.

NUTRITIONAL INFORMATION

Calories	512	Sugars	22g
Protein	10g	Fat	37g
Carbohydrate	37g	Saturates	18g

2¼ hrs — 1 hr 5 mins

SERVES 8

INGREDIENTS

PASTRY

- 150 g /5½ oz plain flour
- 25 g/1 oz caster sugar
- 125 g/4½ oz butter, cut into small pieces
- 1 tbsp water

FILLING

- 350 g/12 oz curd cheese
- 4 tbsp double cream
- 3 eggs
- 125 g/4½ oz caster sugar
- grated rind of 1 orange
- 100 g/3½ oz pine kernels

1 To make the pastry, place the flour and sugar in a bowl and rub in the butter with your fingertips until the mixture resembles breadcrumbs. Add the water and work the mixture together until a soft dough has formed. Wrap in clingfilm and chill in the refrigerator for 30 minutes.

2 Roll out the dough on a lightly floured surface and line a 24-cm/9½-inch loose-bottomed quiche/flan tin. Prick the pastry with a fork and chill in the refrigerator for 30 minutes.

3 Line the pastry case with foil and baking beans and bake in a preheated oven, 190°C/375°F/Gas Mark 5, for 15 minutes. Remove the foil and beans and cook the pastry case for a further 15 minutes.

4 To make the filling, beat together the curd cheese, cream, eggs, sugar, orange rind and half of the pine kernels. Pour the filling into the pastry case and sprinkle over the remaining pine kernels.

5 Lower the oven temperature to 170°C/325°F/Gas Mark 3 and bake the tart for 35 minutes or until just set. Leave to cool before removing the tart from the tin and serving.

1

2

4

VARIATION

Replace the pine nuts with flaked almonds, if you prefer.

Mixed Peel & Nut Tart

This very rich tart is not for the faint-hearted. Serve it in thin slices – even to lovers of desserts and those with a sweet tooth.

NUTRITIONAL INFORMATION

Calories	643	Sugars	34g
Protein	9g	Fat	47g
Carbohydrate	49g	Saturates	23g

2¼ hrs — 20 mins

SERVES 8

INGREDIENTS

PASTRY

- 150 g/5½ oz plain flour
- 25 g/1 oz caster sugar
- 125 g/4½ oz butter, cut into small pieces
- 1 tbsp water

FILLING

- 6 tbsp butter
- 50 g /1¾ oz caster sugar
- 75 g/2¾ oz set honey
- 200 ml/7 fl oz double cream
- 1 egg, beaten
- 200 g/7 oz mixed nuts
- 200 g/7 oz mixed peel

1. To make the pastry, place the flour and sugar in a bowl and rub in the butter with your fingertips until the mixture resembles breadcrumbs. Add the water and work the mixture together until a soft dough has formed. Wrap in clingfilm and chill in the refrigerator for 30 minutes.

2. Roll out the dough on a lightly floured surface and line a 24-cm/9½-inch loose-bottomed quiche/flan tin. Prick the pastry with a fork and chill for 30 minutes.

3. Line the pastry case with foil and baking beans and bake in a preheated oven, 190°C/375°F/Gas Mark 5, for 15 minutes. Remove the foil and baking beans and cook the pastry case for a further 15 minutes.

4. To make the filling, melt the butter, sugar and honey in a small saucepan. Stir in the cream and beaten egg, then add the nuts and mixed peel. Cook over a low heat for 2 minutes until the mixture is a pale golden colour, stirring constantly.

5. Pour the filling into the pastry case and bake the tart for a further 15–20 minutes or until just set. Leave to cool, then serve in slices.

1

2

4

VARIATION

Substitute walnuts or pecan nuts for the mixed nuts, if you prefer.

Apricot & Cranberry Tart

This frangipane tart is ideal for Christmas, when fresh cranberries are in abundance. If liked, brush the warm tart with melted apricot jam.

NUTRITIONAL INFORMATION

Calories	752	Sugars	40g
Protein	9g	Fat	55g
Carbohydrate	59g	Saturates	28g

1 hr 20 mins — 1½ hrs

SERVES 8

INGREDIENTS

PASTRY

- 150 g/5½ oz plain flour
- 25 g/1 oz caster sugar
- 125 g/4½ oz butter, cut into small pieces
- 1 tbsp water

FILLING

- 200 g/7 oz unsalted butter
- 200g/7 oz caster sugar
- 1 egg
- 2 egg yolks
- 5 tbsp plain flour, sieved
- 175 g/6 oz ground almonds
- 4 tbsp double cream
- 410 g/14½ oz canned apricot halves, drained
- 125 g/4½ oz fresh cranberries

1 To make the pastry, place the flour and sugar in a bowl and rub in the butter with your fingertips until the mixture resembles breadcrumbs. Add the water and work the mixture together until a soft dough has formed. Wrap in clingfilm and chill in the refrigerator for 30 minutes.

2 Roll out the dough on a lightly floured surface and line a 24-cm/9½-inch loose-bottomed quiche/flan tin. Prick the base of the pastry case all over with a fork and chill in the refrigerator for 30 minutes.

3 Line the pastry case with foil and baking beans and bake in a preheated oven, 190°C/375°F/Gas Mark 5, for 15 minutes. Remove the foil and baking beans and cook the pastry case for a further 10 minutes.

4 To make the filling, cream together the butter and sugar until light and fluffy. Beat in the egg and egg yolks, then stir in the flour, almonds and cream.

5 Arrange the apricot halves and cranberries over the bottom of the pastry case and spoon the filling mixture over the top.

6 Bake in the oven for about 1 hour or until the topping is just set. Leave to cool slightly, then serve warm or cold.

2

4

5

Mincemeat & Grape Jalousie

This jalousie makes a good Christmas-time dessert. Its festive filling and flavour is a great alternative to mince pies.

NUTRITIONAL INFORMATION

Calories	796	Sugars	73g
Protein	9g	Fat	35g
Carbohydrate	118g	Saturates	3g

1 hr 5 mins — 45 mins

SERVES 4

INGREDIENTS

- butter, for greasing
- 500 g/1lb 2 oz fresh ready-made puff pastry, defrosted if frozen
- 410 g/14½ oz mincemeat
- 100 g/3½ oz grapes, seeded and halved
- 1 egg, lightly beaten, for glazing
- demerara sugar, for sprinkling

1 Lightly grease a baking tray.

2 On a lightly floured surface, roll out the pastry and cut it into 2 rectangles.

3 Place one pastry rectangle on the prepared baking tray and brush the edges with water.

4 Combine the mincemeat and grapes in a mixing bowl. Spread the mixture over the pastry rectangle on the baking tray, leaving a 2.5-cm/1-inch border.

5 Fold the second pastry rectangle in half lengthways, and carefully cut a series of parallel lines across the folded edge, leaving a 2.5-cm/1-inch border.

6 Open out the pastry rectangle and lay it over the mincemeat. Seal the edges of the pastry and press together well.

7 Flute and crimp the edges of the pastry. Lightly brush with the beaten egg and sprinkle with demerara sugar.

8 Bake in a preheated oven, 220°C/425°F/Gas Mark 7, for 15 minutes. Lower the heat to 180°C/350°F/Gas Mark 4 and cook for a further 30 minutes until the jalousie is well risen and golden brown.

9 Carefully transfer the jalousie to a wire rack to cool completely before serving.

4

5

6

COOK'S TIP

For an enhanced festive flavour, stir 2 tablespoons sherry into the mincemeat.

Pear Tarts

These tarts are made with ready-made puff pastry which is available from most supermarkets. The finished pastry is rich and buttery.

NUTRITIONAL INFORMATION

Calories	250	Sugars	15g
Protein	3g	Fat	14g
Carbohydrate	30g	Saturates	3g

35 mins

20 mins

SERVES 6

INGREDIENTS

250 g/9 oz ready-made puff pastry, defrosted if frozen

25 g/1 oz soft brown sugar

2 tbsp butter, plus extra for brushing

1 tbsp finely chopped stem ginger

3 pears, peeled, halved and cored

cream, to serve

2

5
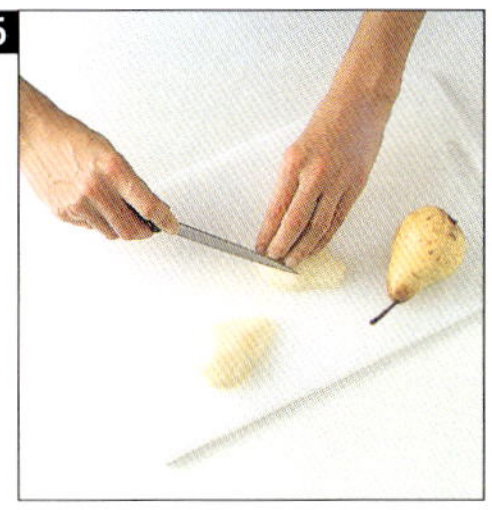

6

1 On a lightly floured surface, roll out the pastry. Cut out six 10-cm/4-inch circles with a plain cutter.

2 Place the circles on a large baking tray and chill in the refrigerator for 30 minutes.

3 Cream together the brown sugar and butter in a small bowl, then stir in the chopped stem ginger.

4 Prick the pastry circles with a fork and spread a little of the ginger mixture on to each one.

5 Slice the pear halves lengthways, keeping the pears intact at the tip. Fan out the slices slightly.

6 Place a fanned-out pear half on top of each pastry circle. Make small flutes around the edge of the pastry circles and brush each pear half with a little melted butter.

7 Bake in a preheated oven, 200°C/400°F/Gas Mark 6, for 15–20 minutes until the pastry is well risen and golden. Allow to cool slightly, then serve warm with a little cream.

COOK'S TIP

If you prefer, serve these tarts with vanilla ice cream for a delicious dessert.

Crème Brûlée Tarts

An unusual dessert, serve these melt-in-the-mouth tarts with fresh mixed summer berries, if wished.

NUTRITIONAL INFORMATION

Calories	635	Sugars	17g
Protein	6g	Fat	53g
Carbohydrate	36g	Saturates	32g

16 hrs 20 mins — 25 mins

SERVES 6

INGREDIENTS

PASTRY

- 150 g/5½ oz plain flour
- 25 g/1 oz caster sugar
- 125 g/4½ oz butter, cut into small pieces
- 1 tbsp water

FILLING

- 4 egg yolks
- 50 g/1¾ oz caster sugar
- 400 ml/14 fl oz double cream
- 1 tsp vanilla essence
- demerara sugar, for sprinkling

2

4

7

1 To make the pastry, place the flour and sugar in a bowl and rub in the butter with your fingertips until the mixture resembles breadcrumbs. Add the water and work the mixture together until a soft dough has formed. Wrap in clingfilm and chill for 30 minutes.

2 Divide the dough into 6 pieces. Roll out each piece on a lightly floured surface to line 6 tart tins 10 cm/4 inches wide. Prick the bottom of the pastry with a fork and chill for 20 minutes.

3 Line the pastry cases with foil and baking beans and bake in a preheated oven, 190°C/375°F/Gas Mark 5, for 15 minutes. Remove the foil and beans and cook the pastry cases for a further 10 minutes until crisp. Leave to cool.

4 Meanwhile, make the filling. In a bowl, beat the egg yolks and sugar until pale. Heat the cream and vanilla essence in a pan until just below boiling point, then pour it on to the egg mixture, whisking constantly.

5 Return the mixture to a clean pan and bring to just below the boil, stirring, until thick. Do not allow the mixture to boil or it will curdle.

6 Leave the mixture to cool slightly, then pour it into the tart tins. Leave to cool and then chill overnight.

7 Sprinkle the tarts with the sugar. Place under a preheated hot grill for a few minutes. Leave to cool, then chill for 2 hours before serving.

Lime Frangipane Tartlets

These little tartlets have an unusual lime-flavoured pastry and are filled with an almond frangipane mixture.

NUTRITIONAL INFORMATION

Calories	149	Sugars	9g
Protein	2g	Fat	9g
Carbohydrate	17g	Saturates	5g

45 mins 15 mins

SERVES 12

INGREDIENTS

- 125 g/4½ oz plain flour
- 100 g/3½ oz butter, softened
- 1 tsp grated lime rind
- 1 tbsp lime juice
- 50 g/1¾ oz caster sugar
- 1 egg
- 25 g/1 oz ground almonds
- 50 g/1¾ oz icing sugar, sifted
- ½ tbsp water

3

5

6

1 Reserve 5 teaspoons of the flour and 3 teaspoons of the butter and set aside until required.

2 Rub the remaining butter into the remaining flour with your fingertips until the mixture resembles fine breadcrumbs. Stir in the lime rind, followed by the lime juice and bring the mixture together to form a soft dough.

3 Roll out the dough thinly on a lightly floured surface. Stamp out 12 x 7.5-cm/3-inch rounds with a fluted cutter and line a bun tin.

4 In a bowl, cream together the reserved butter with the caster sugar.

5 Mix in the egg, then the ground almonds and the reserved flour.

6 Divide the almond mixture between the pastry cases.

7 Bake in a preheated oven, 200°C/400°F/Gas Mark 6, for 15 minutes until set and lightly golden. Remove the tartlets from the tin and and place on a wire rack to cool.

8 Mix the icing sugar with the water. Drizzle a little of the icing over each tartlet and serve.

COOK'S TIP

These tartlets can be made in advance. Store them in an airtight container and ice them just before serving.

Paper-Thin Fruit Pies

Perfect for weight watchers, these crisp pastry cases, filled with fruit and glazed with apricot jam, are best served hot with low-fat custard.

NUTRITIONAL INFORMATION

Calories	158	Sugars	12g
Protein	2g	Fat	10g
Carbohydrate	14g	Saturates	2g

20 mins | 15 mins

SERVES 4

INGREDIENTS

- 1 eating apple
- 1 ripe pear
- 2 tbsp lemon juice
- 55 g/2 oz low-fat spread
- 225 g/8 oz filo pastry, defrosted if frozen
- 2 tbsp low-sugar apricot jam
- 1 tbsp unsweetened orange juice
- 1 tbsp finely chopped pistachio nuts
- 2 tsp icing sugar, for dusting
- low-fat custard, to serve

1 Core and thinly slice the apple and pear and toss them in the lemon juice.

2 Melt the low-fat spread in a small saucepan over a low heat. Cut the sheets of pastry into 4 and cover with a clean, damp tea towel. Brush 4 non-stick Yorkshire pudding tins, measuring 10 cm/4 inch across, with a little of the low-fat spread.

3 Working on each pie separately, brush 4 sheets of pastry with low-fat spread. Press a small sheet of pastry into the base of one tin. Arrange the other sheets of pastry on top at slightly different angles. Repeat with the remaining sheets of pastry to make another 3 pies.

4 Arrange the apple and pear slices alternately in the centre of each pastry case and lightly crimp the edges of the pastry of each pie.

5 Mix the jam and orange juice together until smooth and brush over the fruit. Bake in a preheated oven, 200°C/400°F/Gas Mark 6, for 12–15 minutes.

6 Sprinkle with the pistachio nuts, dust lightly with icing sugar and serve hot with low-fat custard.

2

3

4

VARIATION

Other combinations of fruit are equally delicious. Try peach and apricot, raspberry and apple or pineapple and mango.

Almond Cheesecakes

These creamy cheese desserts are so delicious that it's hard to believe that they are low in fat.

NUTRITIONAL INFORMATION

Calories	361	Sugars	29g
Protein	16g	Fat	15g
Carbohydrate	43g	Saturates	4g

1¼ hrs

10 mins

SERVES 4

INGREDIENTS

12 amaretti biscuits

1 egg white, lightly beaten

225 g/8 oz skimmed-milk soft cheese

½ tsp almond essence

½ tsp finely grated lime rind

25 g/1 oz ground almonds

25 g/1 oz caster sugar

55 g/2 oz sultanas

2 tsp powdered gelatine

2 tbsp boiling water

2 tbsp lime juice

TO DECORATE

25 g/1 oz flaked toasted almonds

strips of lime rind

1 Place the biscuits in a clean plastic bag, seal the bag and, using a rolling pin, crush them into small pieces.

2 Place the crumbs in a bowl and bind together with the egg white.

3 Arrange 4 non-stick pastry rings or poached egg rings, 9 cm/3½ inches across, on a baking tray lined with baking paper. Divide the biscuit mixture into 4 equal portions and spoon it into the rings, pressing down well. Bake in a preheated oven, 180°C/350°F/Gas Mark 4, for 10 minutes until crisp. Remove from the oven and leave to cool in the rings.

4 Beat the soft cheese, then beat in the almond essence, lime rind, ground almonds, sugar and sultanas until thoroughly combined.

5 Dissolve the gelatine in the boiling water and stir in the lime juice. Fold into the cheese mixture and spoon over the biscuit bases. Smooth over the tops and chill for 1 hour or until set.

6 Loosen the cheesecakes from the tins using a small palette knife or spatula and transfer to serving plates. Decorate with flaked toasted almonds and strips of lime rind,and serve.

1

3

5

Brown Sugar Pavlovas

This simple combination of fudgey meringue topped with fromage frais and raspberries is the perfect finale to any meal.

NUTRITIONAL INFORMATION

Calories	155	Sugars	34g
Protein	5g	Fat	0.2g
Carbohydrate	35g	Saturates	0g

1 hr

1 hr

SERVES 4

INGREDIENTS

- 2 large egg whites
- 1 tsp cornflour
- 1 tsp raspberry vinegar
- 100 g/3½ oz light muscovado sugar, crushed free of lumps
- 2 tbsp redcurrant jelly
- 2 tbsp unsweetened orange juice
- 150 ml/5 fl oz low-fat fromage frais
- 175 g/6 oz raspberries, defrosted if frozen
- rose-scented geranium leaves, to decorate (optional)

1 Line a large baking tray with baking paper. Whisk the egg whites until very stiff and dry. Gently fold in the cornflour and vinegar.

2 Gradually whisk in the sugar, a spoonful at a time, until the mixture is thick and glossy.

3 Divide the mixture into 4 and spoon on to the baking tray, spaced well apart. Smooth each portion into a round, about 10 cm/4 inches across and bake in a preheated oven, 150°C/300°C/Gas Mark 2, for 40–45 minutes until lightly browned and crisp. Remove from the oven and leave to cool on the baking tray.

4 Place the redcurrant jelly and orange juice in a small pan and heat, stirring, until melted. Leave to cool for 10 minutes.

5 Using a palette knife, carefully remove each pavlova from the baking paper and transfer to a serving plate. Top with the fromage frais and the raspberries. Brush the fruit with the redcurrant and orange glaze, and decorate with the geranium leaves, if using.

COOK'S TIP

Make a large pavlova by forming the meringue into a single round, measuring 18 cm/7 inches across, on a lined baking tray and bake for 1 hour.

Baked Pears with Cinnamon

This simple, healthy recipe is easy to prepare and cook but is deliciously warming. For a treat, serve hot on a pool of low-fat custard.

NUTRITIONAL INFORMATION

Calories	207	Sugars	35g
Protein	3g	Fat	6g
Carbohydrate	37g	Saturates	2g

10 mins 25 mins

SERVES 4

INGREDIENTS

- 4 ripe pears
- 2 tbsp lemon juice
- 4 tbsp light muscovado sugar
- 1 tsp ground cinnamon
- 55 g/2 oz low-fat spread
- finely shredded lemon rind, to decorate
- low-fat custard, to serve

1 Core and peel the pears, then slice them in half lengthways and brush them all over with the lemon juice to prevent them from discolouring. Place the pears, cored side down, in a small non-stick roasting tin.

2 Place the sugar, cinnamon and low-fat spread in a small saucepan and heat gently, stirring constantly, until the sugar has dissolved. Keep the heat very low to stop too much water evaporating from the low-fat spread as it gets hot. Spoon the mixture over the pears.

3 Bake the pears in a preheated oven, 200°C/400°F/Gas Mark 6, for 20–25 minutes or until they are tender and golden, occasionally spooning the sugar mixture over the fruit during the cooking time.

4 To serve, heat the low-fat custard until it is piping hot and spoon a little over the base of each of 4 warm dessert plates. Then arrange 2 pear halves on each plate.

5 Decorate the pears with a little finely shredded lemon rind and serve immediately.

VARIATION

For alternative flavours, replace the cinnamon with ground ginger and serve the pears sprinkled with chopped stem ginger in syrup. Alternatively, use ground allspice and spoon over some warmed dark rum to serve.

Baked Bananas

The orange-flavoured cream can be prepared in advance but do not make up the banana parcels until just before you need to cook them.

NUTRITIONAL INFORMATION

Calories	380	Sugars	40g
Protein	2g	Fat	18g
Carbohydrate	43g	Saturates	11g

30 mins — 10 mins

SERVES 4

INGREDIENTS

- 4 bananas
- 2 passion fruit
- 4 tbsp orange juice
- 4 tbsp orange-flavoured liqueur

ORANGE-FLAVOURED CREAM

- 150 ml/5 fl oz/ ⅔ cup double cream
- 3 tbsp icing sugar
- 2 tbsp orange-flavoured liqueur

1 

2 

3 

1 To make the orange-flavoured cream, pour the double cream into a mixing bowl and sprinkle over the icing sugar. Whisk the mixture until it is standing in soft peaks. Carefully fold in the orange-flavoured liqueur and chill in the refrigerator until required.

2 Peel the bananas and place each one on to a sheet of kitchen foil.

3 Cut the passion fruit in half and squeeze the juice of each half over each banana. Spoon over the orange juice and liqueur.

4 Fold the kitchen foil over the top of the bananas so that they are completely enclosed.

5 Place the parcels on a baking tray and bake the bananas in a preheated oven, 180°C/350°F/Gas Mark 4, for about 10 minutes or until they are just tender (test by inserting a cocktail stick).

6 Transfer the foil parcels to warm, individual serving plates. Open out the foil parcels at the table and then serve immediately with the chilled orange-flavoured cream.

VARIATION

Leave the bananas in their skins for a really quick dessert. Split the banana skins and pop in 1–2 cubes of chocolate. Wrap the bananas in kitchen foil and bake for 10 minutes or until the chocolate just melts.

Baked Apples with Berries

This winter dessert is a classic dish. Large, fluffy apples are hollowed out and filled with spices, almonds and blackberries.

NUTRITIONAL INFORMATION

Calories	228	Sugars	31g
Protein	1g	Fat	2g
Carbohydrate	31g	Saturates	0.2g

10 mins 45 mins

SERVES 4

INGREDIENTS

- 4 medium cooking apples
- 1 tbsp lemon juice
- 100 g/3½ oz prepared blackberries, defrosted if frozen
- 15 g/½ oz flaked almonds
- ½ tsp ground allspice
- ½ tsp finely grated lemon rind
- 2 tbsp demerara sugar
- 300 ml/10 fl oz ruby port
- 1 cinnamon stick, broken
- 2 tsp cornflour blended with 2 tbsp cold water
- low-fat custard, to serve

1

2

3

1 Wash and dry the apples. Using a small sharp knife, make a shallow cut through the skin around the middle of each apple – this will help the apples to cook through.

2 Core the apples, brush the centres with the lemon juice to prevent them from browning and stand them in an ovenproof dish.

3 In a bowl, mix together the blackberries, almonds, allspice, lemon rind and sugar. Using a teaspoon, spoon the mixture into the centre of each apple.

4 Pour the port into the dish, add the cinnamon stick and bake the apples in a preheated oven, 200°C/400°F/Gas Mark 6, for 35–40 minutes or until tender and soft.

5 Drain the cooking juices into a pan and keep the apples warm.

6 Discard the cinnamon and add the cornflour mixture to the cooking juices. Cook over a medium heat, stirring constantly, until thickened.

7 Heat the custard until piping hot. Pour the sauce over the apples and serve with the custard.

Italian Bread Pudding

This deliciously rich pudding is cooked with cream and apples and is delicately flavoured with orange.

NUTRITIONAL INFORMATION

Calories	387	Sugars	31g
Protein	8g	Fat	20g
Carbohydrate	45g	Saturates	12g

45 mins 25 mins

SERVES 4

INGREDIENTS

- 1 tbsp butter
- 2 small eating apples, peeled, cored and sliced into rings
- 75 g/2¾ oz granulated sugar
- 2 tbsp white wine
- 100 g/3½ oz bread, sliced with crusts removed (slightly stale French baguette is ideal)
- 300 ml/10 fl oz single cream
- 2 eggs, beaten
- pared rind of 1 orange, cut into matchsticks

1 Lightly grease a 1.25-litre/2-pint deep ovenproof dish with the butter.

2 Arrange the apple rings in the base of the dish. Sprinkle half of the sugar over the apples.

3 Pour the wine over the apples. Add the bread slices, pushing them down with your hands to flatten them slightly.

4 Mix the cream with the eggs, the remaining sugar and the orange rind and pour the mixture over the bread. Leave to soak for 30 minutes.

5 Bake the pudding in a preheated oven, 180°C/350°F/Gas Mark 4, for 25 minutes until golden and set. Remove from the oven, leave to cool slightly and serve warm.

2

3

3

VARIATION

For a change, try adding dried fruit, such as apricots, cherries or dates, to the pudding, if you prefer.

Tuscan Pudding

These baked mini-ricotta puddings are delicious served warm or chilled and will keep in the refrigerator for 3–4 days.

NUTRITIONAL INFORMATION

Calories	293	Sugars	28g
Protein	9g	Fat	17g
Carbohydrate	28g	Saturates	9g

20 mins 15 mins

SERVES 4

INGREDIENTS

- 1 tbsp butter
- 75 g/2¾ oz mixed dried fruit
- 250 g/9 oz ricotta cheese
- 3 egg yolks
- 50 g/1¾ oz caster sugar
- 1 tsp cinnamon
- finely grated rind of 1 orange, plus extra to decorate
- crème fraîche, to serve

1 Lightly grease 4 mini pudding basins or ramekin dishes with the butter.

2 Put the dried fruit in a bowl and cover with warm water. Set aside to soak for 10 minutes.

3 Beat the ricotta cheese with the egg yolks in a bowl. Stir in the caster sugar, cinnamon and orange rind and mix to combine.

4 Drain the dried fruit in a sieve set over a bowl. Mix the drained fruit with the ricotta cheese mixture.

5 Spoon the mixture into the basins or ramekin dishes.

6 Bake in a preheated oven, 180°C/350°F/Gas Mark 4, for 15 minutes. The tops should be firm to the touch but should not have turned brown.

7 Decorate the puddings with grated orange rind. Serve warm or chilled with a spoon of crème fraîche, if liked.

COOK'S TIP

Crème fraîche has a slightly sour, nutty taste and is very thick. It is suitable for cooking, but has the same fat content as double cream. It can be made by stirring cultured buttermilk into double cream and refrigerating overnight.

Mascarpone Cheesecake

The lemon and mascarpone give this baked cheesecake a wonderfully tangy flavour. Ricotta cheese could be used as an alternative.

NUTRITIONAL INFORMATION

Calories	327	Sugars	25g
Protein	9g	Fat	18g
Carbohydrate	33g	Saturates	11g

15 mins — 50 mins

SERVES 8

INGREDIENTS

- 1½ tbsp unsalted butter, plus extra for greasing
- 150 g/5½ oz ginger biscuits, crushed
- 25 g/1 oz stem ginger, chopped
- 500 g/1 lb 2 oz mascarpone cheese
- finely grated rind and juice of 2 lemons
- 100 g/3½ oz caster sugar
- 2 large eggs, separated
- fruit coulis (see Cook's Tip), to serve

1 Grease and line the base of a 25-cm/10-inch spring-form cake tin or loose-bottomed tin.

2 Melt the butter in a pan and stir in the crushed biscuits and chopped ginger. Use the mixture to line the tin, pressing the mixture about 5 mm/¼ inch up the sides.

3 Beat together the cheese, lemon rind and juice, sugar and egg yolks until quite smooth.

4 Whisk the egg whites until they are stiff and fold into the cheese and lemon mixture.

5 Pour the mixture into the prepared tin and bake in a preheated oven, 180°C/350°F/Gas Mark 4, for 35–45 minutes until just set. Don't worry if it cracks or sinks – this is quite normal.

6 Leave the cheesecake in the tin to cool. Serve with fruit coulis (see Cook's Tip).

COOK'S TIP

Fruit coulis can be made by cooking 400 g/14 oz fruit, such as blueberries, for 5 minutes with 2 tablespoons of water. Sieve the mixture, then stir in 1 tablespoon (or more to taste) of sifted icing sugar. Leave to cool before serving.

Baked Sweet Ravioli

These scrumptious little parcels are the perfect dessert for anyone with a really sweet tooth and a fancy for something unusual.

NUTRITIONAL INFORMATION

Calories	765	Sugars	56g
Protein	16g	Fat	30g
Carbohydrate	114g	Saturates	15g

1½ hrs

20 mins

SERVES 4

INGREDIENTS

SWEET PASTA DOUGH

425 g/15 oz plain flour

140 g/5 oz butter, plus extra for greasing

140 g/5 oz caster sugar

4 eggs

25 g/1 oz yeast

125 ml/4 fl oz warm milk

FILLING

175 g/6 oz chestnut purée

55 g/2 oz cocoa powder

55 g/2 oz caster sugar

55 g/2 oz chopped almonds

55 g/2 oz crushed amaretti biscuits

175 g/6 oz orange marmalade

1 To make the sweet pasta dough, sieve the flour into a mixing bowl, then mix in the butter, sugar and 3 of the eggs.

2 Mix together the yeast and warm milk in a small bowl and when thoroughly combined, mix into the dough.

3 Knead the dough for 20 minutes, cover with a clean cloth and set aside in a warm place for 1 hour to rise.

4 Mix together the chestnut purée, cocoa powder, sugar, almonds, crushed amaretti biscuits and orange marmalade in a separate bowl.

5 Generously grease a baking tray with some butter.

6 Lightly flour the work surface. Roll out the sweet pasta dough into a thin sheet and cut into 5-cm/2-inch rounds with a plain pastry cutter.

7 Put a spoonful of filling on to one half of each pasta round and then fold in half, pressing the edges firmly together to seal. Transfer the ravioli the prepared baking tray, spacing them out well. Bake in batches, if necessary.

8 Beat the remaining egg and brush all over the ravioli to glaze. Bake in a preheated oven, 180°C/350°F/Gas Mark 4, for 20 minutes. Serve hot.

3

4

8

German Noodle Pudding

This rich and satisfying pudding is a traditional Jewish recipe that will quickly become popular with all the family.

NUTRITIONAL INFORMATION

Calories	719	Sugars	28g
Protein	20g	Fat	45g
Carbohydrate	62g	Saturates	25g

10 mins 45 mins

SERVES 4

INGREDIENTS

- 4 tbsp butter, plus extra for greasing
- 175 g/6 oz ribbon egg noodles
- 115 g/4 oz cream cheese
- 225 g/8 oz cottage cheese
- 85 g/3 oz caster sugar
- 2 eggs, lightly beaten
- 125 ml/4 fl oz soured cream
- 1 tsp vanilla essence
- a pinch of ground cinnamon
- 1 tsp grated lemon rind
- 25 g/1 oz flaked almonds
- 25 g/1 oz dry white breadcrumbs
- icing sugar, for dusting

1 Grease an ovenproof dish with a little butter.

2 Bring a large pan of water to the boil. Add the noodles, bring back to the boil and cook until almost tender. Drain and set aside.

3 Beat together the cream cheese, cottage cheese and caster sugar in a mixing bowl until the mixture is smooth. Beat in the eggs, a little at a time.

4 Stir in the soured cream, vanilla essence, cinnamon and lemon rind and fold in the noodles. Transfer the mixture to the prepared dish and smooth the surface.

5 Melt the butter in a small frying pan over a low heat. Add the almonds and fry, stirring constantly, for about 1–1½ minutes, until they are lightly coloured. Remove the frying pan from the heat and stir the breadcrumbs into the almonds.

6 Sprinkle the almond and breadcrumb mixture evenly over the pudding and bake in a preheated oven, 180°C/350°F/Gas Mark 4, for 35–40 minutes until just set. Dust the top with a little sieved icing sugar and serve immediately.

3

4

6

VARIATION

Although not authentic, you could add 3 tablespoons of raisins with the lemon rind in step 3, if liked.

Honey & Nut Nests

Pistachio nuts and honey are combined with crisp cooked angel hair pasta in this unusual and scrumptious dessert.

NUTRITIONAL INFORMATION

Calories	802	Sugars	53g
Protein	13g	Fat	48g
Carbohydrate	85g	Saturates	16g

10 mins 1 hr

SERVES 4

INGREDIENTS

- 225 g/8 oz angel hair pasta
- 115 g/4 oz butter
- 175 g/6 oz shelled pistachio nuts, chopped
- 115 g/4 oz sugar
- 115 g/4 oz clear honey
- 150 ml/5 fl oz water
- 2 tsp lemon juice
- salt
- Greek-style yogurt, to serve

1 Bring a large saucepan of lightly salted water to the boil. Add the angel hair pasta, bring back to the boil and cook for 8–10 minutes or until tender, but still firm to the bite. Drain the pasta and return to the pan. Add the butter and toss to coat the pasta thoroughly. Set aside to cool completely.

2 Arrange 4 small flan or poaching rings on a baking tray. Divide the angel hair pasta into 8 equal quantities and spoon 4 of them into the rings. Press down lightly. Top the pasta with half of the nuts, then add the remaining pasta.

3 Bake in a preheated oven, 180°C/350°F/Gas Mark 4, for 45 minutes or until golden brown.

4 Meanwhile, put the sugar, honey and water in a saucepan and bring to the boil over a low heat, stirring constantly until the sugar has dissolved completely. Simmer for 10 minutes, add the lemon juice and simmer for 5 minutes.

5 Using a spatula or fish slice, carefully transfer the angel hair nests to a serving dish. Pour over the honey syrup, sprinkle over the remaining nuts and set aside to cool completely before serving. Hand the Greek-style yogurt separately.

2

2

2

COOK'S TIP

Angel hair pasta is also known as *capelli d'Angelo.* Long and very fine, it is usually sold in small bunches that already resemble nests.

Banana Pastries

These pastries require a little time to prepare, but are well worth the effort. A sweet banana filling is wrapped in dough and baked.

NUTRITIONAL INFORMATION

Calories	745	Sugars	24g
Protein	13g	Fat	30g
Carbohydrate	112g	Saturates	15g

45 mins — 25 mins

SERVES 4

INGREDIENTS

PASTRY

- 450 g/1 lb plain flour
- 4 tbsp lard
- 4 tbsp unsalted butter
- 125 ml/4 fl oz water

FILLING

- 2 large bananas
- 75 g/2¾ oz finely chopped no-soak dried apricots
- pinch of nutmeg
- dash of orange juice
- 1 egg yolk, beaten
- icing sugar, for dusting
- cream or ice cream, to serve

1 To make the pastry, sift the flour into a large mixing bowl. Add the lard and butter and rub into the flour with the fingertips until the mixture resembles breadcrumbs. Gradually blend in the water to make a soft dough. Wrap in clingfilm and chill in the refrigerator for 30 minutes.

2 Mash the bananas in a bowl with a fork and stir in the apricots, nutmeg and orange juice, mixing well.

3 Roll the dough out on a lightly floured surface and cut out 16 rounds 10-cm/4-inch in diameter.

4 Spoon a little of the banana filling on to one half of each round and fold the dough over the filling to make semi-circles. Pinch the edges together and seal by pressing with the prongs of a fork.

5 Arrange the pastries on a non-stick baking tray and brush them with the beaten egg yolk. Cut a small slit in each pastry and cook in a preheated oven, 180°C/350°F/Gas Mark 4, for about 25 minutes or until golden brown and crisp.

6 Dust the banana pastries with icing sugar and serve with cream or ice cream.

2

4

5

VARIATION

Use a fruit filling of your choice, such as apple or plum, as an alternative.

Chinese Custard Tarts

These small tarts are irresistible – custard is baked in a rich, sweet pastry. The tarts may be served warm or cold.

NUTRITIONAL INFORMATION

Calories	474	Sugars	30g
Protein	9g	Fat	22g
Carbohydrate	64g	Saturates	12g

20 mins   30 mins

SERVES 4

INGREDIENTS

PASTRY

175 g/6 oz plain flour

3 tbsp caster sugar

4 tbsp unsalted butter

2 tbsp lard

2 tbsp water

CUSTARD

2 small eggs

55 g/2 oz caster sugar

175 ml/6 fl oz milk

½ tsp ground nutmeg, plus extra for sprinkling

cream, to serve

1 To make the pastry, sift the flour into a bowl. Add the caster sugar and rub in the butter and lard with your fingertips until the mixture resembles breadcrumbs. Add the water and mix to form a firm dough.

2 Transfer the dough to a lightly floured surface and knead for about 5 minutes until smooth. Form into a ball, cover with clingfilm and chill in the refrigerator while you prepare the filling.

3 To make the custard, beat the eggs and sugar together. Gradually add the milk and ground nutmeg and beat until well combined.

4 Separate the dough into 15 even-size pieces. Flatten the dough pieces into rounds and press into shallow patty tins.

5 Spoon the custard into the pastry cases and cook in a preheated oven, 150°C/300°F/Gas Mark 2, for 25–30 minutes.

6 Transfer the Chinese custard tarts to a wire rack, leave to cool slightly, then sprinkle with extra ground nutmeg. Serve warm or cold with cream.

3
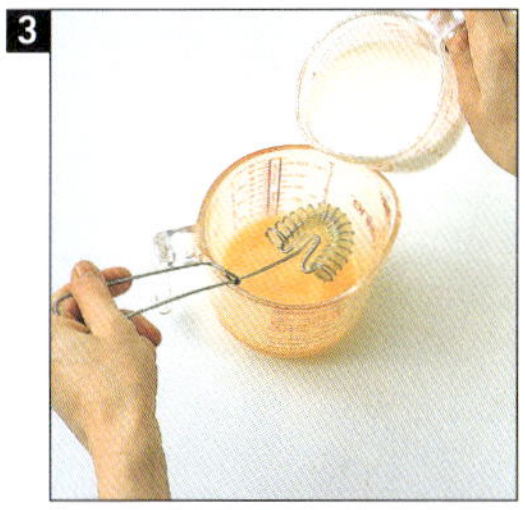

4

6

COOK'S TIP

For extra convenience, make the dough in advance, cover and leave to chill in the refrigerator until required.

Cakes & Bread

There is nothing more traditional than afternoon tea and cakes and this chapter gives a wickedly extravagant twist to some of those delicious tea-time classics – full of chocolate, spice and all things nice, these recipes are a

treat to enjoy. The chapter includes a variety of different cakes depending on the time you have and the effort you want to spend. Small cakes include Fruity Muffins, Almond Slices, and Treacle Scones. These cakes are easier to prepare and cook than larger ones and, in general, are particular favourites.

Teacakes

These popular tea snacks are ideal split in half and toasted, then spread with butter. Use a luxury mix of dried fruit, if possible.

NUTRITIONAL INFORMATION	
Calories 197	Sugars 11g
Protein 6g	Fat 3g
Carbohydrate ... 39g	Saturates 2g

3¼ hrs — 20 mins

SERVES 12

INGREDIENTS

- 2 tbsp butter, cut into small pieces, plus extra for greasing
- 450 g/1 lb strong white bread flour
- 1 sachet easy-blend dried yeast
- 50 g/1¾ oz caster sugar
- 1 tsp salt
- 300 ml/10 fl oz hand-hot milk
- 75 g/2¾ oz luxury dried fruit mix
- honey, for brushing

1 Grease several baking trays with a little butter.

2 Sieve the flour into a large mixing bowl. Stir in the dried yeast, sugar and salt. Rub in the butter with your fingers until the mixture resembles fine breadcrumbs. Add the milk and mix all of the ingredients together to form a soft dough.

3 Place the dough on a lightly floured surface and knead for about 5 minutes. Alternatively, you can knead the dough with an electric mixer with a dough hook.

4 Place the dough in a greased bowl, cover and leave to rise in a warm place for about 1–1½ hours until it has doubled in size.

5 Knead the dough again for a few minutes and knead in the fruit. Divide the dough into 12 rounds and place on the baking trays. Cover and leave for 1 further hour or until springy to the touch.

6 Bake in a preheated oven, 200°C/400°F/Gas Mark 6, for 20 minutes. Brush the teacakes with honey while they are still warm.

7 Transfer the teacakes to a wire rack to cool completely before serving them split in half and toasted, if wished. Spread with butter and serve.

3

5

5

COOK'S TIP

It is important to have the milk at the right temperature: heat it until you can put your little finger into the milk and leave it there for 10 seconds without its feeling too hot.

Cinnamon Swirls

These cinnamon-flavoured buns are delicious if they are served warm a few minutes after they come out of the oven.

NUTRITIONAL INFORMATION

Calories	160	Sugars	10g
Protein	4g	Fat	6g
Carbohydrate	24g	Saturates	4g

1 hr 25 mins · 30 mins

SERVES 12

INGREDIENTS

- 2 tbsp butter, cut into small pieces, plus extra for greasing
- 225 g/8 oz strong white bread flour
- ½ tsp salt
- 1 sachet easy-blend dried yeast
- 1 egg, beaten
- 125 ml/4 fl oz warm milk
- 2 tbsp maple syrup

FILLING

- 4 tbsp butter, softened
- 2 tsp ground cinnamon
- 50 g/1¾ oz soft brown sugar
- 50 g/1¾ oz currants

5

6

6

1 Grease a 23-cm/9-inch square baking tin with a little butter.

2 Sieve the flour and salt into a mixing bowl. Stir in the dried yeast. Rub in the butter with your fingertips until the mixture resembles fine breadcrumbs. Add the egg and milk and mix everything to form a dough.

3 Place the dough in a greased bowl, cover and leave in a warm place for about 40 minutes or until doubled in size.

4 Knead the dough lightly for 1 minute to knock it back, then roll out on a lightly floured surface to a rectangle 30 x 23 cm/12 x 9 inches.

5 To make the filling, cream together the butter, cinnamon and brown sugar until the mixture is light and fluffy. Spread the filling over the dough, leaving a 2.5-cm/1-inch border all round. Sprinkle over the currants.

6 Roll up the dough like a Swiss roll, starting at a long edge, and press down to seal. Cut the roll into 12 slices. Place them in the tin, cover and leave for 30 minutes.

7 Bake in a preheated oven, 190°C/375°F/Gas Mark 5, for 20–30 minutes or until well risen. Brush the swirls with the syrup and leave to cool slightly before serving warm.

Cinnamon & Currant Loaf

This spicy, fruit tea bread is quick and easy to make. Serve it buttered and with a drizzle of honey for an afternoon snack.

NUTRITIONAL INFORMATION

Calories	439	Sugars	33g
Protein	7g	Fat	18g
Carbohydrate	67g	Saturates	11g

1 hr 10 mins — 1 hr 10 mins

SERVES 8

INGREDIENTS

- 150 g/5½ oz butter, cut into small pieces, plus extra for greasing
- 350 g/12 oz plain flour
- pinch of salt
- 1 tbsp baking powder
- 1 tbsp ground cinnamon
- 125 g/4½ oz soft brown sugar
- 175 g/6 oz currants
- finely grated rind of 1 orange
- 5–6 tbsp orange juice
- 6 tbsp milk
- 2 eggs, beaten lightly

1 Grease a 900-g/2-lb loaf tin and line the base with baking paper.

2 Sieve the flour, salt, baking powder and cinnamon into a bowl. Rub in the butter pieces with your fingers until the mixture resembles coarse breadcrumbs.

3 Stir in the sugar, currants and orange rind. Beat the orange juice, milk and eggs together and add to the dry ingredients. Mix well together.

4 Spoon the mixture into the prepared tin. Make a slight dip in the middle of the mixture to help it rise evenly.

5 Bake in a preheated oven, 180°C/350°F/Gas Mark 4, for about 1–1 hour 10 minutes or until a fine metal skewer inserted into the centre of the loaf comes out clean.

6 Leave the loaf to cool before turning out of the tin. Transfer to a wire rack and leave to cool completely before slicing and serving.

COOK'S TIP

Once you have added the liquid to the dry ingredients, work as quickly as possible because the baking powder is activated by the liquid.

Banana & Cranberry Loaf

The addition of chopped nuts, mixed peel, fresh orange juice and dried cranberries makes this a rich, moist tea bread.

NUTRITIONAL INFORMATION

Calories	388	Sugars	40g
Protein	5g	Fat	17g
Carbohydrate	57g	Saturates	2g

45 mins 1 hr

SERVES 8

INGREDIENTS

- butter, for greasing
- 175 g/6 oz self-raising flour
- ½ tsp baking powder
- 150 g/5½ oz soft brown sugar
- 2 bananas, mashed
- 50 g/1¾ oz chopped mixed peel
- 25 g/1 oz chopped mixed nuts
- 50 g/1¾ oz dried cranberries
- 5–6 tbsp orange juice
- 2 eggs, beaten
- 150 ml/5 fl oz sunflower oil
- 75 g/2¾ oz icing sugar, sifted
- grated rind of 1 orange

2

3

3

1 Grease a 900-g/2-lb loaf tin and line the base with baking paper.

2 Sieve the flour and baking powder into a mixing bowl. Stir in the sugar, bananas, chopped mixed peel, nuts and dried cranberries.

3 Stir the orange juice, eggs and sunflower oil together until well combined. Add the mixture to the dry ingredients and mix until well blended. Spoon the mixture into the prepared loaf tin and smooth the top.

4 Bake in a preheated oven, 180°C/350°F/Gas Mark 4, for about 1 hour until firm to the touch or until a fine skewer inserted into the centre of the loaf comes out clean.

5 Turn out the loaf and leave it to cool on a wire rack.

6 Mix the icing sugar with a little water and drizzle the icing over the loaf. Sprinkle the orange rind over the top. Leave the icing to set before serving the loaf in slices.

COOK'S TIP

This tea bread will keep for a couple of days. Wrap it carefully and store in a cool, dry place.

Banana & Date Loaf

This tea bread is excellent for afternoon tea or coffee time with its moist texture and more-ish flavour.

NUTRITIONAL INFORMATION

Calories	432	Sugars	41g
Protein	7g	Fat	16g
Carbohydrate	70g	Saturates	10g

15 mins 1 hr

SERVES 6

INGREDIENTS

- 100 g/3½ oz butter, cut into small pieces, plus extra for greasing
- 225 g/8 oz self-raising flour
- 75 g/2¾ oz caster sugar
- 125 g/4½ oz stoned dates, chopped
- 2 bananas, roughly mashed
- 2 eggs, lightly beaten
- 2 tbsp honey

1 Grease a 900-g/2-lb loaf tin and line the base with baking paper.

2 Sieve the flour into a mixing bowl. Rub the butter into the flour with your fingertips until the mixture resembles fine breadcrumbs.

3 Stir the sugar, chopped dates, bananas, beaten eggs and honey into the dry ingredients. Mix together to form a soft dropping consistency.

4 Spoon the mixture into the prepared loaf tin and level the surface with the back of a knife.

5 Bake in a preheated oven, 160°C/325°F/Gas Mark 3, for about 1 hour or until golden and a fine metal skewer inserted into the centre comes out clean.

6 Leave the loaf to cool in the tin before turning out and transferring to a wire rack to cool completely.

7 Serve the loaf warm or cold, cut into thick slices.

COOK'S TIP

This tea bread will keep for several days if stored in an airtight container and kept in a cool, dry place.

Crown Loaf

This is a rich sweet bread combining alcohol, nuts and fruit in a decorative wreath shape. It is ideal for serving at Christmas.

NUTRITIONAL INFORMATION	
Calories 164	Sugars 14g
Protein 3g	Fat 6g
Carbohydrate ...25g	Saturates 3g

1½ hrs

30 mins

1 LOAF

INGREDIENTS

- 2 tbsp butter, cut into small pieces, plus extra for greasing
- 225 g/8 oz strong white bread flour
- ½ tsp salt
- 1 sachet easy-blend dried yeast
- 125 ml/4 fl oz hand-hot milk
- 1 egg, beaten

FILLING

- 4 tbsp butter, softened
- 50 g/1¾ oz soft brown sugar
- 25 g/1 oz chopped hazelnuts
- 25 g/1 oz stem ginger, chopped
- 50 g/1¾ oz mixed peel
- 1 tbsp rum or brandy
- 100 g/3½ oz icing sugar
- 2 tbsp lemon juice

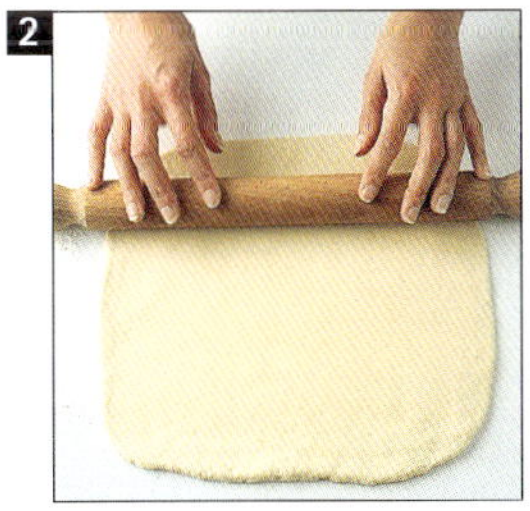

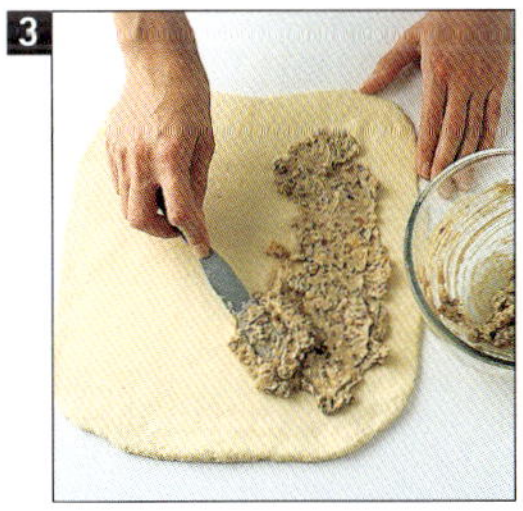

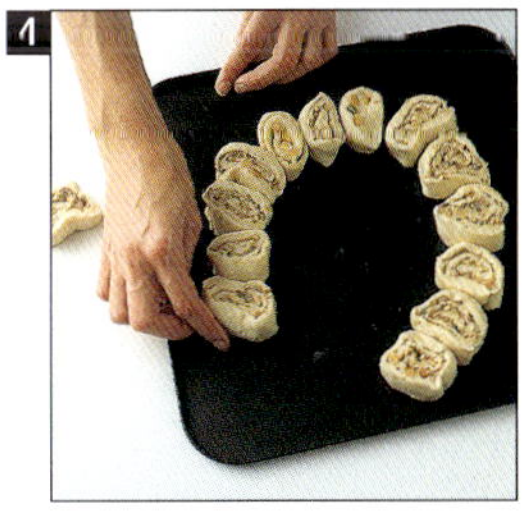

1 Grease a baking sheet. Sieve the flour and salt into a bowl. Stir in the yeast. Rub in the butter with your fingers. Add the milk and egg and mix to a dough.

2 Place the dough in a greased bowl, cover and leave in a warm place for 40 minutes until doubled in size. Knead the dough lightly for 1 minute to knock it back. Roll out to a rectangle 30 x 23 cm/ 12 x 9 inches.

3 To make the filling, cream together the butter and sugar until the mixture is light and fluffy. Stir in the hazelnuts, ginger, mixed peel and rum or brandy. Spread the filling over the dough, leaving a 2.5-cm/1-inch border.

4 Roll up the dough, starting from the long edge, to form a sausage shape. Cut the dough roll into slices at 5-cm/ 2-inch intervals and place on the baking tray in a circle with the slices just touching. Cover and set aside to rise in a warm place for 30 minutes.

5 Bake in a preheated oven, 190°C/ 325°F/Gas Mark 5, for 20–30 minutes or until golden. Meanwhile, mix the icing sugar with enough lemon juice to form a thin icing.

6 Leave the loaf to cool slightly before drizzling with icing. Allow the icing to set slightly before serving the loaf.

Date & Honey Loaf

This bread is full of good things – chopped dates, sesame seeds and honey. Toast thick slices and spread with soft cheese for a light snack.

NUTRITIONAL INFORMATION

Calories	240	Sugars	14g
Protein	6g	Fat	6g
Carbohydrate	44g	Saturates	1g

2 hrs 40 mins   30 mins

1 LOAF

INGREDIENTS

- butter, for greasing
- 250 g/9 oz strong white bread flour
- 75 g/2¾ oz strong brown bread flour
- ½ tsp salt
- 1 sachet easy-blend dried yeast
- 200 ml/7 fl oz hand-hot water
- 3 tbsp sunflower oil
- 3 tbsp honey
- 75 g/2¾ oz dried dates, chopped
- 2 tbsp sesame seeds

1 Grease a 900-g/2-lb loaf tin with butter. Sieve the white and brown flours into a large mixing bowl and stir in the salt and dried yeast.

2 Pour in the hand-hot water, oil and honey. Mix everything together to form a dough.

3 Place the dough on a lightly floured surface and knead for about 5 minutes until smooth.

4 Place the dough in a greased bowl, cover and leave to rise in a warm place for about 1 hour or until doubled in size.

5 Knead in the dates and sesame seeds. Shape the dough and place in the tin.

3
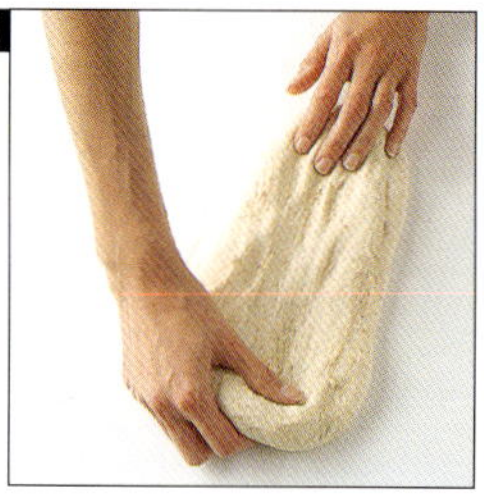

5

5

6 Cover and leave in a warm place for a further 30 minutes or until springy to the touch.

7 Bake in a preheated oven, 220°C/425°F/Gas Mark 7, for 30 minutes or until a hollow sound is heard when the base of the loaf is tapped.

8 Transfer the loaf to a wire rack and leave to cool completely. Serve cut into thick slices.

COOK'S TIP

If you cannot find a warm place, sit a bowl with the dough in it over a saucepan of warm water and cover.

Pumpkin Loaf

The pumpkin purée in this loaf makes it beautifully moist. It is delicious eaten at any time of the day.

NUTRITIONAL INFORMATION

Calories	456	Sugars	33g
Protein	7g	Fat	21g
Carbohydrate	62g	Saturates	12g

1½ hrs — 2 hrs 10 mins

SERVES 6

INGREDIENTS

- vegetable oil, for greasing
- 450 g/1 lb pumpkin flesh
- 125 g/ 4½ oz butter, softened, plus extra for greasing
- 175 g /6 oz caster sugar
- 2 eggs, beaten
- 225 g /8 oz plain flour, sieved
- 1½ tsp baking powder
- ½ tsp salt
- 1 tsp ground mixed spice
- 25 g/1 oz pumpkin seeds

1 Grease a 900-g/2-lb loaf tin with vegetable oil.

2 Chop the pumpkin into large pieces and wrap in buttered foil. Cook in a preheated oven, 200°C/400°F/ Gas Mark 6, for 30–40 minutes until they are tender.

3 Leave the pumpkin to cool completely before mashing well to make a thick purée.

4 In a bowl, cream the butter and sugar together until light and fluffy. Add the eggs a little at a time.

5 Stir in the pumpkin purée. Fold in the flour, baking powder, salt and mixed spice.

6 Fold the pumpkin seeds gently through the mixture. Spoon the mixture into the loaf tin.

7 Bake in a preheated oven, 160°C/325°F/Gas Mark 3, for about 1¼–1½ hours or until a skewer inserted into the centre of the loaf comes out clean.

8 Leave the loaf to cool and serve buttered, if wished.

2

4

5

COOK'S TIP

To ensure that the pumpkin purée is dry, place it in a saucepan over a medium heat for a few minutes, stirring frequently, until it is thick.

Tropical Fruit Bread

The flavours in this bread will bring a touch of sunshine to your breakfast table. The mango can be replaced with other dried fruits.

NUTRITIONAL INFORMATION

Calories	228	Sugars	10g
Protein	6g	Fat	7g
Carbohydrate	37g	Saturates	5g

1¼ hrs

30 mins

1 LOAF

INGREDIENTS

- 2 tbsp butter, cut into small pieces, plus extra for greasing
- 350 g/12 oz strong white bread flour
- 50 g /1¾ oz bran
- ½ tsp salt
- ½ tsp ground ginger
- 1 sachet easy-blend dried yeast
- 25 g/1 oz soft brown sugar
- 250 ml/9 fl oz tepid water
- 75 g/2¾ oz glacé pineapple, finely chopped
- 25 g/1 oz dried mango, finely chopped
- 50 g/1¾ oz desiccated coconut, toasted
- 1 egg, beaten
- 2 tbsp coconut shreds

1

1

1

1 Grease a baking tray. Sieve the flour into a large mixing bowl. Stir in the bran, salt, ginger, dried yeast and sugar. Rub in the butter with your fingers, then add the water and mix to form a dough.

2 On a lightly floured surface, knead the dough for 5–8 minutes until smooth. Alternatively, use an electric mixer with a dough hook. Place the dough in a greased bowl, cover and leave to rise in a warm place for 30 minutes, until doubled in size.

3 Knead the pineapple, mango and desiccated coconut into the dough. Shape into a round and place on the baking tray. Score the top with the back of a knife. Cover and leave for a further 30 minutes in a warm place.

4 Brush the loaf with the egg and sprinkle with the 2 tablespoons of coconut. Bake in a preheated oven, 220°C/425°F/Gas Mark 7, for 30 minutes or until golden.

5 Leave the bread to cool on a wire rack before serving.

COOK'S TIP

To test the bread after the second rising, gently poke the dough with your finger –it should spring back if it has risen enough.

Citrus Bread

This sweet loaf is flavoured with citrus fruits. As with Tropical Fruit Bread (see page 190), it is excellent served at breakfast.

NUTRITIONAL INFORMATION

Calories	195	Sugars	10g
Protein	5g	Fat	4g
Carbohydrate	37g	Saturates	2g

1 hr 55 mins · 35 mins

1 LOAF

INGREDIENTS

- 4 tbsp butter, cut into small pieces, plus extra for greasing
- 450 g/1 lb strong white bread flour
- ½ tsp salt
- 50 g/1¾ oz caster sugar
- 1 sachet easy-blend dried yeast
- 5–6 tbsp orange juice
- 4 tbsp lemon juice
- 3–4 tbsp lime juice
- 150 ml/5 fl oz hand-hot water
- 1 orange
- 1 lemon
- 1 lime
- 2 tbsp clear honey

1 Lightly grease a baking tray with a little butter.

2 Sieve the flour and salt into a mixing bowl. Stir in the sugar and dried yeast.

3 Rub the butter into the mixture using your fingertips. Add the orange, lemon and lime juice and the water and mix to form a dough.

4 Place the dough on a lightly floured working surface and knead for 5 minutes. Alternatively, use an electric mixer with a dough hook. Place the dough in a greased bowl, cover and leave to rise in a warm place for 1 hour.

5 Meanwhile, grate the rind of the orange, lemon and lime. Knead the fruit rinds into the dough.

6 Divide the dough into 2 balls, making one slightly bigger than the other.

7 Place the larger ball on the baking tray and set the smaller one on top.

8 Push a floured finger through the centre of the dough. Cover and leave to rise for about 40 minutes or until springy to the touch.

9 Bake in a preheated oven, 220°C/425°F/Gas Mark 7, for 35 minutes. Remove from the oven and transfer to a wire rack. Glaze with the clear honey.

5

7

8

Chocolate Bread

For the chocoholics among us, this bread is not only great fun to make, but it is also even better to eat.

NUTRITIONAL INFORMATION			
Calories	228	Sugars	4g
Protein	8g	Fat	3g
Carbohydrate	46g	Saturates	1g

2 hrs 40 mins — 30 Mins

1 LOAF

INGREDIENTS

- butter, for greasing
- 450 g/1 lb strong white bread flour
- 25 g/1 oz cocoa powder
- 1 tsp salt
- 1 sachet easy-blend dried yeast
- 25 g/1 oz soft brown sugar
- 1 tbsp oil
- 300 ml/10 fl oz hand-hot water

1 Lightly grease a 900-g/2-lb loaf tin with a little butter.

2 Sieve the flour and cocoa powder into a large mixing bowl. Stir in the salt, dried yeast and brown sugar.

3 Pour in the oil along with the hand-hot water and mix the ingredients together to make a dough.

4 Knead the dough on a lightly floured surface for 5 minutes. Alternatively, use an electric mixer with a dough hook.

5 Place the dough in a greased bowl, cover and leave to rise in a warm place for about 1 hour or until the dough has doubled in size.

6 Knock back the dough and shape it into a loaf. Place the dough in the prepared tin, cover and leave to rise in a warm place for a further 30 minutes.

7 Bake in a preheated oven, 200°C/400°F/Gas Mark 6, for 25–30 minutes, or until a hollow sound is heard when the base of the bread is tapped.

8 Transfer the bread to a wire rack and leave to cool. Cut into slices to serve with butter.

2

3

6

COOK'S TIP

This bread can be sliced and spread with butter or it can be lightly toasted.

Mango Twist Bread

This is a sweet bread which has puréed mango mixed into the dough, resulting in a moist loaf with an exotic flavour.

NUTRITIONAL INFORMATION

Calories	228	Sugars	18g
Protein	6g	Fat	4g
Carbohydrate	46g	Saturates	2g

2 hrs 50 mins | 30 mins

1 LOAF

INGREDIENTS

- 3 tbsp butter, cut into small pieces, plus extra for greasing
- 450 g/1 lb strong white bread flour
- 1 tsp salt
- 1 sachet easy-blend dried yeast
- 1 tsp ground ginger
- 50 g/1¾ oz soft brown sugar
- 1 small mango, peeled, stoned and puréed
- 250 ml/9 fl oz hand-hot water
- 2 tbsp clear honey
- 125 g/4½ oz sultanas
- 1 egg, beaten
- icing sugar, for dusting

1

1

2

1 Grease a baking tray with a little butter. Sieve the flour and salt into a large mixing bowl, stir in the dried yeast, ground ginger and brown sugar. Rub in the butter with your fingertips.

2 Stir in the mango purée, water and clear honey and mix together to form a dough.

3 Place the dough on a lightly floured surface and knead for 5 minutes until smooth. Alternatively, use an electric mixer with a dough hook. Place the dough in a greased bowl, cover and leave to rise in a warm place for about 1 hour until it has doubled in size.

4 Knead in the sultanas and shape the dough into 2 sausage shapes, each 25 cm/10 inches long. Carefully twist the 2 pieces together and pinch the ends to seal. Place the dough on the baking tray, cover and leave in a warm place for a further 40 minutes.

5 Brush the loaf with the egg and bake in a preheated oven, 220°C/425°F/Gas Mark 7, for 30 minutes or until golden brown. Leave to cool on a wire rack. Dust with icing sugar before serving.

COOK'S TIP

You can tell when the bread is cooked as it will sound hollow when tapped on the bottom.

Olive Oil, Fruit & Nut Cake

It is worth using a good quality olive oil for this cake as this will determine its flavour. The cake will keep well in an airtight tin.

NUTRITIONAL INFORMATION

Calories	309	Sugars	17g
Protein	4g	Fat	17g
Carbohydrate	38g	Saturates	3g

10 mins | 45 mins

SERVES 8

INGREDIENTS

- butter, for greasing
- 225 g/8 oz self-raising flour
- 50 g/1¾ oz caster sugar
- 125 ml/4 fl oz milk
- 4 tbsp orange juice
- 150 ml/5 fl oz olive oil
- 100 g/3½ oz mixed dried fruit
- 25 g/1 oz pine kernels

3

4

5

1 Grease an 18-cm/7-inch cake tin and line with baking paper.

2 Sieve the flour into a mixing bowl and stir in the caster sugar.

3 Make a well in the centre of the dry ingredients and pour in the milk and orange juice. Stir the mixture with a wooden spoon, gradually beating in the flour and sugar.

4 Pour in the olive oil, stirring well so that all of the ingredients are thoroughly mixed.

5 Stir the mixed dried fruit and pine kernels into the mixture and spoon into the prepared tin. Smooth the top with a palette knife.

6 Bake in a preheated oven, 180°C/350°F/Gas Mark 4, for about 45 minutes, until the cake is golden and firm to the touch.

7 Leave the cake to cool in the tin for a few minutes before transferring to a wire rack to cool completely.

8 Serve the cake warm or cold and cut into slices.

COOK'S TIP

Pine kernels are best known as the flavouring ingredient in the classic Italian pesto, but here they give a delicate, slightly resinous flavour to this cake.

Caraway Madeira

This is a classic Madeira cake made in the traditional way with caraway seeds. If you do not like their flavour, they can be omitted.

NUTRITIONAL INFORMATION

Calories	479	Sugars	24g
Protein	7g	Fat	26g
Carbohydrate	57g	Saturates	16g

1¼ hrs

1 hr

SERVES 8

INGREDIENTS

- 225 g/8 oz butter, softened, plus extra for greasing
- 175 g/6 oz soft brown sugar
- 3 eggs, beaten
- 350 g/12 oz self-raising flour
- 1 tbsp caraway seeds
- grated rind of 1 lemon
- 6 tbsp milk
- 1 or 2 strips of citron peel

1 Grease and line a 900 g/2 lb loaf tin.

2 In a bowl, cream together the butter and soft brown sugar until the mixture is pale and fluffy.

3 Gradually add the beaten eggs to the creamed mixture, beating thoroughly after each addition.

4 Sieve the flour into the bowl and gently fold into the creamed mixture in a figure-of-eight movement.

5 Add the caraway seeds, lemon rind and the milk and fold in until thoroughly blended.

6 Spoon the mixture into the prepared tin and level the surface.

7 Bake in a preheated oven, 160°C/325°F/Gas Mark 3, for 20 minutes.

8 Remove the cake from the oven, place the pieces of citron peel on top of the cake and return it to the oven for a further 40 minutes or until the cake is well risen and a fine skewer inserted into the centre comes out clean.

9 Leave the cake to cool in the tin before turning out and transferring to a wire rack to cool completely. Serve in slices when cold.

2

4

5

COOK'S TIP

Citron peel is available in the baking section of supermarkets. If it is unavailable, you can substitute chopped mixed peel.

Clementine Cake

This cake is flavoured with clementine rind and juice, creating a rich buttery cake but one full of fresh fruit flavour.

NUTRITIONAL INFORMATION	
Calories 427	Sugars 32g
Protein 6g	Fat 25g
Carbohydrate ...48g	Saturates 13g

5 mins — 1 hr

SERVES 8

INGREDIENTS

175 g/6 oz butter, softened, plus extra for greasing
2 clementines
175 g/6 oz caster sugar
3 eggs, beaten
175 g/6 oz self-raising flour
3 tbsp ground almonds
3 tbsp single cream

GLAZE AND TOPPING

6 tbsp clementine juice
2 tbsp caster sugar
3 white sugar cubes, crushed

2

4

7

1 Grease an 18-cm/7-inch round cake tin with butter and line the base with baking paper.

2 Pare the rind from the clementines and chop the rind finely. In a bowl, cream together the butter, sugar and clementine rind until pale and fluffy.

3 Gradually add the beaten eggs to the mixture, beating thoroughly after each addition.

4 Gently fold in the self-raising flour followed by the ground almonds and the single cream. Spoon the mixture into the prepared tin.

5 Bake in a preheated oven, 180°C/350°F/Gas Mark 4, for 55–60 minutes or until a fine skewer inserted into the centre comes out clean. Leave in the tin to cool slightly.

6 Meanwhile, make the glaze. Put the clementine juice into a small saucepan with the caster sugar. Bring to the boil and simmer for 5 minutes.

7 Transfer the cake to a wire rack. Drizzle the glaze over the cake until it has been absorbed and sprinkle with the crushed sugar cubes.

COOK'S TIP

If you prefer, chop the rind from the clementines in a food processor or blender together with the sugar in step 2. Tip the mixture into a bowl with the butter and begin to cream the mixture.

Glacé Fruit Cake

This cake is extremely colourful; you can choose any mixture of glacé fruits or stick to just one type if you prefer.

NUTRITIONAL INFORMATION

Calories	398	Sugars	34g
Protein	5g	Fat	20g
Carbohydrate	53g	Saturates	12g

1 hr   1 hr 10 mins

SERVES 8

INGREDIENTS

- 175 g/6 oz butter, softened, plus extra for greasing
- 175 g/6 oz caster sugar
- 3 eggs, beaten
- 175 g/6 oz self-raising flour, sieved
- 25 g/1 oz ground rice
- finely grated rind of 1 lemon
- 4 tbsp lemon juice
- 125 g/4½ oz glacé fruits, chopped
- icing sugar, for dusting (optional)

1. Lightly grease an 18-cm/7-inch cake tin and line with baking parchment.
2. In a bowl, whisk together the butter and caster sugar until light and fluffy.
3. Add the beaten eggs, a little at a time. Fold in the flour and ground rice.
4. Add the grated lemon rind and juice, followed by the chopped glacé fruits. Lightly mix all the ingredients together.
5. Spoon the mixture into the prepared tin and level the surface with the back of a spoon or a knife.
6. Bake the cake in a preheated oven, 180°C/350°F/Gas Mark 4, for about 1–1 hour 10 minutes until well risen or until a fine skewer inserted into the centre of the cake comes out clean.
7. Leave the cake to cool in the tin for 5 minutes, then turn out on to a wire rack to cool completely.
8. Dust well with icing sugar, if using, before serving.

2

3

4

COOK'S TIP

Wash and dry the glacé fruits before chopping them. This will prevent the fruits from sinking to the bottom of the cake while it is cooking.

Crunchy Fruit Cake

Polenta adds texture to this fruit cake, as well as a golden yellow colour. It also acts as a flour, binding the ingredients together.

NUTRITIONAL INFORMATION

Calories	328	Sugars	33g
Protein	59g	Fat	15g
Carbohydrate	47g	Saturates	7g

5–10 mins 1 hr

SERVES 8

INGREDIENTS

- 100 g/3½ oz butter, softened, plus extra for greasing
- 100g/3½ oz caster sugar
- 2 eggs, beaten
- 50 g/1¾ oz self-raising flour, sieved
- 1 tsp baking powder
- 100 g/3½ oz polenta
- 225 g/8 oz mixed dried fruit
- 25 g/1 oz pine kernels
- grated rind of 1 lemon
- 4 tbsp lemon juice
- 2 tbsp milk

2

3

5

1 Grease an 18-cm/7-inch cake tin with a little butter and line the base with baking paper.

2 In a bowl, whisk together the butter and sugar until light and fluffy.

3 Whisk in the beaten eggs, a little at a time, whisking thoroughly after each addition.

4 Gently fold the flour, baking powder and polenta into the mixture until totally incorporated.

5 Stir in the mixed dried fruit, pine kernels, grated lemon rind, lemon juice and milk.

6 Spoon the mixture into the prepared tin and level the surface.

7 Bake in a preheated oven, 180°C/350°F/Gas Mark 4, for about 1 hour or until a fine skewer inserted into the centre of the cake comes out clean.

8 Leave the cake to cool in the tin before turning out.

VARIATION

To give a crumblier light fruit cake, omit the polenta and use 150 g/5½ oz self-raising flour instead.

Carrot Cake

This classic favourite is always popular with children and adults alike when it is served for afternoon tea.

NUTRITIONAL INFORMATION

Calories	294	Sugars	32g
Protein	3g	Fat	15g
Carbohydrate	40g	Saturates	5g

5–10 mins 25 mins

12 BARS

INGREDIENTS

- butter, for greasing
- 125 g/4½ oz self-raising flour
- pinch of salt
- 1 tsp ground cinnamon
- 125 g/4½ oz soft brown sugar
- 2 eggs
- 100 ml/3½ fl oz sunflower oil
- 125 g/4½ oz carrots, peeled and finely grated
- 25 g/1 oz desiccated coconut
- 25 g/1 oz walnuts, chopped
- walnut pieces, for decoration

FROSTING

- 4 tbsp butter, softened
- 50 g/1¾ oz full-fat soft cheese
- 225 g/8 oz icing sugar, sieved
- 1 tsp lemon juice

1 Lightly grease a 20-cm/8-inch square cake tin and line with baking paper.

2 Sieve the flour, salt and ground cinnamon into a large bowl and stir in the brown sugar. Add the eggs and oil to the dry ingredients and mix well.

3 Stir in the grated carrot, desiccated coconut and chopped walnuts.

4 Pour the mixture into the prepared tin and bake in a preheated oven, 180°C/350°F/Gas Mark 4, for 20–25 minutes or until just firm to the touch. Leave to cool in the tin.

5 Meanwhile, make the cheese frosting. In a bowl, beat together the butter, full-fat soft cheese, icing sugar and lemon juice until the mixture is fluffy and creamy.

6 Turn the cake out of the tin and cut into 12 bars or slices. Spread with the frosting and then decorate with walnut pieces.

2

3

5

VARIATION

For a moister cake, replace the coconut with 1 roughly mashed banana.

Lemon Syrup Cake

The lovely light and tangy flavour of the sponge is balanced by the lemony syrup poured over the top of the cake.

NUTRITIONAL INFORMATION	
Calories 424	Sugars 38g
Protein 6g	Fat 21g
Carbohydrate ...58g	Saturates 5g

1 hr 5 mins | 1 hr

SERVES 8

INGREDIENTS

- butter, for greasing
- 200 g/7 oz plain flour
- 2 tsp baking powder
- 200 g/7 oz caster sugar
- 4 eggs
- 150 ml/5 fl oz soured cream
- grated rind 1 large lemon
- 4 tbsp lemon juice
- 150 ml/5 fl oz sunflower oil

SYRUP

- 4 tbsp icing sugar
- 3 tbsp lemon juice

3

4

7

1 Lightly grease a 20-cm/8-inch loose-bottomed round cake tin with a little butter and line the base with baking paper.

2 Sieve the flour and baking powder into a mixing bowl and stir in the caster sugar.

3 In a separate bowl, whisk the eggs, soured cream, lemon rind, lemon juice and oil together.

4 Pour the egg mixture into the dry ingredients and mix thoroughly until evenly combined.

5 Pour the mixture into the prepared tin and bake in a preheated oven, 180°C/350°F/Gas Mark 4, for about 45–60 minutes until well risen and golden brown on top.

6 Meanwhile, to make the syrup, mix together the icing sugar and lemon juice in a small saucepan. Stir over a low heat until just beginning to bubble and turn syrupy.

7 As soon as the cake comes out of the oven prick the surface with a fine skewer, then brush the syrup over the top. Leave the cake to cool completely in the tin before turning out and serving.

COOK'S TIP

Pricking the surface of the hot cake with a skewer ensures that the syrup seeps right into the cake and the full flavour is absorbed.

Orange Kugelhopf Cake

Baking in a deep, fluted kugelhopf tin ensures that you create a cake with a stunning shape. The moist cake is full of fresh orange flavour.

NUTRITIONAL INFORMATION

Calories	877	Sugars	82g
Protein	12g	Fat	35g
Carbohydrate	137g	Saturates	21g

25 mins | 55 mins

SERVES 4

INGREDIENTS

- 225 g/8 oz butter, softened, plus extra for greasing
- 425 g/15 oz plain flour, plus extra for dusting
- 225 g/8 oz caster sugar
- 4 eggs, separated
- 3 tsp baking powder
- 300 ml/10 fl oz fresh orange juice
- 1 tbsp orange flower water
- 1 tsp grated orange rind
- salt

SYRUP

- 200 ml/7 fl oz orange juice
- 200 g/7 oz granulated sugar

1 Grease and flour a 25-cm/10-inch kugelhopf tin or deep ring mould.

2 In a bowl, cream together the butter and caster sugar until the mixture is light and fluffy. Add the egg yolks, one at a time, whisking the mixture thoroughly after each addition.

3 Sieve together the flour, a pinch of salt and the baking powder into a separate bowl. Gently fold the dry ingredients and the orange juice alternately into the creamed mixture with a metal spoon, working as lightly as possible. Stir in the orange flower water and orange rind.

4 Whisk the egg whites until they form soft peaks and then fold them into the mixture in a figure-of-eight movement.

5 Pour the mixture into the prepared tin or ring mould and bake in a preheated oven, 180°C/350°F/Gas Mark 4, for about 50–55 minutes or until a metal skewer inserted into the centre of the cake comes out clean.

6 In a saucepan, bring the orange juice and sugar to the boil over a low heat, then simmer for 5 minutes until the sugar has dissolved.

7 Remove the cake from the oven and leave to cool in the tin for 10 minutes. Prick the top of the cake with a fine skewer and brush over half of the syrup. Leave the cake to cool for another 10 minutes. Invert the cake on to a wire rack placed over a deep plate and brush the syrup over the cake until it is entirely covered. Serve warm or cold.

3

4

7

Apple Cake with Cider

This can be eaten as a cake at tea time or with a cup of coffee, or it can be warmed through and served with cream for a dessert.

NUTRITIONAL INFORMATION

Calories	263	Sugars	22g
Protein	4g	Fat	9g
Carbohydrate	43g	Saturates	5g

1 hr 5 mins — 40 mins

SERVES 8

INGREDIENTS

- 75 g/2¾ oz butter, cut into small pieces, plus extra for greasing
- 225 g/8 oz self-raising flour
- 1 tsp baking powder
- 75 g/2¾ oz caster sugar
- 50 g/1¾ oz dried apple, chopped
- 75 g/2¾ oz raisins
- 150 ml/5 fl oz sweet cider
- 1 egg, beaten
- 175 g/6 oz raspberries

1 Grease a 20-cm/8-inch cake tin and line with baking paper.

2 Sieve the flour and baking powder into a mixing bowl and rub in the butter with your fingertips until the mixture resembles fine breadcrumbs.

3 Stir in the caster sugar, chopped dried apple and raisins.

4 Pour in the sweet cider and egg and mix together until thoroughly blended. Stir in the raspberries very gently so they do not break up.

5 Pour the mixture into the prepared cake tin.

6 Bake in a preheated oven, 190°C/375°F/Gas Mark 5, for about 40 minutes until risen and lightly golden.

7 Leave the cake to cool in the tin, then turn out on to a wire rack. Leave until completely cold before serving.

VARIATION

If you don't want to use cider, replace it with clear apple juice, if you prefer.

Spiced Apple Ring

The addition of pieces of fresh apple and crunchy almonds to the cake mixture makes this beautifully moist yet with a crunch to it.

NUTRITIONAL INFORMATION

Calories	379	Sugars	27g
Protein	5g	Fat	22g
Carbohydrate	43g	Saturates	13g

1 hr 5 mins 30 mins

SERVES 8

INGREDIENTS

- 175 g/6 oz butter, softened, plus extra for greasing
- 175 g/6 oz caster sugar
- 3 eggs, beaten
- 175 g/6 oz self-raising flour
- 1 tsp ground cinnamon
- 1 tsp ground mixed spice
- 2 dessert apples, cored and grated
- 2 tbsp apple juice or milk
- 25 g/1 oz flaked almonds

1 Lightly grease a 25-cm/10-inch ovenproof ring mould.

2 In a mixing bowl, cream together the butter and sugar until light and fluffy. Gradually add the beaten eggs, beating well after each addition.

3 Sieve the flour and spices together, then carefully fold them into the creamed mixture.

4 Stir in the grated apples and the apple juice or milk and mix to a soft dropping consistency.

5 Sprinkle the flaked almonds around the base of the mould and spoon the cake mixture on top. Level the surface with the back of the spoon.

6 Bake the cake in a preheated oven, 180°C/350°F/Gas Mark 4, for about 30 minutes until well risen and a fine skewer inserted into the centre comes out clean.

7 Leave the cake to cool in the tin before turning out and transferring to a wire rack to cool completely. Serve the spiced apple ring cut into slices.

4

5

5

COOK'S TIP

This cake can also be made in an 18-cm/7-inch round cake tin if you do not have an ovenproof ring mould.

Coffee Streusel Cake

This cake has a moist coffee and almond sponge on the bottom, covered with a crisp crunchy, spicy topping.

NUTRITIONAL INFORMATION

Calories	409	Sugars	21g
Protein	8g	Fat	19g
Carbohydrate	55g	Saturates	10g

10 mins — 1 hr

SERVES 8

INGREDIENTS

- butter, for greasing
- 275 g/9½ oz plain flour
- 1 tbsp baking powder
- 75 g/2¾ oz caster sugar
- 150 ml/5 fl oz milk
- 2 eggs
- 100 g/3½ oz butter, melted and cooled
- 2 tbsp instant coffee mixed with 1 tbsp boiling water
- 50 g/1¾ oz almonds, chopped
- icing sugar, for dusting

TOPPING

- 75 g/2¾ oz self-raising flour
- 75 g/2¾ oz demerara sugar
- 2 tbsp butter, cut into small pieces
- 1 tsp ground mixed spice
- 1 tbsp water

1 Grease a 23-cm/9-inch loose-bottomed round cake tin with a little butter and line with baking paper. Sieve together the flour and baking powder into a large mixing bowl, then stir in the caster sugar.

2 Whisk the milk, eggs, butter and coffee mixture together and pour on to the dry ingredients. Add the chopped almonds and mix lightly together. Spoon the mixture into the tin.

3 To make the topping, mix the flour and demerara sugar together in a separate bowl.

4 Add the butter and rub it in with your fingertips until the mixture is crumbly. Sprinkle in the ground mixed spice and the water and bring the mixture together in loose crumbs. Sprinkle the topping evenly over the surface of the cake mixture in the tin.

5 Bake in a preheated oven, 190°C/375°F/Gas Mark 5, for about 1 hour. Cover loosely with foil if the topping starts to brown too quickly. Leave to cool in the tin, then turn out. Dust with icing sugar just before serving.

2

2

4

Sugar-free Fruit Cake

This cake is full of flavour from the mixed fruits. The fruit gives the cake its sweetness so there is no need for extra sugar.

NUTRITIONAL INFORMATION

Calories	423	Sugars	34g
Protein	8g	Fat	16g
Carbohydrate	68g	Saturates	9g

1 hr 5 mins

1 hr

SERVES 8

INGREDIENTS

- 125 g/4½ oz butter, cut into small pieces, plus extra for greasing
- 350 g/12 oz plain flour
- 2 tsp baking powder
- 1 tsp ground mixed spice
- 75 g/2¾ oz no-soak dried apricots, chopped
- 75 g/2¾ oz dried dates, chopped
- 75 g/2¾ oz glacé cherries, chopped
- 100 g/3½ oz raisins
- 125 ml/4 fl oz milk
- 2 eggs, beaten
- grated rind of 1 orange
- 5–6 tbsp orange juice
- 3 tbsp clear honey

3

4

5

1 Grease a 20-cm/8-inch round cake tin with a little butter and line the base with baking paper.

2 Sieve the flour, baking powder and ground mixed spice into a large mixing bowl.

3 Rub in the butter with your fingertips until the mixture resembles fine breadcrumbs.

4 Carefully stir in the apricots, dates, glacé cherries and raisins with the milk, beaten eggs, grated orange rind and orange juice.

5 Stir in the honey and mix everything together to form a soft dropping consistency. Spoon into the prepared cake tin and level the surface.

6 Bake in a preheated oven, 180°C/350°F/Gas Mark 4, for 1 hour until a fine skewer inserted into the centre of the cake comes out clean.

7 Leave the cake to cool in the tin before turning out.

VARIATION

For a fruity alternative, replace the honey with 1 mashed ripe banana, if you prefer.

Almond Cake

Being glazed with a honey syrup after baking gives this cake a lovely moist texture, but it can be eaten without the glaze, if preferred.

NUTRITIONAL INFORMATION

Calories	324	Sugars	27g
Protein	5g	Fat	16g
Carbohydrate	43g	Saturates	4g

2 hrs 5 mins — 50 mins

SERVES 8

INGREDIENTS

- 100 g/3½ oz soft tub margarine, plus extra for greasing
- 50 g/1¾ oz soft brown sugar
- 2 eggs
- 175 g/6 oz self-raising flour
- 1 tsp baking powder
- 4 tbsp milk
- 2 tbsp clear honey
- 50 g/1¾ oz flaked almonds

SYRUP

- 150 ml/5 fl oz clear honey
- 2 tbsp lemon juice

1 Grease an 18-cm/7-inch round cake tin and line with baking paper.

2 Place the margarine, brown sugar, eggs, flour, baking powder, milk and honey in a large mixing bowl and beat well with a wooden spoon for about 1 minute until all of the ingredients are thoroughly mixed together.

3 Spoon into the prepared tin, level the surface with the back of a spoon or a knife and sprinkle with the almonds.

4 Bake in a preheated oven, 180°C/350°F/Gas Mark 4, for about 50 minutes or until the cake is well risen and a fine skewer inserted into the centre comes out clean.

5 Meanwhile, make the syrup. Combine the honey and lemon juice in a small saucepan and simmer for about 5 minutes or until the syrup starts to coat the back of a spoon.

6 As soon as the cake comes out of the oven, pour over the syrup, allowing it to seep into the middle of the cake.

7 Leave the cake to cool for at least 2 hours before slicing.

2

3

6

COOK'S TIP

Experiment with different flavoured honeys for the syrup glaze until you find one that you think tastes best.

Gingerbread

This wonderfully spicy gingerbread is made even moister by the addition of chopped fresh apples.

NUTRITIONAL INFORMATION

Calories	248	Sugars	21g
Protein	3g	Fat	11g
Carbohydrate	36g	Saturates	7g

1¼ hrs

35 mins

12 BARS

INGREDIENTS

- 150 g/5½ oz butter, plus extra for greasing
- 175 g/6 oz soft brown sugar
- 2 tbsp black treacle
- 225 g/8 oz plain flour
- 1 tsp baking powder
- 2 tsp bicarbonate of soda
- 2 tsp ground ginger
- 150 ml/5 fl oz milk
- 1 egg, beaten
- 2 dessert apples, peeled, chopped and coated with 1 tbsp lemon juice

2

4

5

1 Grease a 23-cm/9-inch square cake tin and line with baking paper.

2 Melt the butter, sugar and treacle in a saucepan over a low heat and set the mixture aside to cool.

3 Sieve the flour, baking powder, bicarbonate of soda and ginger into a mixing bowl.

4 Stir in the milk, beaten egg and cooled buttery liquid, followed by the chopped apples coated with the lemon juice.

5 Mix everything together gently, then pour the mixture into the prepared tin and smooth the surface.

6 Bake in a preheated oven, 170°C/325°F/Gas Mark 3, for 30–35 minutes until the cake has risen and a fine skewer inserted into the centre comes out clean.

7 Leave the cake to cool in the tin before turning out and cutting into 12 bars.

VARIATION

If you enjoy the flavour of ginger, try adding 25 g/1 oz finely chopped stem ginger to the mixture in step 3.

Apple Shortcakes

This American-style dessert is a sweet scone, split and filled with sliced apples and whipped cream. The shortcakes can be eaten warm or cold.

NUTRITIONAL INFORMATION

Calories	511	Sugars	44g
Protein	5g	Fat	24g
Carbohydrate	73g	Saturates	15g

25 mins | 15 mins

MAKES 4

INGREDIENTS

- 2 tbsp butter, cut into small pieces, plus extra for greasing
- 150 g/5½ oz plain flour
- ½ tsp salt
- 1 tsp baking powder
- 1 tbsp caster sugar
- 50 ml/2 fl oz milk
- icing sugar, for dusting (optional)

FILLING

- 3 dessert apples, peeled, cored and sliced
- 100 g/3½ oz caster sugar
- 1 tbsp lemon juice
- 1 tsp ground cinnamon
- 300 ml/10 fl oz water
- 150 ml/5 fl oz double cream, lightly whipped

2

2

4

1 Lightly grease a baking tray. Sieve the flour, salt and baking powder into a mixing bowl. Stir in the sugar, then rub in the butter with your fingers until the mixture resembles fine breadcrumbs.

2 Pour in the milk and mix to a soft dough. On a lightly floured surface, knead the dough lightly, then roll out to 1 cm/½ inch thick. Stamp out 4 rounds, using a 5-cm/2-inch cutter. Transfer the rounds to the prepared baking tray.

3 Bake in a preheated oven, 220°C/425°F/Gas Mark 7, for about 15 minutes until the shortcakes are well risen and lightly browned. Leave to cool.

4 To make the filling, place the apple slices, sugar, lemon juice and cinnamon in a saucepan. Add the water, bring to the boil and simmer, uncovered, for 5-10 minutes until the apples are tender. Leave to cool a little, then remove the apples from the pan.

5 To serve, split the shortcakes in half. Place each bottom half on an individual serving plate and spoon on a quarter of the apple slices, then the cream. Place the other half of the shortcake on top. Serve dusted with icing sugar, if wished.

Treacle Scones

These scones are light and buttery like traditional scones, but they have a deliciously rich flavour which comes from the black treacle.

NUTRITIONAL INFORMATION

Calories	208	Sugars	9g
Protein	4g	Fat	9g
Carbohydrate	30g	Saturates	6g

15 mins 10 mzins

SERVES 8

INGREDIENTS

- 6 tbsp butter, cut into small pieces, plus extra for greasing
- 225 g/8 oz self-raising flour
- 1 tbsp caster sugar
- pinch of salt
- 1 dessert apple, peeled, cored and chopped
- 1 egg, beaten
- 2 tbsp black treacle
- 5 tbsp milk

1 Lightly grease a baking tray with a little butter.

2 Sieve the flour, sugar and salt into a mixing bowl.

3 Add the butter and rub it in with your fingertips until the mixture resembles fine breadcrumbs.

4 Stir the chopped apple into the mixture until thoroughly combined.

5 Mix the beaten egg, treacle and milk together in a jug. Add to the dry ingredients and mix well to form a soft dough.

6 On a lightly floured working surface, roll out the dough to a thickness of 2cm/¾ inch and cut out 8 scones, using a 5-cm/2-inch cutter.

7 Arrange the scones on the prepared baking tray and bake in a preheated oven, 220°C/425°F/Gas Mark 7, for 8–10 minutes.

8 Transfer the scones to a wire rack and leave to cool slightly.

9 Serve split in half and spread with butter.

4

5

6

COOK'S TIP

These scones can be frozen, but are best defrosted and eaten within 1 month.

Cherry Scones

These are an alternative to traditional scones, using sweet glacé cherries which not only create colour but add a distinct flavour.

NUTRITIONAL INFORMATION

Calories	211	Sugars	10g
Protein	4g	Fat	9g
Carbohydrate	31g	Saturates	6g

10 mins | 30 mins

MAKES 8

INGREDIENTS

- 6 tbsp butter, cut into small pieces, plus extra for greasing
- 225 g/8 oz self-raising flour
- 15 g/½ oz caster sugar
- pinch of salt
- 40 g/1½ oz glacé cherries, chopped
- 40 g/1½ oz sultanas
- 1 egg, beaten
- 50 ml/2 fl oz milk

1 Lightly grease a baking tray with a little butter.

2 Sieve the flour, sugar and salt into a mixing bowl and rub in the butter with your fingertips until the scone mixture resembles breadcrumbs.

3 Stir in the glacé cherries and sultanas. Add the egg.

4 Reserve 1 tablespoon of the milk for glazing, then add the remainder to the mixture. Mix well together to form a soft dough.

5 On a lightly floured surface, roll out the dough to a thickness of 2 cm/¾ inch and cut out 8 scones, using a 5cm/2-inch cutter.

6 Place the scones on the prepared baking tray and brush the tops with the reserved milk.

7 Bake in a preheated oven, 220°C/425°F/Gas Mark 7, for 8–10 minutes or until the scones are golden brown.

8 Leave to cool on a wire rack, then serve split and buttered.

COOK'S TIP

These scones will freeze very successfully but they are best defrosted and eaten within 1 month.

3

4

5

Cranberry Muffins

These savoury muffins are an ideal accompaniment to soup, or they make a nice change from sweet cakes for serving with coffee.

NUTRITIONAL INFORMATION

Calories	96	Sugars	4g
Protein	3g	Fat	4g
Carbohydrate	14g	Saturates	2g

1 hr 5 mins 20 Mins

SERVES 18

INGREDIENTS

butter, for greasing
225 g/8 oz plain flour
2 tsp baking powder
½ tsp salt
50 g/1¾ oz caster sugar
4 tbsp butter, melted
2 eggs, beaten
200 ml/7 fl oz milk
100 g/3½ oz fresh cranberries
35 g/1¼ oz Parmesan cheese, freshly grated

1 Lightly grease 2 bun tins. Sieve the flour, baking powder and salt into a mixing bowl. Stir in the caster sugar.

2 In a separate bowl, mix the butter, beaten eggs and milk together, then pour into the bowl of dry ingredients. Mix lightly together until all of the ingredients are evenly combined. Finally, stir in the fresh cranberries.

3 Divide the mixture between the prepared tins.

4 Sprinkle the grated Parmesan cheese over the top of each portion of the muffin mixture.

1

2

4

5 Bake in a preheated oven, 200°C/400°F/Gas Mark 6, for about 20 minutes or until the muffins are well risen and a golden brown colour.

6 Leave the muffins to cool in the tins. Transfer the muffins to a wire rack and leave to cool completely before serving them.

VARIATION

For a sweet alternative to this recipe, replace the Parmesan cheese with demerara sugar in step 4 if you prefer.

Fruit Loaf with Apple Spread

This sweet, fruity loaf is ideal served for tea or as a healthy snack. The fruit spread can be made quickly while the cake is in the oven.

NUTRITIONAL INFORMATION

Calories	733	Sugars	110g
Protein	12g	Fat	5g
Carbohydrate	171g	Saturates	1g

1¼ hrs — 2 hrs

SERVES 4

INGREDIENTS

- butter, for greasing
- 175 g/6 oz porridge oats
- 100 g/3½ oz light muscovado sugar
- 1 tsp ground cinnamon
- 125 g/4½ oz sultanas
- 175 g/6 oz seedless raisins
- 2 tbsp malt extract
- 300 ml/10 fl oz unsweetened apple juice
- 175 g/6 oz wholemeal self-raising flour
- 1½ tsp baking powder
- strawberries and apple wedges, to serve

FRUIT SPREAD

- 225 g/8 oz strawberries, washed and hulled
- 2 eating apples, cored, chopped and mixed with 1 tbsp lemon juice to prevent them from browning
- 300 ml/10 fl oz unsweetened apple juice

1

5

5

1 Grease and line a 900-g/2-lb loaf tin. Place the porridge oats, sugar, cinnamon, sultanas, raisins and malt extract in a mixing bowl. Pour in the apple juice, stir well and leave to soak for 30 minutes.

2 Sift in the flour and baking powder, adding any bran that remains in the sieve, and fold in using a metal spoon.

3 Spoon the mixture into the prepared tin and bake in a preheated oven, 180°C/350°F/Gas Mark 4, for 1½ hours until firm or until a skewer inserted into the centre comes out clean.

4 Leave to cool for 10 minutes, then turn on to a rack and leave to cool.

5 Meanwhile, make the fruit spread. Place the strawberries and apples in a saucepan and pour in the apple juice. Bring to the boil over a low heat, cover and simmer gently for 30 minutes. Beat the sauce well and spoon into a sterilized warmed jar. Leave to cool, then seal and label.

6 Serve the loaf, cut into slices with 1–2 tablespoons of the fruit spread and an assortment of strawberries and apple wedges.

Banana & Lime Cake

A substantial cake that is ideal served for tea. The mashed bananas help to keep the cake moist and the lime icing gives it extra zing and zest.

NUTRITIONAL INFORMATION

Calories	235	Sugars	31g
Protein	5g	Fat	1g
Carbohydrate	55g	Saturates	0.3g

35 mins 45 mins

SERVES 10

INGREDIENTS

- butter, for greasing
- 300 g/10½ oz plain flour
- 1 tsp salt
- 1½ tsp baking powder
- 175 g/6 oz light muscovado sugar
- 1 tsp lime rind, grated
- 1 egg, beaten
- 1 banana, mashed with 1 tbsp lime juice
- 150 ml/5 fl oz low-fat natural fromage frais
- 115 g/4 oz sultanas

TOPPING

- 115 g/4 oz icing sugar
- 1–2 tsp lime juice
- ½ tsp finely grated lime rind

TO DECORATE

- banana chips
- finely grated lime rind

1 Grease and line a deep 18-cm/7-inch round cake tin with baking paper.

2 Sift the flour, salt and baking powder into a mixing bowl and stir in the sugar and lime rind.

3 Make a well in the centre of the dry ingredients and add the egg, banana, fromage frais and sultanas. Mix well until thoroughly incorporated.

4 Spoon the mixture into the tin and smooth the surface. Bake in a preheated oven, 180°C/350°F/Gas Mark 4, for 40–45 minutes until firm to the touch or until a skewer inserted in the centre comes out clean.

5 Leave the cake to cool for 10 minutes, then turn out on to a wire rack.

6 To make the topping, sift the icing sugar into a small bowl and mix with the lime juice to form a soft, but not too runny icing. Stir in the grated lime rind. Drizzle the icing over the cake, letting it run down the sides.

7 Decorate the cake with banana chips and lime rind. Let the cake stand for 15 minutes so that the icing sets.

1

3

4

VARIATION

For a delicious alternative, replace the lime rind and juice with orange and the sultanas with chopped apricots.

Crispy-Topped Fruit Bake

The sugar cubes give a lovely crunchy taste to this easy-to-make cake, which, served with cream, makes a splendid dessert.

NUTRITIONAL INFORMATION

Calories	227	Sugars	30g
Protein	5g	Fat	1g
Carbohydrate	53g	Saturates	0.2g

15 mins — 1 hr

SERVES 10

INGREDIENTS

- butter, for greasing
- 350 g/12 oz cooking apples
- 3 tbsp lemon juice
- 300 g/10½ oz wholemeal self-raising flour
- ½ tsp baking powder
- 1 tsp ground cinnamon, plus extra for dusting
- 175 g/6 oz prepared blackberries, defrosted if frozen, plus extra to decorate
- 175 g/6 oz light muscovado sugar
- 1 egg, beaten
- 200 ml/7 fl oz low-fat natural fromage frais
- 55 g/2 oz white or brown sugar cubes, lightly crushed
- sliced eating apple, to decorate

1 Grease and line a 900-g/2-lb loaf tin. Core, peel and finely dice the apples. Place them in a saucepan with the lemon juice, bring to the boil, cover and simmer gently for 10 minutes until soft and pulpy. Beat thoroughly and set aside to cool.

1

2 Sift the flour, baking powder and 1 teaspoon of cinnamon into a bowl, adding any bran that remains in the sieve. Stir in 115 g/4 oz blackberries and the sugar.

2

3 Make a well in the centre of the ingredients and add the egg, fromage frais and cooled apple purée. Mix well to incorporate thoroughly. Spoon the mixture into the prepared loaf tin and smooth over the top.

4 Sprinkle with the remaining blackberries, pressing them down into the cake mixture, and top with the crushed sugar lumps. Bake in a preheated oven, 190°C/375°F/Gas Mark 5, for 40–45 minutes. Leave to cool in the tin.

4

5 Remove the cake from the tin and peel away the lining paper. Serve dusted with cinnamon and decorated with extra blackberries and apple slices.

VARIATION

Try replacing the blackberries with blueberries. Use canned or frozen blueberries if the fresh fruit is unavailable.

Rich Fruit Cake

Serve this moist, fruit-laden cake for a special occasion. It would also make an excellent Christmas or birthday cake.

NUTRITIONAL INFORMATION

Calories	772	Sugars	137g
Protein	14g	Fat	5g
Carbohydrate	179g	Saturates	1g

35 mins · 1¾ hrs

SERVES 4

INGREDIENTS

- butter, for greasing
- 175 g/6 oz stoned unsweetened dates
- 125 g/4½ oz no-soak dried prunes
- 200 ml/7 fl oz unsweetened orange juice
- 2 tbsp black treacle
- 1 tsp finely grated lemon rind
- 1 tsp finely grated orange rind
- 225 g/8 oz wholemeal self-raising flour
- 1 tsp mixed spice
- 125 g/4½ oz seedless raisins
- 125 g/4½ oz golden sultanas
- 125 g/4½ oz currants
- 125 g/4½ oz dried cranberries
- 3 large eggs, separated

TO DECORATE

- 1 tbsp apricot jam, warmed
- icing sugar, to dust
- 175 g/6 oz sugarpaste
- strips of orange rind
- strips of lemon rind

1

2

3

1 Grease and line a deep 20.5-cm/8 inch round cake tin. Chop the dates and prunes and place in a pan. Pour over the orange juice and simmer for 10 minutes. Remove the pan from the heat and beat the fruit mixture until puréed. Add the treacle and rinds and set aside to cool.

2 Sift the flour and spice into a bowl, adding any bran that remains in the sieve. Add the dried fruits. When the date and prune mixture is cool, whisk in the egg yolks. In a clean bowl, whisk the egg whites until stiff. Spoon the fruit mixture into the dry ingredients and mix together.

3 Gently fold in the egg whites. Transfer to the prepared tin and bake in a preheated oven, 170°C/325°F/Gas Mark 3, for 1½ hours. Leave to cool in the tin.

4 Remove the cake from the tin and brush the top with jam. Dust the work surface with icing sugar and roll out the sugarpaste thinly. Lay the sugarpaste over the top of the cake and trim the edges. Decorate with orange and lemon rind.

Carrot & Ginger Cake

This melt-in-the-mouth version of a favourite cake has a fraction of the fat of the traditional cake.

NUTRITIONAL INFORMATION

Calories	249	Sugars	28g
Protein	7g	Fat	6g
Carbohydrate	46g	Saturates	1g

15 mins

1¼ hrs

SERVES 10

INGREDIENTS

- butter, for greasing
- 225 g/8 oz plain flour
- 1 tsp baking powder
- 1 tsp bicarbonate of soda
- 2 tsp ground ginger
- ½ tsp salt
- 175 g/6 oz light muscovado sugar
- 225 g/8 oz carrots, grated
- 2 pieces chopped stem ginger
- 25 g/1 oz grated fresh root ginger
- 60 g/2 oz seedless raisins
- 2 medium eggs, beaten
- 3 tbsp corn oil
- juice of 1 orange

FROSTING

- 225 g/8 oz low-fat soft cheese
- 4 tbsp icing sugar
- 1 tsp vanilla essence

TO DECORATE

- grated carrot
- finely chopped stem ginger
- ground ginger

2

2

4

1 Preheat the oven to 180°C/350°F/Gas Mark 4. Grease and line a 20.5-cm/8-inch round cake tin with baking paper.

2 Sift the flour, baking powder, bicarbonate of soda, ground ginger and salt into a bowl. Stir in the sugar, carrots, stem ginger, fresh root ginger and raisins. Beat together the eggs, oil and orange juice, then pour into the bowl. Mix the ingredients together well.

3 Spoon the mixture into the tin and bake in the oven for 1–1¼ hours until firm to the touch, or until a skewer inserted into the centre of the cake comes out clean.

4 To make the frosting, place the soft cheese in a bowl and beat to soften. Sift in the icing sugar and add the vanilla essence. Mix well.

5 Remove the cake from the tin and smooth the frosting over the top. Decorate the cake and serve.

Strawberry Roulade

Serve this moist, light sponge rolled up with an almond and strawberry fromage frais filling for a delicious tea-time treat.

NUTRITIONAL INFORMATION

Calories	166	Sugars	19g
Protein	6g	Fat	3g
Carbohydrate	30g	Saturates	1g

30 mins 10 mins

SERVES 8

INGREDIENTS

3 large eggs

125 g/4½ oz caster sugar

125 g/4½ oz plain flour

1 tbsp hot water

FILLING

200 ml/7 fl oz low-fat fromage frais

1 tsp almond essence

225 g/8 oz small strawberries

TO DECORATE

1 tbsp flaked almonds, toasted

1 tsp icing sugar

1 Line a 35 x 25-cm/14 x 10-inch Swiss roll tin with baking paper. Place the eggs in a mixing bowl with the caster sugar. Place the bowl over a pan of hot, but not boiling water and whisk until pale and thick.

2 Remove the bowl from the pan. Sieve in the flour and fold into the eggs with the hot water. Pour the mixture into the tin and bake in a preheated oven, 220°C/425°F/Gas Mark 7, for about 8–10 minutes, until golden and set.

3 Transfer the mixture to a sheet of baking paper. Peel off the lining paper and roll up the sponge tightly along with the baking paper. Wrap in a tea towel and set aside to cool.

4 Mix together the fromage frais and the almond essence. Reserving a few strawberries for decoration, wash, hull and slice the remainder. Leave the fromage frais mixture and strawberries to chill in the refrigerator until required.

5 Unroll the sponge, spread the fromage frais mixture over the sponge and sprinkle with the sliced strawberries. Roll the sponge up again and transfer to a serving plate. Sprinkle with almonds and lightly dust with icing sugar. Decorate with the reserved strawberries.

1

3

5

Fruity Muffins

Perfect for those on a low-fat diet and for weight watchers, these little cakes contain no butter, just a little corn oil.

NUTRITIONAL INFORMATION

Calories	162	Sugars	11g
Protein	4g	Fat	4g
Carbohydrate	28g	Saturates	1g

10 mins 30 mins

MAKES 10

INGREDIENTS

- 225 g/8 oz wholemeal self-raising flour
- 2 tsp baking powder
- 25 g/1 oz light muscovado sugar
- 100 g/3½ oz no-soak dried apricots, finely chopped
- 1 medium banana, mashed with 1 tbsp orange juice
- 1 tsp orange rind, finely grated
- 300 ml/10 fl oz skimmed milk
- 1 egg, beaten
- 3 tbsp corn oil
- 2 tbsp porridge oats
- fruit spread, honey or maple syrup, to serve

1 Place 10 paper muffin cases in a deep patty tin. Sieve the flour and baking powder into a mixing bowl, adding any bran that remains in the sieve. Stir in the sugar and chopped apricots.

2 Make a well in the centre of the dry ingredients and add the mashed banana, grated orange rind, milk, beaten egg and corn oil. Mix together well to form a thick batter.

3 Divide the batter evenly between the 10 paper cases. Sprinkle the tops with a few porridge oats and bake in a preheated oven, 200°C/400°F/Gas Mark 6, for 25–30 minutes until well risen and firm to the touch or until a skewer inserted into the centre comes out clean. Transfer the muffins to a wire rack to cool slightly. Serve the muffins while they are warm with a little fruit spread, honey or maple syrup.

VARIATION

If you like dried figs, they make a deliciously crunchy alternative to the apricots; they also go very well with the flavour of the orange. Other no-soak dried fruits, chopped up finely, can be used as well.

2

3

3

Orange & Almond Cake

This light and tangy citrus cake from Sicily is better eaten as a dessert than as a cake. It is especially good served after a large meal.

NUTRITIONAL INFORMATION

Calories	399	Sugars	20g
Protein	8g	Fat	31g
Carbohydrate	23g	Saturates	13g

30 mins · 40 mins

SERVES 8

INGREDIENTS

- butter, for greasing
- 4 eggs, separated
- 125 g/4½ oz caster sugar, plus 2 tsp for the cream
- finely grated rind and juice of 2 oranges
- finely grated rind and juice of 1 lemon
- 125 g/4½ oz ground almonds
- 2½ tbsp self-raising flour
- 200 ml/7 fl oz whipping cream
- 1 tsp cinnamon

TO DECORATE

- 25 g/1 oz flaked almonds, toasted
- icing sugar, to dust

1 Grease and line the base of an 18-cm/7-inch round deep cake tin.

2 Blend the egg yolks with the sugar until the mixture is thick and creamy. Whisk half of the orange rind and all of the lemon rind into the egg yolks.

3 Mix the orange and lemon juice with the ground almonds and stir into the egg yolks. The mixture will be quite runny. Fold in the flour.

4 Whisk the egg whites until stiff and gently fold into the egg yolk mixture.

5 Pour the mixture into the tin and bake in a preheated oven, 180°C/350°F/Gas Mark 4, for 35–40 minutes until golden and springy to the touch. Leave to cool in the tin for 10 minutes and then turn out.

6 Whip the cream to form soft peaks. Stir in the remaining orange rind, cinnamon and sugar. Once the cake is cold, cover with the almonds, dust with icing sugar and serve with the cream.

VARIATION

You could serve this cake with a syrup. Boil the juice and finely grated rind of 2 oranges, 75 g/2¾ oz caster sugar and 2 tablespoons of water for 5–6 minutes until slightly thickened. Stir in 1 tablespoon of orange liqueur just before serving.

Coconut Cake

This is a great family favourite. I was always delighted to find it included in my lunch box and considered it a real treat!

NUTRITIONAL INFORMATION

Calories	464	Sugars	20g
Protein	8g	Fat	26g
Carbohydrate	54g	Saturates	18g

10 mins 30 mins

MAKES 6–8

INGREDIENTS

- 100 g/3½ oz butter, cut into small pieces, plus extra for greasing
- 225 g/8 oz self-raising flour
- 100 g/3½ oz demerara sugar
- 100 g/3½ oz desiccated coconut, plus extra for sprinkling
- 2 eggs, beaten
- 4 tbsp milk
- salt

1 Grease a 900-g/2-lb loaf tin and line the base with baking paper.

2 Sieve the flour and a pinch of salt into a mixing bowl and rub in the butter with your fingertips until the mixture resembles fine breadcrumbs.

3 Stir in the demerara sugar, coconut, eggs and milk and mix to a soft dropping consistency.

4 Spoon the mixture into the prepared tin and level the surface. Bake in a preheated oven, 160°C/325°F/Gas Mark 3, for 30 minutes.

5 Remove the cake from the oven and sprinkle with the extra coconut. Return the cake to the oven and cook for a further 30 minutes until well risen and golden and a fine skewer inserted into the centre comes out clean.

6 Leave the cake to cool in the tin before turning it out and transferring it to a wire rack to cool completely before serving.

COOK'S TIP

The flavour of this cake is enhanced by storing it in a cool dry place for a few days before eating.

Pear & Ginger Cake

This deliciously buttery pear and ginger cake is ideal for tea-time or you can serve it with cream for a delicious dessert.

NUTRITIONAL INFORMATION

Calories	531	Sugars	41g
Protein	6g	Fat	30g
Carbohydrate	62g	Saturates	19g

15 mins 40 mins

SERVES 6

INGREDIENTS

- 200 g/7 oz unsalted butter, softened, plus extra for greasing
- 175 g/6 oz caster sugar
- 175 g/6 oz self-raising flour
- 3 tsp ground ginger
- 3 eggs, beaten
- 450 g/1 lb dessert pears, peeled, cored and thinly sliced, then brushed with lemon juice to prevent them from browning
- 1 tbsp soft brown sugar
- ice cream or double cream, lightly whipped, to serve (optional)

2

3

4

1 Lightly grease and line the base of a deep 20-cm/8-inch cake tin.

2 Put175 g/6 oz of the butter and the caster sugar into a bowl. Sieve in the flour and ground ginger and add the eggs. Beating well with a whisk, mix to form a smooth consistency.

3 Spoon the cake mixture into the prepared tin, levelling out the surface with a palette knife.

4 Arrange the pear slices over the cake mixture. Sprinkle with the brown sugar and dot with the remaining butter.

5 Bake in a preheated oven, 180°C/350°F/Gas Mark 4, for 35–40 minutes or until the cake is golden and feels springy to the touch.

6 Serve the pear and ginger cake warm, with ice cream or cream, if you wish.

COOK'S TIP

Soft brown sugar is often known as Barbados sugar. It is a darker form of light brown soft sugar.

Almond Slices

A mouth-watering dessert that is sure to impress your guests, especially if it is served with whipped cream.

NUTRITIONAL INFORMATION

Calories	416	Sugars	37g
Protein	11g	Fat	26g
Carbohydrate	38g	Saturates	12g

5 mins 5 mins

SERVES 8

INGREDIENTS

3 eggs
75 g/2¾ oz ground almonds
200 g/7 oz milk powder
200 g/7 oz sugar
½ tsp saffron strands
100 g/3½ oz unsalted butter
flaked almonds, to decorate

2

3

4

1 Beat the eggs together in a bowl and set aside.

2 Place the ground almonds, milk powder, sugar and saffron in a large mixing bowl and stir to mix well.

3 Melt the butter in a small saucepan over a low heat. Pour the melted butter over the dry ingredients and mix well until thoroughly combined.

4 Add the reserved beaten eggs to the mixture and stir to blend well.

5 Spread the mixture in a shallow 15–20-cm/7–9-inch ovenproof dish and bake in a preheated oven, 160°C/325°F/Gas Mark 3, for 45 minutes. Test whether the cake is cooked through by piercing with the tip of a sharp knife or a skewer – it will come out clean if it is cooked thoroughly.

6 Cut the almond cake into slices. Decorate the almond slices with flaked almonds and transfer to serving plates. Serve hot or cold.

COOK'S TIP

These almond slices are best eaten hot, but they may also be served cold. They can be made a day or even a week in advance and re-heated. They also freeze beautifully.

Soda Bread

This variation of traditional Irish soda bread is best eaten on the day it has been baked, when it is deliciously fresh.

NUTRITIONAL INFORMATION

Calories	203	Sugars	7g
Protein	8g	Fat	2g
Carbohydrate	42g	Saturates	0g

1 hr 10 mins   40 mins

1 LOAF

INGREDIENTS

- butter, for greasing
- 300 g/10½ oz plain white flour, plus extra for dusting
- 300 g/10½ oz plain wholemeal flour
- 2 tsp baking powder
- 1 tsp bicarbonate of soda
- 25 g/1 oz caster sugar
- 1 tsp salt
- 1 egg, beaten
- 425 ml/15 fl oz natural yogurt

1 Grease a baking tray with butter and dust with flour.

2 Sieve the flours, baking powder, bicarbonate of soda, sugar and salt into a large bowl and add any bran remaining in the sieve.

3 In a mixing jug, beat together the egg and yogurt and pour the mixture into the dry ingredients. Mix everything together to make a soft and sticky dough.

4 On a lightly floured surface, knead the dough for a few minutes until it is smooth, then shape the dough into a round about 5 cm/2 inches deep.

5 Transfer the dough to the baking tray. Mark a cross shape in the centre of the top of the dough.

6 Bake in a preheated oven, 190°C/375°F/Gas Mark 5, for about 40 minutes or until the bread is golden brown all over.

7 Transfer the loaf to a wire rack and leave to cool completely. Cut into slices to serve.

3

3

5

VARIATION

For a fruity version of this soda bread, add 125g/4½ oz raisins to the dry ingredients in step 2.

Spicy Bread

Serve this spicy bread fresh from the oven with your favourite soup or a fresh tomato and onion salad for a light lunch or supper.

NUTRITIONAL INFORMATION

Calories	122	Sugars	1g
Protein	4g	Fat	3g
Carbohydrate	22g	Saturates	2g

1 hr 10 mins — 45 mins

1 LOAF

INGREDIENTS

- 2 tbsp butter, cut into small pieces, plus extra for greasing
- 225 g/8 oz self-raising flour
- 100 g/3½ oz plain flour
- 1 tsp baking powder
- ¼ tsp salt
- ¼ tsp cayenne pepper
- 2 tsp curry powder
- 2 tsp poppy seeds
- 150 ml/5 fl oz milk
- 1 egg, beaten

1 Lightly grease a baking tray with a little butter.

2 Sieve the self-raising flour and the plain flour into a mixing bowl along with the baking powder, salt, cayenne pepper, curry powder and poppy seeds.

3 Rub in the butter with your fingertips until everything is thoroughly mixed together and resembles breadcrumbs.

4 Add the milk and the beaten egg and mix to a soft dough.

5 Turn the dough out on to a lightly floured surface, then knead lightly for a few minutes.

6 Shape the dough into a round and mark it with a cross shape in the centre of the top.

7 Bake in a preheated oven, 190°C/375°F/Gas Mark 5, for 45 minutes.

8 Transfer the bread to a wire rack and leave to cool slightly. Serve in chunks or slices.

COOK'S TIP

If the bread looks as though it is browning too much, cover it with a piece of foil for the remainder of the cooking time.

Chilli Corn Bread

This Mexican-style corn bread makes a great accompaniment to chilli or it can be eaten on its own as a tasty snack.

NUTRITIONAL INFORMATION

Calories	179	Sugars	1g
Protein	3g	Fat	14g
Carbohydrate	10g	Saturates	3g

5 mins · 25 mins

SERVES 12

INGREDIENTS

- butter, for greasing
- 125 g/4½ oz plain flour
- 125 g/4½ oz polenta
- 1 tbsp baking powder
- ½ tsp salt
- 1 green chilli, deseeded and finely chopped
- 5 spring onions, finely chopped
- 2 eggs
- 142 ml/4½ fl oz soured cream
- 125 ml/4 fl oz sunflower oil

1 Grease a 20-cm/8-inch square cake tin with butter and line the base with baking paper.

2 In a large bowl, mix the flour, polenta, baking powder and salt together.

3 Add the finely chopped green chilli and the spring onions to the dry ingredients and mix well.

4 In a mixing jug, beat the eggs together with the soured cream and sunflower oil. Pour the mixture into the bowl of dry ingredients. Mix everything together quickly and thoroughly.

5 Pour the mixture into the prepared cake tin.

6 Bake in a preheated oven, 200°C/400°F/Gas Mark 6, for 20–25 minutes or until the loaf has risen and is lightly browned on top.

7 Leave the bread to cool slightly before turning out of the tin on to a wire rack to cool completely. Cut into bars or squares to serve.

3

4

4

VARIATION

Add 125 g/4½ oz of sweetcorn kernels to the mixture in step 3, if you prefer.

Cheese & Ham Loaf

This recipe is a quick way to make tasty bread, using self-raising flour and baking powder to ensure a good rising.

NUTRITIONAL INFORMATION

Calories	360	Sugars	2g
Protein	14g	Fat	21g
Carbohydrate	31g	Saturates	13g

25–30 mins 1 hr

SERVES 6

INGREDIENTS

- 75 g/2¾ oz butter, cut into small pieces, plus extra for greasing
- 225 g/8 oz self-raising flour
- 1 tsp salt
- 2 tsp baking powder
- 1 tsp paprika
- 125 g/4½ oz mature cheese, grated
- 75 g/ 2¾ oz smoked ham, chopped
- 2 eggs, beaten
- 150 ml/5 fl oz milk

1 Grease a 450-g/1-lb loaf tin with butter and line the base with baking paper.

2 Sieve the flour, salt, baking powder and paprika into a mixing bowl.

3 Add the butter and rub it in with your fingertips until the mixture resembles fine breadcrumbs. Stir in the cheese and ham.

4 Add the beaten eggs and milk to the dry ingredients in the bowl and combine well.

5 Spoon the cheese and ham mixture into the prepared loaf tin.

6 Bake in a preheated oven, 180°C/350°F/Gas Mark 4, for about 1 hour or until the loaf is well risen.

7 Leave the bread to cool in the tin, then turn out and transfer to a wire rack to cool completely.

8 Serve the bread cut into thick slices.

COOK'S TIP

This tasty bread is best eaten on the day it is made as it does not keep for very long.

Cheese & Chive Bread

This is a quick bread to make. It is fully of a wonderful cheese flavour and, to enjoy it at its best, it should be eaten as fresh as possible.

NUTRITIONAL INFORMATION

Calories	190	Sugars	1g
Protein	7g	Fat	9g
Carbohydrate	22g	Saturates	5g

25 mins 30 mins

SERVES 8

INGREDIENTS

- butter, for greasing
- 225 g/8 oz self-raising flour
- 1 tsp salt
- 1 tsp mustard powder
- 100 g/3½ oz mature cheese, grated
- 2 tbsp chopped fresh chives
- 1 egg, beaten
- 2 tbsp butter, melted
- 150 ml/5 fl oz milk

4

5

6

1 Grease a 23-cm/9-inch square cake tin with a little butter and line the base with baking parchment.

2 Sieve the flour, salt and mustard powder into a large mixing bowl.

3 Reserve 3 tablespoons of the grated mature cheese for sprinkling over the top of the loaf before baking in the oven.

4 Stir the remaining grated cheese into the bowl, together with the chopped fresh chives. Mix well together.

5 Add the beaten egg, melted butter and milk to the dry ingredients and stir the mixture thoroughly to combine.

6 Pour the mixture into the prepared tin and spread with a knife. Sprinkle over the reserved grated cheese.

7 Bake in a preheated oven, 190°C/375°F/Gas Mark 5, for about 30 minutes.

8 Leave the bread to cool slightly in the tin. Turn out on to a wire rack to cool completely. Cut into triangles to serve.

COOK'S TIP

You can use any hard mature cheese of your choice for this recipe.

Garlic Bread Rolls

This bread is not at all like the shop-bought, ready-made garlic bread. Instead it has a subtle flavour and a soft texture.

NUTRITIONAL INFORMATION

Calories	265	Sugars	3g
Protein	10g	Fat	6g
Carbohydrate	46g	Saturates	2g

1¾ hrs

35 mins

SERVES 8

INGREDIENTS

- butter, for greasing
- 12 cloves garlic, peeled
- 350 ml/12 fl oz milk
- 450 g/1 lb strong white bread flour
- 1 tsp salt
- 1 sachet easy-blend dried yeast
- 1 tbsp dried mixed herbs
- 2 tbsp sunflower oil
- 1 egg, beaten
- milk, for brushing
- rock salt, for sprinkling

1 Lightly grease a baking tray with a little butter.

2 Place the garlic cloves and milk in a saucepan, bring to the boil and simmer gently for 15 minutes. Leave to cool slightly, then process in a blender or food processor to purée the garlic.

3 Sieve the flour and salt into a large mixing bowl and stir in the dried yeast and mixed herbs.

4 Add the garlic-flavoured milk, sunflower oil and beaten egg to the dry ingredients and mix everything thoroughly to form a dough.

5 Place the dough on a lightly floured work surface and knead lightly for a few minutes until smooth and soft.

6 Place the dough in a lightly greased bowl, cover and leave to rise in a warm place for about 1 hour or until doubled in size.

7 Knock back the dough by kneading it for 2 minutes. Shape into 8 rolls and place on the baking tray. Score the top of each roll with a knife, cover and leave for 15 minutes.

8 Brush the rolls with milk and sprinkle rock salt over the top.

9 Bake in a preheated oven, 220°C/425°F/Gas Mark 7, for 15–20 minutes. Transfer the rolls to a wire rack and leave to cool before serving.

2

4

5

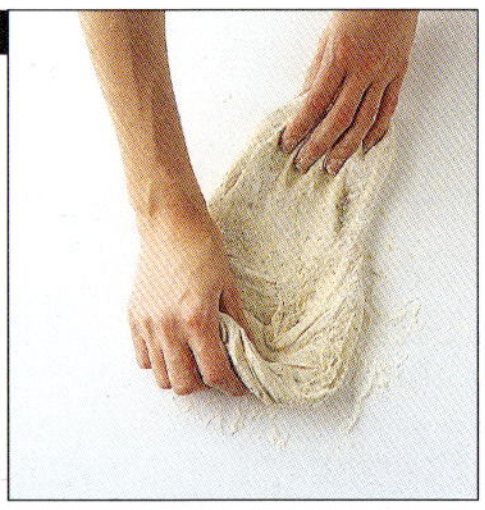

Mini Focaccia

This is a delicious Italian bread made with olive oil. The topping of red onions and thyme is particularly flavorsome.

NUTRITIONAL INFORMATION

Calories	439	Sugars	3g
Protein	9g	Fat	15g
Carbohydrate	71g	Saturates	2g

2¼ hrs — 25 mins

SERVES 4

INGREDIENTS

- 2 tbsp olive oil, plus extra for brushing
- 2½ cups white bread flour
- ½ tsp salt
- 1 sachet active dry yeast
- 1 cup lukewarm water
- 1 cup pitted green or black olives, halved

TOPPING

- 2 red onions, sliced
- 2 tbsp olive oil
- 1 tsp sea salt
- 1 tbsp fresh thyme leaves

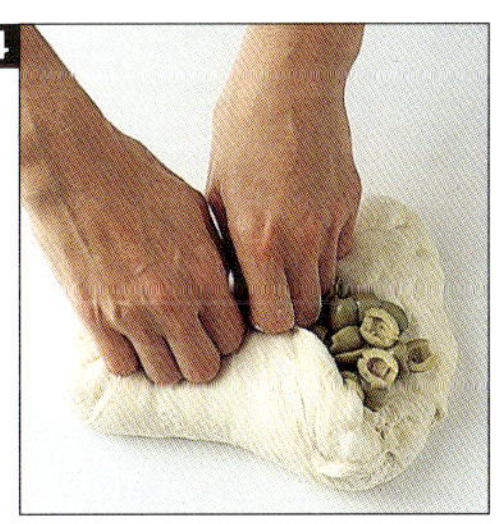

1 Lightly brush several cookie sheets with olive oil and set aside.

2 Strain the flour and salt into a large bowl, then stir in the yeast. Pour in the olive oil and lukewarm water and mix together to form a dough.

3 Turn the dough out onto a lightly floured counter and knead it for about 5 minutes. Alternatively, use an electric mixer with a dough hook and knead for 7–8 minutes.

4 Place the dough in a greased bowl, cover, and let stand in a warm place for about 1–1½ hours or until it has doubled in size. Punch down the dough by kneading it again for 1–2 minutes.

5 Knead half of the olives into the dough. Divide the dough into quarters and then shape the quarters into circles. Place them on the cookie sheets and push your fingers into the dough to achieve a dimpled effect.

6 To make the topping, sprinkle the red onions and remaining olives over the dough circles. Drizzle the olive oil over the top and sprinkle with the sea salt and thyme leaves. Cover and let rise for 30 minutes.

7 Bake in a preheated oven, 375°F/190°C, for 20–25 minutes or until the focaccia are golden.

8 Transfer to a wire rack and let cool before serving.

VARIATION

Use this quantity of dough to make 1 large focaccia, if you prefer.

Sun-dried Tomato Rolls

These white rolls have the addition of finely chopped sun-dried tomatoes. The tomatoes are sold in jars and are available at most supermarkets.

NUTRITIONAL INFORMATION

Calories	214	Sugars	1g
Protein	5g	Fat	12g
Carbohydrate	22g	Saturates	7g

2¼ hrs

15 mins

SERVES 8

INGREDIENTS

- butter, for greasing
- 225 g/8 oz strong white bread flour
- ½ tsp salt
- 1 sachet easy-blend dried yeast
- 100 g/3½ oz butter, melted and cooled slightly
- 3 tbsp milk, warmed
- 2 eggs, beaten
- 50 g/1¾ oz sun-dried tomatoes, well drained and finely chopped
- milk, for brushing

3

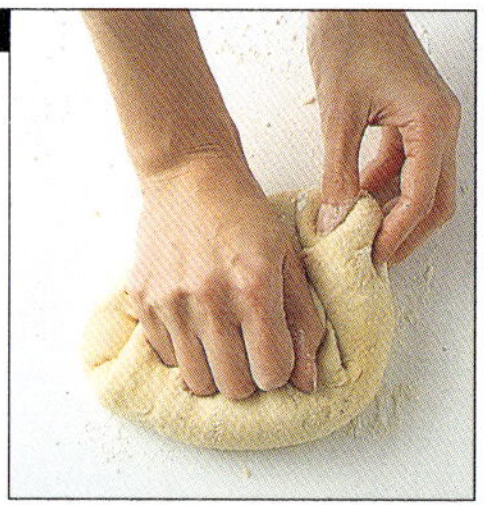

5

6

1 Lightly grease a baking tray.

2 Sieve the flour and salt into a large mixing bowl. Stir in the yeast, then pour in the butter, milk and eggs. Mix together to form a dough.

3 Turn the dough on to a lightly floured surface and knead for about 5 minutes. Alternatively, use an electric mixer with a dough hook.

4 Place the dough in a greased bowl, cover and leave to rise in a warm place for 1–1½ hours or until the dough has doubled in size. Knock back the dough for 2–3 minutes.

5 Knead the sun-dried tomatoes into the dough, sprinkling the work surface with a little extra flour as the tomatoes are quite oily.

6 Divide the dough into 8 equal-size balls and place them on the prepared baking tray. Cover and leave to rise for about 30 minutes or until the rolls have doubled in size.

7 Brush the rolls with milk and bake in a preheated oven, 230°C/450°F/Gas Mark 8, for 10–15 minutes or until the rolls are golden brown.

8 Transfer the rolls to a wire rack and leave to cool slightly before serving.

VARIATION

Add some finely chopped anchovies or olives to the dough in step 5 for extra flavour, if wished.

Thyme Crescents

These savoury crescent snacks are perfect for a quick and tasty bite to eat. They can also be shaped into twists, if preferred.

NUTRITIONAL INFORMATION

Calories	209	Sugars	0g
Protein	2g	Fat	18g
Carbohydrate	12g	Saturates	7g

10 mins — 15 mins

SERVES 8

INGREDIENTS

- 100 g/3½ oz butter, softened, plus extra for greasing
- 250 g/9 oz ready-made puff pastry, defrosted if frozen
- 1 garlic clove, crushed
- 1 tsp lemon juice
- 1 tsp dried thyme
- salt and pepper

1 Lightly grcasc a baking tray.

2 On a lightly floured surface, roll out the pastry to form a 25-cm/10-inch round and cut into 8 wedges.

3 In a small bowl, mix the softened butter, garlic clove, lemon juice and dried thyme together until soft. Season with salt and pepper to taste.

COOK'S TIP

Dried herbs have a stronger flavour than fresh ones, which makes them perfect for these pastries. The crescents can be made with other dried herbs of your choice, such as rosemary and sage, or mixed herbs.

4 Spread a little of the butter and thyme mixture on to each wedge of pastry, dividing it equally between them.

5 Carefully roll up each wedge, starting from the wide end.

6 Arrange the crescents on the prepared baking tray and chill in the refrigerator for 30 minutes.

7 Dampen the baking tray with cold water. This will create a steamy atmosphere in the oven while the crescents are baking and help the pastries to rise.

8 Bake in a preheated oven, 200°C/400°F/Gas Mark 6, for 10–15 minutes until the crescents are well risen and golden brown.

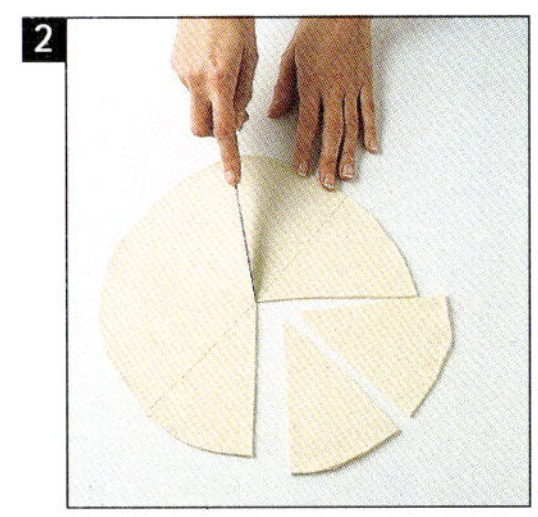

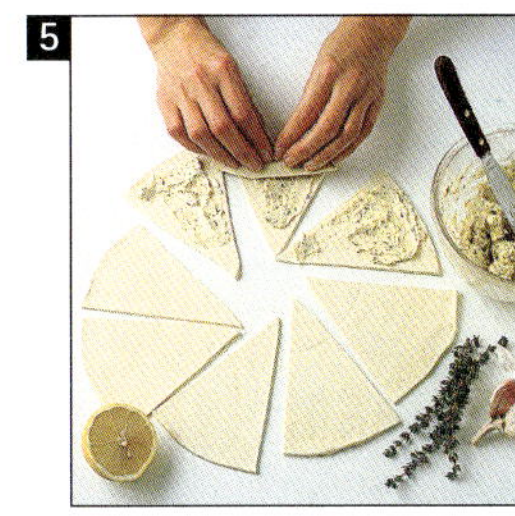

Cheese & Mustard Scones

These home-made scones are given an interesting flavour by adding grated mature cheese and mustard to the mixture.

NUTRITIONAL INFORMATION

Calories	218	Sugars	1g
Protein	7g	Fat	12g
Carbohydrate	22g	Saturates	7g

15 mins 15 mins

MAKES 8

INGREDIENTS

- 4 tbsp butter, cut into small pieces, plus extra for greasing
- 225 g/8 oz self-raising flour
- 1 tsp baking powder
- pinch of salt
- 125 g/4½ oz mature cheese, grated
- 1 tsp mustard powder
- 150 ml/5 fl oz milk
- pepper

1 Lightly grease a baking tray with a little butter.

2 Sieve the flour, baking powder and salt into a mixing bowl. Rub in the butter with your fingertips until the mixture resembles breadcrumbs.

3 Stir in the grated cheese, mustard and enough milk to form a soft dough.

4 On a lightly floured surface, knead the dough very lightly, then flatten it out with the palm of your hand to a depth of about 2.5 cm/1 inch.

5 Cut the dough into 8 wedges with a knife. Brush each one with a little milk and sprinkle with pepper to taste.

2

3

5

6 Bake in a preheated oven, 220°C/ 425°F/Gas Mark 7, for 10–15 minutes until the scones are golden brown.

7 Transfer the scones to a wire rack and leave to cool slightly before serving.

COOK'S TIP

Scones should be eaten on the day they are made as they quickly go stale. Serve them split in half and spread with butter.

Cheese & Chive Scones

These tea-time classics have been given a healthy twist by the use of low-fat soft cheese and reduced-fat Cheddar cheese.

NUTRITIONAL INFORMATION			
Calories	297	Sugars	3g
Protein	13g	Fat	7g
Carbohydrate	49g	Saturates	4g

10 mins

20 mins

MAKES 10

INGREDIENTS

- 225 g/8 oz self-raising flour
- 1 tsp powdered mustard
- ½ tsp cayenne pepper
- ½ tsp salt
- 100 g/3½ oz low-fat soft cheese with added herbs
- 2 tbsp fresh snipped chives, plus extra to garnish
- 100 ml/3½ fl oz skimmed milk, plus extra for brushing
- 55 g/2 oz reduced-fat mature Cheddar cheese, grated
- low-fat soft cheese, to serve

1 Sift the flour, mustard, cayenne and salt into a large mixing bowl.

2 Add the soft cheese to the mixture and mix together until well incorporated. Stir in the snipped chives.

3 Make a well in the centre of the ingredients and gradually pour in 100 ml/3½ fl oz milk, stirring as you pour, until the mixture forms a soft dough.

4 Turn the dough on to a floured surface and knead lightly. Roll out until 2 cm/¾ inch thick and use a 5-cm/2-inch plain pastry cutter to stamp out as many rounds as you can. Transfer the rounds to a baking sheet.

5 Re-knead the dough trimmings together and roll out again. Stamp out more rounds – you should be able to make 10 scones in total.

6 Brush the scones with milk and sprinkle with the grated cheese. Bake in a preheated oven, 200°C/400°F/Gas Mark 6, for 15–20 minutes until risen and golden. Transfer to a wire rack to cool. Serve warm with low-fat soft cheese, garnished with chives.

2

4

6

VARIATION

For sweet scones, omit the mustard, cayenne pepper, chives and grated cheese. Replace the flavoured soft cheese with plain low-fat soft cheese. Add 75 g/2¾ oz currants and 25 g/1 oz caster sugar. Serve with low-fat soft cheese and fruit spread.

Savoury Pepper Bread

This flavoursome bread contains only the minimum amount of fat. Serve with a bowl of hot soup for a filling and nutritious light meal.

NUTRITIONAL INFORMATION

Calories	468	Sugars	11g
Protein	16g	Fat	5g
Carbohydrate	97g	Saturates	1g

2 hrs — 50 mins

SERVES 4

INGREDIENTS

- butter, for greasing
- 1 small red pepper
- 1 small green pepper
- 1 small yellow pepper
- 55 g/2 oz dry pack of sun-dried tomatoes
- 50 ml/2 fl oz boiling water
- 2 tsp dried yeast
- 1 tsp caster sugar
- 150 ml/5 fl oz hand-hot water
- 450 g/1 lb strong white bread flour
- 2 tsp dried rosemary
- 2 tbsp tomato purée
- 150 ml/5 fl oz low-fat natural fromage frais
- 1 tbsp coarse salt
- 1 tbsp olive oil

1 Lightly grease a 23-cm/9-inch round springform cake tin. Halve and deseed the peppers, arrange on the grill rack and cook under a preheated hot grill until the skin is charred. Leave to cool for 10 minutes, peel off the skin and chop the flesh. Slice the tomatoes into strips, place in a bowl and pour over the boiling water. Leave to soak.

2 Place the yeast and sugar in a small jug, pour over the hand-hot water and leave for 10–15 minutes until frothy. Sieve the flour into a bowl and add 1 teaspoon of dried rosemary. Make a well in the centre and pour in the yeast mixture.

3 Add the tomato purée, tomatoes and soaking liquid, peppers, fromage frais and half the salt. Mix to form a soft dough. Turn out on to a lightly floured surface and knead for 3–4 minutes until smooth and elastic. Place in a lightly floured bowl, cover and leave in a warm room for 40 minutes until doubled in size.

4 Knead the dough again and place in the prepared tin. Using a wooden spoon, form 'dimples' in the surface. Cover and leave for 30 minutes. Brush with olive oil and sprinkle with rosemary and salt. Bake for 35–40 minutes, cool for 10 minutes and then release from the tin. Cool on a rack and serve.

2

3

4

COOK'S TIP

For a quick, filling snack serve the bread with a bowl of hot soup in winter, or a crisp leaf salad in summer.

Olive Oil Bread with Cheese

This flat cheese bread is is very similar to Italian focaccia. It is delicious served with *antipasto* or simply on its own. This recipe makes one loaf.

NUTRITIONAL INFORMATION

Calories	586	Sugars	3g
Protein	22g	Fat	26g
Carbohydrate	69g	Saturates	12g

1 hr

30 mins

SERVES 4

INGREDIENTS

- 15 g/½ oz dried yeast
- 1 tsp sugar
- 250 ml/9 fl oz hand-hot water
- 350 g/12 oz strong flour
- 1 tsp salt
- 3 tbsp olive oil
- 200 g/7 oz pecorino cheese, cubed
- ½ tbsp fennel seeds, lightly crushed

1 Mix the yeast with the sugar and 100 ml/3½ fl oz of the water. Leave to ferment in a warm place for about 15 minutes.

2 Mix the flour with the salt. Add 1 tablespoon of the oil, the yeast mixture and the remaining water to form a smooth dough. Knead the dough for 4 minutes.

3 Divide the dough into 2 equal portions. Roll out each portion to a form a round 5 mm/¼ inch thick. Place 1 round on a baking tray.

4 Scatter the cheese and half of the fennel seeds evenly over the round.

5 Place the second round on top and squeeze the edges together to seal so that the filling does not leak during the cooking time.

6 Using a sharp knife, make a few slashes in the top of the dough and brush with the remaining olive oil.

7 Sprinkle with the remaining fennel seeds and leave the dough to rise for 20–30 minutes.

8 Bake in a preheated oven, 200°C/400°F/Gas Mark 6, for 30 minutes or until golden brown. Serve immediately while it is still hot.

3
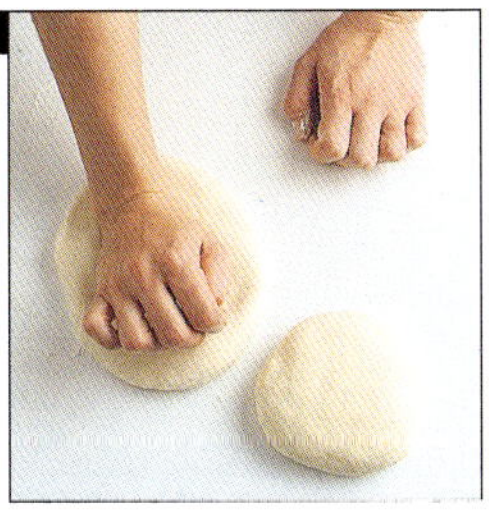

4

5

COOK'S TIP

Pecorino is a hard, quite salty cheese, which is sold in most large supermarkets and Italian delicatessens. If you cannot obtain pecorino, use strong Cheddar or Parmesan cheese instead.

Biscuits

Nothing can compare with a home-made biscuit for bringing a touch of pleasure to a coffee break or tea-time. This selection of delicious biscuits and after-dinner treats will tantalize your tastebuds and keep you coming back for more.

More-ish biscuits like Citrus Crescents, Meringues, Rock Drops, and Gingernuts are quick, easy and satisfying to make. You can easily vary any of the ingredients listed to suit your taste – the possibilities for inventiveness when making biscuits are endless and this chapter shows you how.

Cheese Sables

These savoury biscuits have a delicious buttery flavour. Make sure you use a mature cheese for the best flavour.

NUTRITIONAL INFORMATION

Calories	67	Sugars	0g
Protein	2g	Fat	5g
Carbohydrate	3g	Saturates	3g

50 mins | 20 mins

MAKES 35

INGREDIENTS

- 150 g/5½ oz butter, cut into small pieces, plus extra for greasing
- 150 g/5½ oz plain flour
- 150 g/5½ oz mature cheese, grated
- 1 egg yolk
- sesame seeds, for sprinkling

1 Lightly grease several baking trays with a little butter.

2 Mix the flour and cheese together in a bowl.

3 Add the butter to the cheese and flour mixture and mix with your fingertips until combined.

4 Stir in the egg yolk and mix to form a dough. Wrap the dough and leave to chill in the refrigerator for about 30 minutes.

5 On a lightly floured surface, roll out the cheese dough thinly. Cut out 6-cm/2½-inch rounds, re-rolling the trimmings to make about 35 rounds.

6 Place the rounds on to the prepared baking trays and sprinkle the sesame seeds over the top of them.

3

5

6

7 Bake in a preheated oven, 200°C/400°F/Gas Mark 6, for 20 minutes until the sables are lightly golden.

8 Carefully transfer the cheese sables to a wire rack and leave to cool slightly before serving.

COOK'S TIP

Cut out any shape you like for your savoury biscuits. Children will enjoy them cut into animal or other fun shapes.

Savoury Curried Biscuits

When making these biscuits, try different types of curry powder strengths until you find the one that suits your own taste.

NUTRITIONAL INFORMATION

Calories	48	Sugars	0g
Protein	2g	Fat	4g
Carbohydrate	2g	Saturates	2g

45 mins   15 mins

MAKES 13

INGREDIENTS

- 100 g/3½ oz butter, softened, plus extra for greasing
- 100 g/3½ oz plain flour
- 1 tsp salt
- 2 tsp curry powder
- 100 g/3½ oz Cheshire cheese, grated
- 100 g/3½ oz Parmesan cheese, freshly grated

3 

4 

5 

1 Lightly grease about 4 baking trays with a little butter.

2 Sieve the plain flour and salt into a mixing bowl.

3 Stir in the curry powder and the grated Cheshire and Parmesan cheeses. Rub in the softened butter with your fingertips until the mixture comes together to form a soft dough.

4 On a lightly floured surface, roll out the dough thinly to form a rectangle.

5 Using a 5-cm/2-inch biscuit cutter, cut out 40 round biscuits.

6 Arrange the biscuits on the prepared baking trays.

7 Bake in a preheated oven, 180°C/350°F/Gas Mark 4, for 10–15 minutes until golden brown.

8 Leave the biscuits to cool slightly on the baking trays. Carefully transfer the biscuits to a wire rack until leave until completely cold and crisp, then serve.

COOK'S TIP

These biscuits can be stored for several days in an airtight tin or plastic container.

Spiced Biscuits

These spicy biscuits are perfect to serve with fruit salad or ice cream for a very easy instant dessert.

NUTRITIONAL INFORMATION

Calories	117	Sugars	8g
Protein	1g	Fat	6g
Carbohydrate	15g	Saturates	4g

35 mins 12 mins

MAKES 12

INGREDIENTS

- 175 g/6 oz unsalted butter, plus extra for greasing
- 175 g/6 oz dark muscovado sugar
- 225 g/8 oz plain flour
- ½ tsp bicarbonate of soda
- 1 tsp ground cinnamon
- ½ tsp ground coriander
- ½ tsp ground nutmeg
- ¼ tsp ground cloves
- 2 tbsp dark rum
- salt

2

3

5

1 Lightly grease 2 baking trays with a little butter.

2 Cream together the butter and sugar and whisk until light and fluffy.

3 Sieve the flour, a pinch of salt, the bicarbonate of soda, cinnamon, coriander, nutmeg and cloves into the creamed mixture.

4 Stir the dark rum into the creamed mixture.

5 Using 2 teaspoons, place small mounds of the mixture, on to the baking trays, placing them 7 cm/3 inches apart to allow for spreading during cooking. Flatten each one slightly with the back of a spoon.

6 Bake in a preheated oven, 180°C/350°F/Gas Mark 4, for 10–12 minutes until golden.

7 Carefully transfer the biscuits to wire racks to cool completely and crispen before serving.

COOK'S TIP

Use the back of a fork to flatten the biscuits slightly before baking.

Cinnamon & Seed Squares

These are moist cake-like squares with a lovely spicy flavour. They smell simply wonderful while they are cooking.

NUTRITIONAL INFORMATION

Calories	397	Sugars	23g
Protein	6g	Fat	25g
Carbohydrate	40g	Saturates	14g

1 hr 10 mins 45 mins

MAKES 12

INGREDIENTS

- 250 g/9 oz butter, softened, plus extra for greasing
- 250 g/9 oz caster sugar
- 3 eggs, beaten
- 250 g/9 oz self-raising flour
- ½ tsp bicarbonate of soda
- 1 tbsp ground cinnamon
- 150 ml/5 fl oz soured cream
- 100 g/3½ oz sunflower seeds

1 Grease a 23-cm/9-inch square cake tin with butter and line the base with baking paper.

2 In a large mixing bowl, cream together the butter and caster sugar until the mixture is light and fluffy.

3 Gradually add the beaten eggs to the mixture, beating thoroughly after each addition.

4 Sieve the self-raising flour, bicarbonate of soda and ground cinnamon into the creamed mixture and fold in gently, using a metal spoon.

5 Spoon in the soured cream and sunflower seeds and gently mix until well combined.

6 Spoon the mixture into the prepared cake tin and level the surface with the back of a spoon or a knife.

7 Bake in a preheated oven, 180°C/350°F/Gas Mark 4, for about 45 minutes until the mixture is firm to the touch when pressed with a finger.

8 Loosen the edges with a round-bladed knife, then turn out on to a wire rack to cool completely. Slice into 12 squares.

3

4

5

COOK'S TIP

These moist squares will freeze well and will keep for up to 1 month.

Gingernuts

Nothing compares to the taste of these freshly baked authentic gingernuts which have a lovely hint of orange flavour.

NUTRITIONAL INFORMATION

Calories	106	Sugars	9g
Protein	1g	Fat	4g
Carbohydrate	18g	Saturates	2g

10 mins 20 mins

MAKES 30

INGREDIENTS

- 125 g/4½ oz butter, plus extra for greasing
- 350 g/12 oz self-raising flour
- pinch of salt
- 200 g/7 oz caster sugar
- 1 tbsp ground ginger
- 1 tsp bicarbonate of soda
- 75 g/2¾ oz golden syrup
- 1 egg, beaten
- 1 tsp grated orange rind

4

4

7

1 Lightly grease several baking trays with a little butter.

2 Sieve the flour, salt, sugar, ginger and bicarbonate of soda into a large mixing bowl.

3 Heat the butter and golden syrup together in a saucepan over a very low heat until the butter has melted.

4 Remove the pan from the heat and leave the butter and syrup mixture to cool slightly, then pour it on to the dry ingredients.

5 Add the egg and orange rind and mix thoroughly to a dough.

6 Using your hands, carefully shape the dough into 30 even-size balls.

7 Place the balls well apart on the prepared baking trays, then flatten them slightly with your fingers.

8 Bake in a preheated oven, 160°C/325°F/Gas Mark 3, for 15–20 minutes, then carefully transfer the biscuits to a wire rack to cool.

COOK'S TIP

Store these biscuits in an airtight container and eat them within 1 week.

Peanut Butter Cookies

These crunchy biscuits will be popular with children of all ages as they contain their favourite food – peanut butter.

NUTRITIONAL INFORMATION

Calories	186	Sugars	13g
Protein	4g	Fat	11g
Carbohydrate	19g	Saturates	5g

40 mins 15 mins

MAKES 20

INGREDIENTS

- 125 g/4½ oz butter, softened, plus extra for greasing
- 150 g/5½ oz chunky peanut butter
- 225 g/8 oz granulated sugar
- 1 egg, lightly beaten
- 150 g/5½ oz plain flour
- ½ tsp baking powder
- pinch of salt
- 75 g/2¾ oz natural unsalted peanuts, chopped

1 Lightly grease 2 baking trays with a little butter.

2 In a large mixing bowl, beat together the butter and peanut butter.

3 Gradually add the granulated sugar and beat well.

4 Add the beaten egg, a little at a time, beating well after each addition until it is thoroughly combined.

5 Sieve the flour, baking powder and salt into the peanut butter mixture.

6 Add the chopped peanuts and bring all of the ingredients together to form a soft dough. Wrap the dough in clingfilm and chill in the refrigerator for about 30 minutes.

7 Form the dough into 20 balls and place them on the prepared baking trays about 5 cm/2 inches apart to allow for spreading. Flatten them slightly with your hand.

8 Bake in a preheated oven, 190°C/375°F/Gas Mark 5, for 15 minutes, until golden brown. Transfer the biscuits to a wire rack and leave to cool.

2

6

7

COOK'S TIP

For a crunchy bite and sparkling appearance, sprinkle the biscuits with demerara sugar before baking.

Hazelnut Squares

These can be made quickly and easily for an afternoon tea treat. The chopped hazelnuts can be replaced by any other nut of your choice.

NUTRITIONAL INFORMATION

Calories	163	Sugars	10g
Protein	2g	Fat	10g
Carbohydrate	18g	Saturates	4g

15 mins — 25 mins

MAKES 16

INGREDIENTS

- 100 g/3½ oz butter, cut into small pieces, plus extra for greasing
- 150 g/5½ oz plain flour
- 1 tsp baking powder
- 150 g/5½ oz soft brown sugar
- 1 egg, beaten
- 4 tbsp milk
- 100 g/3½ oz hazelnuts, halved
- demerara sugar, for sprinkling (optional)
- salt

3

4

5

1 Grease a 23-cm/9-inch square cake tin with butter and line the base with baking parchment.

2 Sieve the flour, together with a pinch of salt and the baking powder into a large mixing bowl.

3 Add the butter and rub it in with your fingertips until the mixture resembles fine breadcrumbs. Add the soft brown sugar and stir to mix.

4 Add the beaten egg, milk and halved hazelnuts to the dry ingredients and stir well until thoroughly combined and a soft consistency.

5 Spoon the mixture into the prepared cake tin and level the surface. Sprinkle with demerara sugar, if using.

6 Bake in a preheated oven, 180°C/350°F/Gas Mark 4, for about 25 minutes or until the mixture is firm to the touch when pressed with a finger.

7 Leave to cool for 10 minutes, then loosen the edges with a round-bladed knife and turn out on to a wire rack. Cut into squares.

VARIATION

For a coffee time biscuit, replace the milk with the same amount of cold strong black coffee – the stronger the better!

Coconut Flapjacks

Freshly baked, these chewy flapjacks are always a favourite for after-school snacks and just the thing for tea-time.

NUTRITIONAL INFORMATION

Calories	269	Sugars	19g
Protein	3g	Fat	16g
Carbohydrate	32g	Saturates	10g

45 mins 30 mins

MAKES 16

INGREDIENTS

- 200 g/7 oz butter, plus extra for greasing
- 200 g /7 oz demerara sugar
- 2 tbsp golden syrup
- 275 g/9½ oz porridge oats
- 100 g/3½ oz desiccated coconut
- 75 g/2¾ oz glacé cherries, chopped

1 Grease a 30 x 23-cm/12 x 9-inch baking tray with a little butter.

2 Heat the butter, demerara sugar and golden syrup in a large saucepan over a low heat until just melted.

3 Stir in the oats, desiccated coconut and glacé cherries and mix well until evenly combined.

4 Spread the mixture evenly on to the prepared baking tray and press down with the back of a spatula to make a smooth surface.

5 Bake in a preheated oven, 170°C/325°F/Gas Mark 3, for about 30 minutes.

6 Remove from the oven and leave to cool on the baking tray for about 10 minutes.

7 Cut the flapjack into squares using a sharp knife.

8 Carefully transfer the flapjack squares to a wire rack and set aside to cool completely.

COOK'S TIP

The flapjacks are best stored in an airtight container and eaten within 1 week. They can also be frozen for up to 1 month.

Oat & Raisin Biscuits

These oaty, fruity biscuits couldn't be easier to make and are delicious with a well-earned cup of tea!

NUTRITIONAL INFORMATION

Calories	227	Sugars	22g
Protein	4g	Fat	7g
Carbohydrate	39g	Saturates	3g

50 mins 15 mins

MAKES 10

INGREDIENTS

- 4 tbsp butter, plus extra for greasing
- 125 g/4½ oz caster sugar
- 1 egg, beaten
- 50 g/1¾ plain flour
- ½ tsp salt
- ½ tsp baking powder
- 175 g/6 oz porridge oats
- 125 g/4½ oz raisins
- 2 tbsp sesame seeds

4

4

5

1 Lightly grease 2 baking trays with a little butter.

2 In a large mixing bowl, cream together the butter and sugar until light and fluffy.

3 Gradually add the beaten egg, beating well after each addition, until thoroughly combined.

4 Sieve the flour, salt and baking powder into the creamed mixture. Mix gently to combine. Add the porridge oats, raisins and sesame seeds and mix together thoroughly.

5 Place spoonfuls of the mixture, spaced well apart on the prepared baking trays to allow room to expand during cooking, and flatten them slightly with the back of a spoon.

6 Bake the biscuits in a preheated oven, 180°C/350°F/Gas Mark 4, for 15 minutes.

7 Leave the biscuits to cool slightly on the baking trays.

8 Carefully transfer the biscuits to a wire rack and leave to cool completely before serving.

COOK'S TIP

To enjoy these biscuits at their best, store them in an airtight container.

Rosemary Biscuits

Do not be put off by the idea of herbs being used in these crisp biscuits – try them and you will be pleasantly surprised.

NUTRITIONAL INFORMATION

Calories	58	Sugars	4g
Protein	1g	Fat	2g
Carbohydrate	10g	Saturates	1g

1 hr 10 mins | 15 mins

MAKES 25

INGREDIENTS

- 4 tbsp butter, softened, plus extra for greasing
- 4 tbsp caster sugar
- grated rind of 1 lemon
- 4 tbsp lemon juice
- 1 egg, separated
- 2 tsp finely chopped fresh rosemary
- 200 g/7 oz plain flour, sieved
- caster sugar, for sprinkling (optional)

1 Lightly grease 2 baking trays with a little butter.

2 In a large mixing bowl, cream together the butter and sugar until pale and fluffy.

3 Add the lemon rind and juice, then the egg yolk and beat until they are thoroughly combined. Stir in the chopped fresh rosemary.

4 Add the sieved flour, mixing well until a soft dough is formed. Wrap in clingfilm and leave to chill in the refrigerator for 30 minutes.

5 On a lightly floured surface, roll out the dough thinly and stamp out about 25 circles with a 6-cm/2½-inch biscuit cutter. Arrange the dough circles on the prepared baking trays.

6 In a bowl, lightly whisk the egg white. Gently brush the egg white over the surface of each biscuit, then sprinkle with a little caster sugar, if using.

7 Bake in a preheated oven, 180°C/350°F/Gas Mark 4, for about 15 minutes.

8 Transfer the biscuits to a wire rack and leave to cool before serving.

4

5

6

VARIATION

In place of the fresh rosemary, use 1½ teaspoons of dried rosemary, if you prefer.

Citrus Crescents

For a sweet treat, try these attractive crescent-shaped biscuits, which have a lovely citrus tang to them.

NUTRITIONAL INFORMATION

Calories	72	Sugars	3g
Protein	1g	Fat	4g
Carbohydrate	10g	Saturates	2g

10 mins 15 mins

MAKES 25

INGREDIENTS

- 100 g/3½ oz butter, softened, plus extra for greasing
- 75 g/2¾ oz caster sugar, plus extra for dusting (optional)
- 1 egg, separated
- 200 g/7 oz plain flour
- grated rind of 1 orange
- grated rind of 1 lemon
- grated rind of 1 lime
- 2–3 tbsp orange juice

3

4

5

1 Lightly grease 2 baking trays with a little butter.

2 In a mixing bowl, cream together the butter and sugar until light and fluffy, then gradually beat in the egg yolk.

3 Sieve the flour into the creamed mixture and mix until evenly combined. Add the orange, lemon and lime rinds to the mixture with enough of the orange juice to make a soft dough.

4 Roll out the dough on a lightly floured surface. Stamp out rounds using a 7.5-cm/3-inch biscuit cutter. Make crescent shapes by cutting away a quarter of each round. Re-roll the trimmings to make about 25 crescents.

5 Place the crescents on the prepared baking trays. Prick the surface of each crescent with a fork.

6 Lightly whisk the egg white in a small bowl and brush it over the biscuits. Dust with extra caster sugar, if using.

7 Bake in a preheated oven, 200°C/400°F/Gas Mark 6, for 12–15 minutes. Carefully transfer the biscuits to a wire rack and allow to cool completely and crispen before serving.

COOK'S TIP

Store the citrus crescents in an airtight container. Alternatively, they can be frozen for up to 1 month.

Lemon Jumbles

These lemony, melt-in-the-mouth biscuits are made extra special by dredging with icing sugar just before serving.

NUTRITIONAL INFORMATION

Calories	50	Sugars	3g
Protein	1g	Fat	2g
Carbohydrate	8g	Saturates	1g

10 mins 20 mins

MAKES 50

INGREDIENTS

- 100 g/3½ oz butter, softened, plus extra for greasing
- 125 g/4½ oz caster sugar
- grated rind of 1 lemon
- 1 egg, beaten
- 4 tbsp lemon juice
- 350 g/12 oz plain flour
- 1 tsp baking powder
- 1 tbsp milk
- icing sugar, for dredging

1 Lightly grease several baking trays with a little butter.

2 In a mixing bowl, cream together the butter, caster sugar and lemon rind until pale and fluffy.

3 Add the beaten egg and lemon juice, a little at a time, beating well after each addition.

4 Sieve the flour and baking powder into the creamed mixture and blend together. Add the milk, mixing to form a soft dough.

5 Turn the dough out on to a lightly floured work surface and divide into about 50 equal-size pieces.

2

4

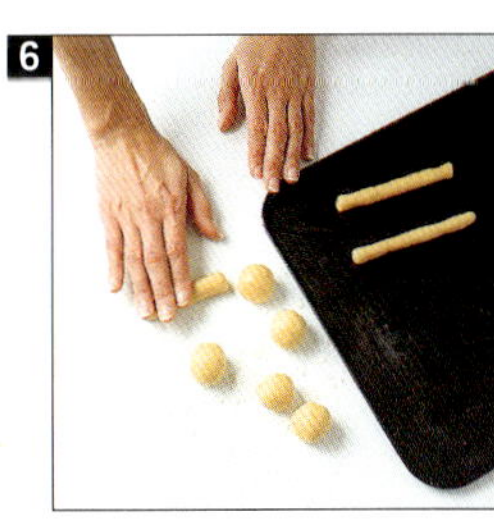

6

6 Roll each piece into a sausage shape with your hands and twist in the middle to make an 'S' shape.

7 Place on the prepared baking trays and bake in a preheated oven, 170°C/325°F/Gas Mark 3, for 15–20 minutes. Carefully transfer to a wire rack and set aside to cool completely. Dredge with icing sugar to serve.

VARIATION

If you prefer, shape the dough into other shapes – letters of the alphabet or geometric shapes – or just make into round biscuits.

Shortbread Fantails

These elegant biscuits are perfect for afternoon tea or they can be served with ice cream for a delicious dessert.

NUTRITIONAL INFORMATION

Calories	248	Sugars	10g
Protein	3g	Fat	13g
Carbohydrate	32g	Saturates	9g

40 mins   35 mins

MAKES 8

INGREDIENTS

- 125 g/4½ oz butter, softened, plus extra for greasing
- 40 g/1½ oz granulated sugar
- 25 g/1 oz icing sugar
- 225 g/8 oz plain flour
- 2 tsp orange flower water
- caster sugar, for sprinkling
- salt

4
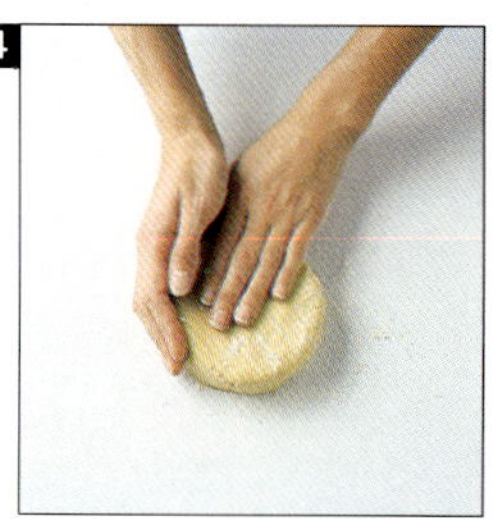

4

4

1 Lightly grease a 20-cm/8-inch shallow round cake tin with butter.

2 In a large mixing bowl, cream together the butter, the granulated sugar and the icing sugar until the mixture is light and fluffy.

3 Sieve the flour and a pinch of salt into the creamed mixture. Add the orange flower water and bring everything together to form a soft dough.

4 On a lightly floured surface, roll out the dough to a 20-cm/8-inch round and place in the prepared tin. Prick the dough well and score into 8 triangles with a round-bladed knife.

5 Bake in a preheated oven, 150°C/300°F/Gas Mark 2, for 30-35 minutes or until the shortbread is crisp and a pale golden colour.

6 Sprinkle with caster sugar, then cut along the marked lines to make the 8 fantails.

7 Leave the shortbread to cool before removing the pieces from the tin. Store in an airtight container.

COOKS TIP

For a crunchy addition, sprinkle 2 tablespoons of chopped mixed nuts over the top of the fantails before baking.

Vanilla Hearts

This is a classic shortbread biscuit which melts in the mouth. Here the biscuits are made in pretty heart shapes which will appeal to everyone.

NUTRITIONAL INFORMATION

Calories	150	Sugars	9g
Protein	1g	Fat	8g
Carbohydrate	20g	Saturates	5g

40 mins | 30 mins

MAKES 16

INGREDIENTS

- 150 g/5½ oz butter, cut into small pieces, plus extra for greasing
- 225 g/8 oz plain flour
- 125 g/4½ oz caster sugar, plus extra for dusting
- 1 tsp vanilla essence

2

3

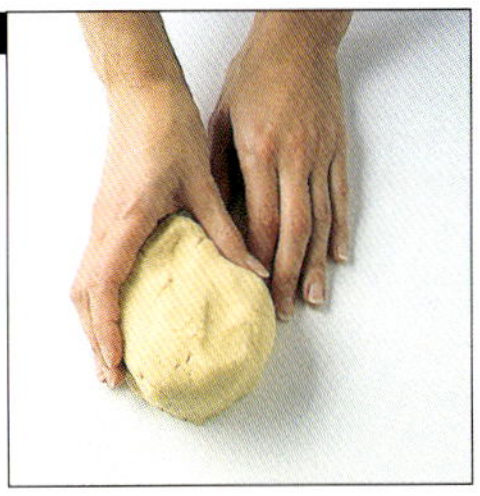

4

1 Lightly grease a baking tray with a little butter.

2 Sieve the flour into a large mixing bowl and rub in the butter with your fingertips until the mixture resembles fine breadcrumbs.

3 Stir in the caster sugar and vanilla essence and bring the mixture together with your hands to make a firm dough.

4 On a lightly floured surface, roll out the dough to a thickness of 2.5 cm/ 1 inch. Stamp out 12 hearts with a heart-shaped biscuit cutter measuring about 5 cm/2 inches across and 2.5 cm/ 1 inch deep.

5 Arrange the hearts on the prepared baking tray. Bake in a preheated oven, 180°C/350°F/Gas Mark 4, for about 15-20 minutes until the hearts are a light golden colour.

6 Transfer the vanilla hearts to a wire rack and leave to cool completely. Dust them with a little caster sugar just before serving.

COOK'S TIP

Place a fresh vanilla pod in your caster sugar and keep it in a storage jar for several weeks to give the sugar a delicious vanilla flavour.

Rock Drops

These rock drops are more substantial than a crisp biscuit. Serve them fresh from the oven to enjoy them at their best.

NUTRITIONAL INFORMATION

Calories	270	Sugars	21g
Protein	4g	Fat	11g
Carbohydrate	41g	Saturates	7g

5–10 mins

20 mins

MAKES 8

INGREDIENTS

- 100 g/3½ oz butter, cut into small pieces, plus extra for greasing
- 200 g/7 oz plain flour
- 2 tsp baking powder
- 75 g/2¾ oz demerara sugar
- 100 g/3½ oz sultanas
- 25 g/1 oz glacé cherries, finely chopped
- 1 egg, beaten
- 2 tbsp milk

1. Lightly grease a baking tray with a little butter.
2. Sieve the flour and baking powder into a mixing bowl. Rub in the butter with your fingertips until the mixture resembles breadcrumbs.
3. Stir in the sugar, sultanas and chopped glacé cherries.
4. Add the beaten egg and the milk to the mixture and mix to form a soft dough.
5. Spoon 8 mounds of the mixture on to the prepared baking tray, spacing them well apart as they will spread while they are cooking.
6. Bake in a preheated oven, 200°C/400°F/Gas Mark 6, for 15–20 minutes until firm to the touch when pressed with a finger.
7. Remove the rock drops from the baking tray. Either serve piping hot from the oven or transfer to a wire rack and leave to cool before serving.

2

3

5

COOK'S TIP

For convenience, prepare the dry ingredients in advance and just before cooking stir in the liquid.

Meringues

These are just as meringues should be – as light as air and at the same time crisp and melt-in-the-mouth.

NUTRITIONAL INFORMATION

Calories	183	Sugars	21g
Protein	1g	Fat	11g
Carbohydrate	21g	Saturates	7g

15 mins

1½ hrs

MAKES 13

INGREDIENTS

- 4 egg whites
- 125 g/4½ oz granulated sugar
- 125 g/4½ oz caster sugar
- salt
- 300 ml/10 fl oz double cream, lightly whipped, to serve

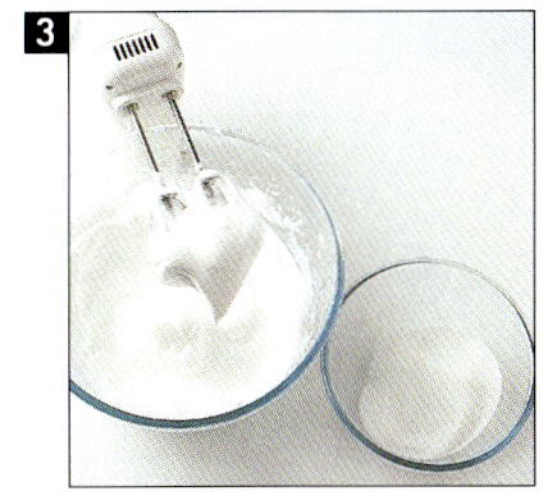

1 Line 3 baking trays with sheets of baking paper.

2 In a large clean bowl, whisk together the egg whites and a pinch of salt until they are stiff, using an electric hand-held whisk or a balloon whisk. (You should be able to turn the bowl upside down without any movement from the whisked egg whites.)

3 Whisk in the granulated sugar, a little at a time; the meringue should start to look glossy at this stage.

4 Sprinkle in the caster sugar, a little at a time and continue whisking until all the sugar has been incorporated and the meringue is thick, white and forms peaks.

5 Transfer the meringue mixture to a piping bag fitted with a 2-cm/¾-inch star nozzle. Pipe about 26 small whirls on to the prepared baking trays.

6 Bake in a preheated oven, 120°C/250°F/Gas Mark ½, for 1½ hours or until the meringues are pale golden in colour and can be easily lifted off the paper. Leave them to cool in the turned-off oven overnight.

7 Just before serving, sandwich the meringues together in pairs with the cream and arrange on a serving plate.

VARIATION

For a finer texture, replace the granulated sugar with caster sugar.

A

B

C